Chemistry and Numbers

Volume 1

The Online Dating Guide

By

Steve Monas

Copyright ©2006 Steve Monas.

All rights reserved. This book, or parts thereof, may not be reproduced in any form without permission from the publisher; exceptions are made for brief excerpts used in published reviews.

ISBN # 1-4196-5123-4

Printed in the United States of America
Library of Congress Control Number: 2006909176
Publisher: BookSurge, LLC
North Charleston , South Carolina
Monas, Steve
Chemistry and Numbers 1 / Steve Monas
ISBN # 1-4196-5123-4

This publication is designed to provide accurate and authoritive information with regard to the subject matter covered. It is sold with the understanding that the publisher is not engaged in rendering legal, accounting, or other proofessional advice. If legal advice or other expert assistance is required, the services of a competent professional person should be sought.

—From a Declaration of Principles jointly adopted by a Committee of the American Bar Association and a Committee of Publishers and Associations.

Table Of Contents

*The names of all the websites used in this book are the trademarks of their respective owners.

Why Did You Create An Online Dating Profile?

As a computer savvy and gregarious person, I took it upon myself to experiment with the online dating realm. The internet has been used as a vehicle to link people from all walks of life. There are numerous websites that promote online dating such as match.com and eharmony.com. There is a social utility website called facebook that helps college students network with each other. Facebook isn't a dating site but it is geared towards connecting friends. It helps friends communicate with each other. Students can create their own profile in facebook and share their interests and personal information with their networks. I met my ex boyfriend through facebook. I randomly added him as my friend and then we met each other in person and started to date. We only dated for a month but if it wasn't for facebook, we would have never crossed paths. These sites allow people to showcase their interests and personality traits. These sites also facilitate the dating process because they determine whether or not a couple is compatible based on surveys.

My best friend introduced me to the online dating websites. She praised these sites for their impressive networking capacities. I was reluctant at first to register for services like match.com but her persuasive demeanor convinced me that this was the right site for me. I'll never forget what she once told me about online dating. She stated, "You meet people online that you normally don't meet on the streets." There is some truth to this statement because online dating filters the a-list guys from the b-list guys. To be politically correct, the a-list guys are the ones who would be suitable match ups for single women.

After tossing and turning in bed, I finally decided to create an online dating profile in order to market my wonderful attributes and showcase them. When you look at the big picture, profiles are all about selling yourself. The information that you enter in a profile may or may not be the selling point. The profile that I created consisted of a list of adjectives and phrases that I would use to describe myself. I also included my hobbies and my preferences in a dating relationship.

My friend is the main reason why I created an online profile. If it wasn't for her, I probably wouldn't be experiencing the dating world. Online dating is worthwhile despite the expensive fees that they charge. Online dating is not free but you get your money's worth when you meet the right person.

Dating is a challenge in general. It is hard to meet people in person because of their busy lives. Online dating is an alternative for the conventional dating trends. We are living in the 21st century and everyone has busy lives. People go to college and work not to mention they have family commitments, etc. Online dating is a convenience for those who don't have time to arrange blind dates. It doesn't really matter where you cross paths with someone as long as the two people have a healthy dating experience. You can cross paths with a person on the street but doing it online is like an escapade.

–Sabrine H.

Introduction

An Online Dating service, also known as internet dating or net dating, is an example of a dating system and allows individuals, couples and groups to meet online and possibly develop a romantic or intimate relationship. Net dating services provide un-moderated matchmaking through the use of personal computers, the Internet, or even cell phones.

Such services generally allow people to provide personal information, and then search for other individuals using criteria such as age range, gender and location. Most sites allow members to upload photos of themselves and browse the photos of others. Sites may offer additional services, such as webcasts, online chat, and message boards. Sites sometimes allow people to register for free but may offer services which require a monthly fee.

Many sites are broad-based, with members from a variety of backgrounds looking for different types of relationships. Other sites are more specific, based on the type of members, interests, location, or relationship desired.

U.S. residents spent $469.5 million on online dating and personals in 2004, the largest segment of "paid content" on the web, according to a study conducted by the Online Publishers Association (OPA) and comScore Networks.

At the end of November 2004, there were 844 lifestyle and dating sites, a 38 percent increase since the start of the year, according to Hitwise Inc. However, market share was increasingly being dominated by several large commercial services, including Yahoo Personals, Match.com, American Singles, and eHarmony. eHarmony CEO Greg Forgatch noted that despite the growing number of sites catering to specific niches, "to become a major player, it still takes a large number of people."

In 2002, a Wired magazine article forecast that, "Twenty years from now, the idea that someone looking for love without looking for it online will be silly, akin to skipping the card catalog to instead wander the stacks because 'the right books are found only by accident.' ...serendipity is the hallmark of inefficient markets, and the marketplace of love, like it or not, is becoming more efficient."

Source: www.wikipedia.org

Tips For Online Dating

The dynamics of online dating differ drastically from real-world dating. In order to have the best chance of a successful match, remember the following tips:

- Do not get discouraged. This is especially true for men, because women can receive hundreds of responses in a short period of time. Be patient, and don't give up!

- Don't look for the one perfect match right away, but consider multiple singles. You can narrow the matches down as you get to know them.

- Consider your profile as a resume. When human resources is looking to hire a new employee, they are faced with a large stack of nearly-identical resumes. Their first goal is to get rid of many as possible for any reason. Same thing with your profile- it needs to stand out or it will be cut.

- Be honest. You might get more responses by telling a creative lie, but if you meet your perfect match, the truth will eventually come out.

- Don't get too personal too fast. Unless the match specifies "casual dating" or "intimate dating", sex should not be brought up until the other person is ready to discuss it.

- Include a photo. Although most sites let you skip this step, members with photos are up to 15 times more likely to have a successful match.

- Most of all, keep an open mind. You may have traditionally preferred a particular race or hair color, but online dating gives you an opportunity to gain perspective and to meet millions of people that you may have avoided in person.

Online Dating And Safety

The pseudo-anonymous nature of the internet gives many singles a false sense of security. They may feel that they can chat freely, and fail to consider their personal safety.

Most online dating sites offer several forms of communication built in to the site. This can be an asset and a liability. If the site offers email and instant messaging, using that instead of your personal accounts can help maintain your privacy. However, it is still important to consider what information you reveal, especially in chat. Under no circumstances should you feel compelled to give your full name, address, employer or school until you feel ready.

Always keep in mind that, as in real life, not everyone online is exactly as the portray themselves. Be wary of singles that try to rush you into meetings or off-site communication, especially if they knowingly push you beyond your level of comfort. If a user persists, report them to the site administrator, as this is a violation of most sites' terms of service, and possibly state or federal law.

Always remember to trust your gut. If you are uncomfortable with a situation, you have every right to simply leave. Especially in online dating, you should always leave yourself a way out.

Choosing Your Photo

One of the most important aspects of your online dating profile is your photo. In order to have the best chance possible to attract your perfect match, consider the following tips:

- Your primary photo should clearly show your features, especially your smile. Preferably, use a head-and-shoulders shot.
- Try to avoid photos with other people, unless that is critical to your personality. For instance, if your children are very important to you, and you want to attract a match that feels the same way, it is advisable to include them in one of your photos.
- Try to avoid pictures with a member of the opposite sex, even if it's a relative. You want other singles to picture themselves with you, not someone else.
- Remember that if you enlarge small photos, you can lose detail.
- Remember to select photos that are sideways. Be sure to rotate the image before posting.
- Use an accurate photo, especially regarding weight and hair.
- Consider what information can be gained from your photo. Can you see your house number? License plate? Workplace?

I live in a part of the USA which, for several reasons, lacks "eligible" men. Furthermore, as a female over 25, I have difficulty finding a classy hang-out, or even an unmarried female friend to be my wing woman. Because moving is not an immediate option, I thought that online dating would provide a few possible men. This is why I joined match.com.

- Zeno J.

member login

match.com the #1 site for love

Age 34
San Diego, CA

Age 38
Cupertino, CA

Age 37
San Jose, CA

Age 30
North Hollywood, CA

Age 33
San Marcos, CA

Meet some of the millions of members looking for love on match.com.

I'm a: M seeking: F age: 25 to 45 near zip:

SHOW ME MY MATCHES

FREE! LISTEN TO TODAY'S LIFE NOTE

Search Now How It Works Subscribe Now FREE Starter Kit MindFindBind with Dr. Phil

Looking for more in a relationship and a dating site?

With over 10 years of experience in online dating and relationships, Match.com is the worldwide leader in online dating and relationships. Where else can you find millions of singles looking for love, just like you? We don't offer just online personals, we are personal in our offerings - to help you find a date, a relationship, a marriage.

Match.com

Quick facts:

Year Established:	1996
Number of members:	8 million
Number of photos allowed:	1
Best Feature:	Many users
Biggest Complaint:	Business practices currently in debate
Cost:	$29.99/month for one month, $14.99/month for 6 months (6 month plan offers guarantee, promising a free 6 months if you don't find someone special within your first 6 months)
Services offered:	Online dating and singles search
Wikipedia reference:	http://en.wikipedia.org/wiki/Match.com

Match.com was founded in 1993 by Gary Kremen (The entrepreneur who gained notoriety by being the first to register the domain name sex.com in 1994), and was one of the first online dating sites in the world.

In 1994, Guinness World Records named Match.com as the largest dating site in the world with 42 million members up to that time, and 15 million active members at that time.

Currently, match.com offices operate over 6 continents and maintains 30 regional dating sites.

Check it out: *In 2005, a class action lawsuit was filed alleging that match.com was engaging in fraudulent business practices by employing people to date or flirt with subscribers. While this suit is still pending, the resulting media backlash has provoked the creation of free competitor sites such as OkCupid and PlentyOfFish.*

Trivia: *In 2002 and early 2003, Match.com's then CEO, Barry Diller, tried to expand Match.com reach by expanding into the local dating scene with a service called MatchLive. Daters would meet in a public location sponsored by Match.com in order to engage in social activities such as speed dating. The idea was scrapped by the parent company.*

Signing up for Match.com

1. On the match.com Home Page, click "Subscribe now"

member login

match.com the #1 site for love

Age 40
San Pedro, CA

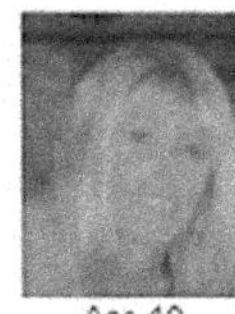

Age 40
Corona del Mar, CA

Age 29
Ladera Ranch, CA

Age 27
Antelope Acres, CA

Age 31
Fresno, CA

Meet some of the millions of members looking for love on match.com.

I'm a: M seeking: F age: 25 to 45 near zip:

SHOW ME MY MATCHES

FREE! LISTEN TO TODAY'S LIFE NOTE

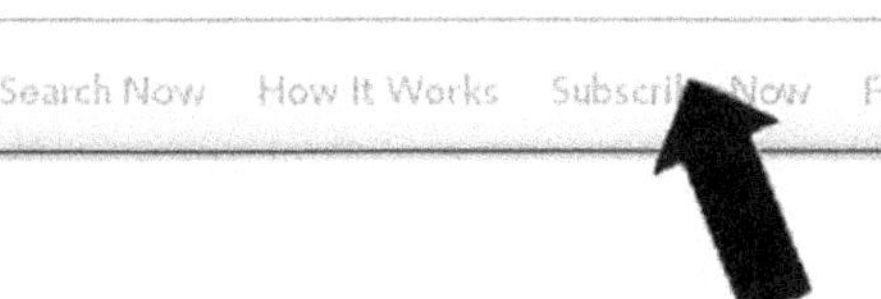

2. Create your free profile.

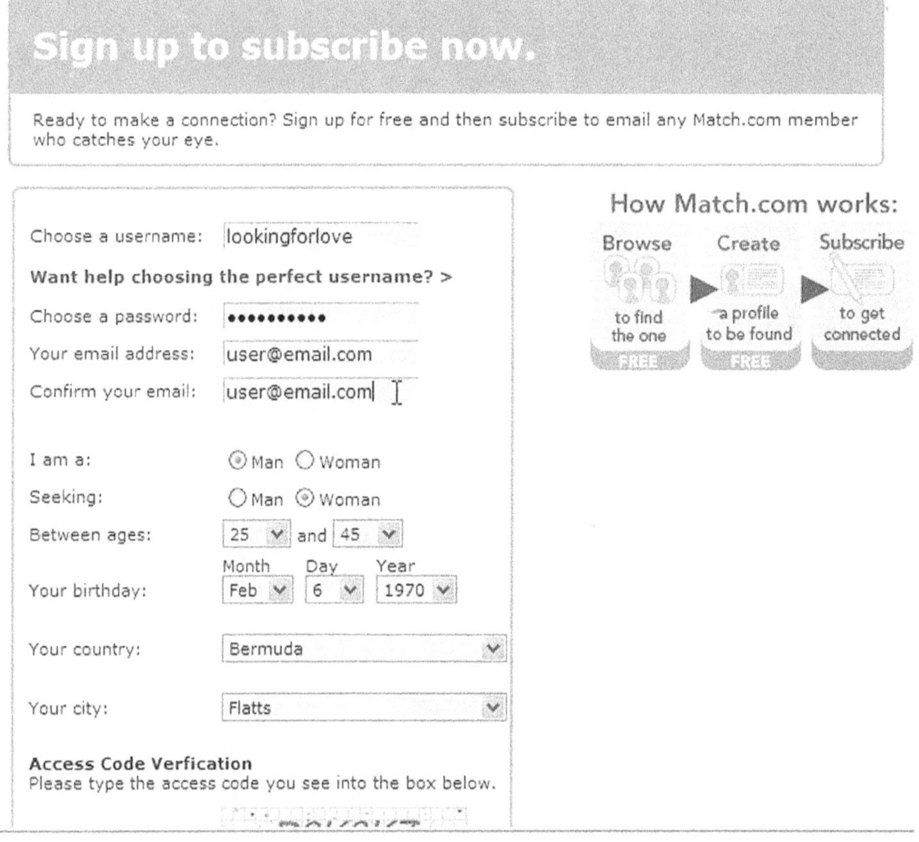

Note: *Creating an account and searching for members is free. However, you must register to contact members.*

3. At this point you will be prompted to subscribe. Note that it is not necessary to subscribe to view or search matches.

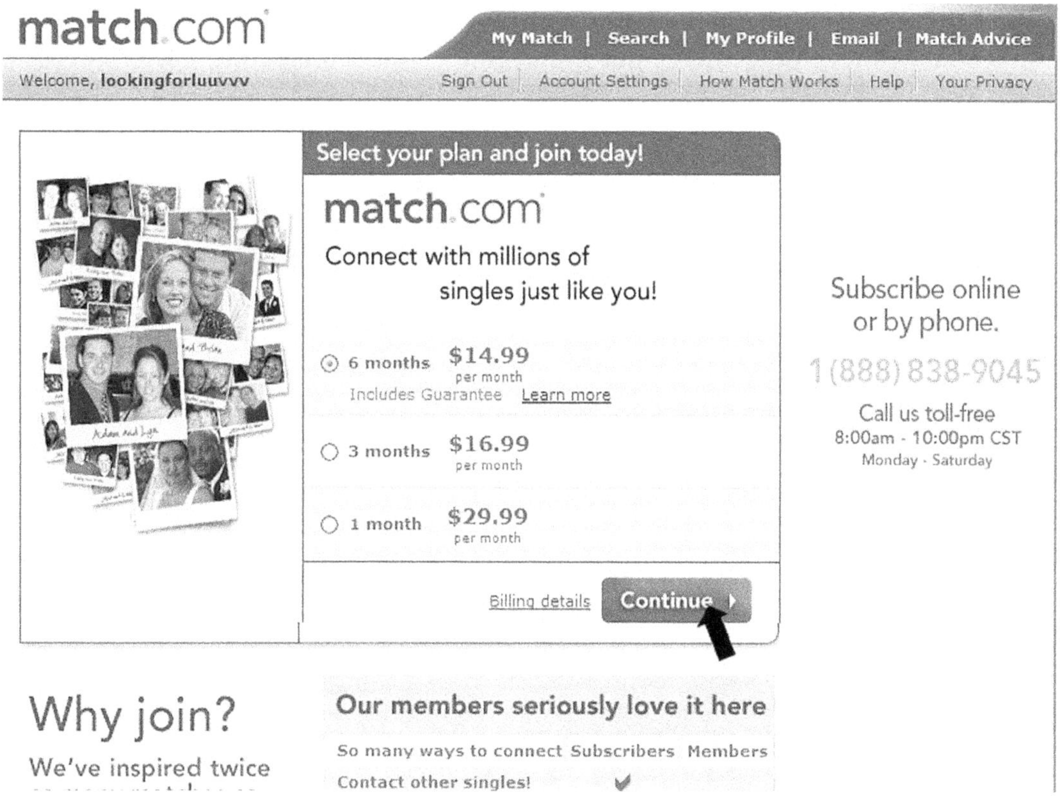

match.com

My Match | Search | My Profile | Email | Match Advice

Welcome, **lookingforluuvvv**

Sign Out | Account Settings | How Match Works | Help | Your Privacy

Select your plan and join today!

match.com

Connect with millions of singles just like you!

6 months $14.99 per month
Includes Guarantee Learn more

3 months $16.99 per month

1 month $29.99 per month

Billing details Continue

Subscribe online or by phone.

1 (888) 838-9045

Call us toll-free
8:00am - 10:00pm CST
Monday - Saturday

Why join?

We've inspired twice

Our members seriously love it here

So many ways to connect Subscribers Members

Contact other singles!

Using Match.com

1. Clicking on "My Match" will access your user control panel.

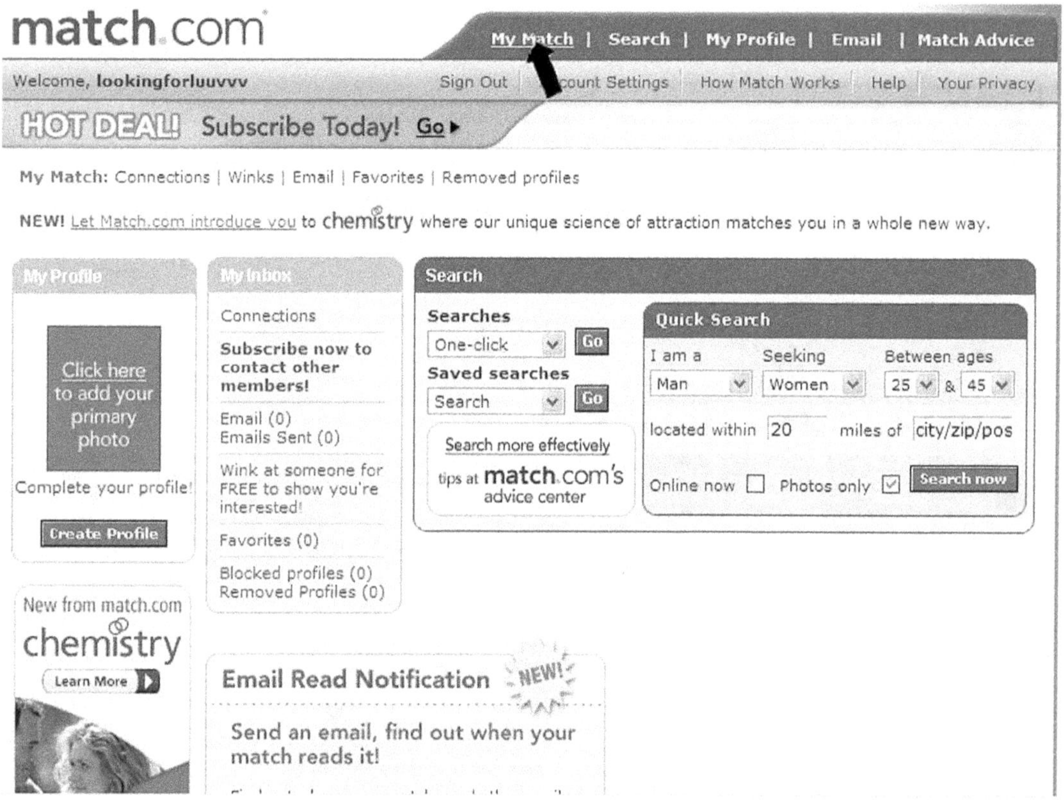

match.com
My Match | Search | My Profile | Email | Match Advice
Welcome, lookingforluuvvv
Sign Out | Account Settings | How Match Works | Help | Your Privacy
HOT DEAL! Subscribe Today! Go
My Match: Connections | Winks | Email | Favorites | Removed profiles
NEW! Let Match.com introduce you to chemistry where our unique science of attraction matches you in a whole new way.
My Profile
Click here to add your primary photo
Complete your profile!
Create Profile
New from match.com
chemistry
Learn More
My Inbox
Connections
Subscribe now to contact other members!
Email (0)
Emails Sent (0)
Wink at someone for FREE to show you're interested!
Favorites (0)
Blocked profiles (0)
Removed Profiles (0)
Search
Searches
One-click Go
Saved searches
Search Go
Search more effectively
tips at match.com's advice center
Quick Search
I am a Man
Seeking Women
Between ages 25 & 45
located within 20 miles of city/zip/pos
Online now Photos only Search now
Email Read Notification NEW!
Send an email, find out when your match reads it!

Check it out: *The "My Profile" panel allows you to complete your profile and add a photo. The profile must be approved by customer service, and can take up to 48 hours for approval.*

Check it out: *The "My Inbox" panel allows you to view and send emails. Remember that you must subscribe in order to send or receive emails.*

2. Use the search panel to perform quick or custom searches.

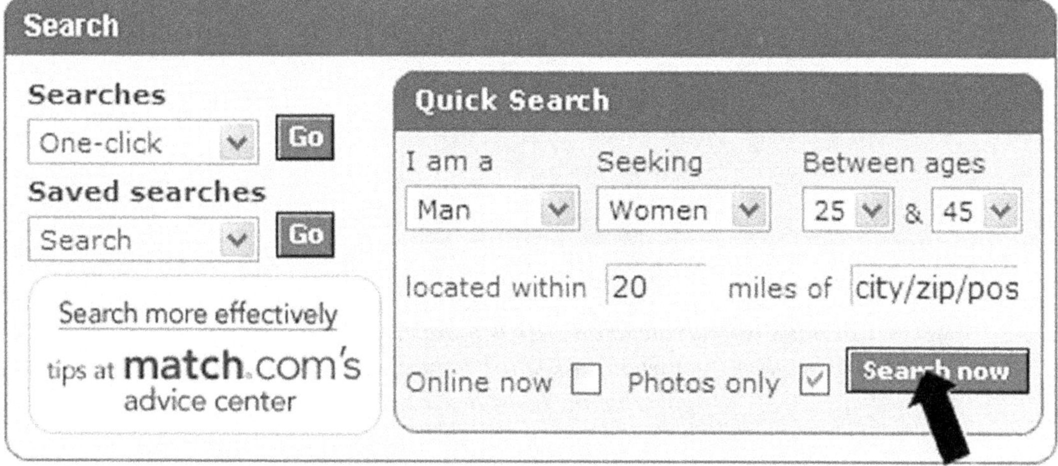

Note: *Your profile must be approved before you can perform custom searches.*

To think is to create and to ask is to receive! I updated my profile when I got what I asked for, I changed my life when I got what my heart deserved!

- Victoria D.

eHarmony®

Already a Member? Log in Here

Experience the eHarmony Difference

Get your FREE Personality Profile®
No need to search – we bring compatible matches to you
Meet quality singles today

Register to Begin

First Name:
I'm a: Please select...
Postal Code:
Country: United States
Email:
Confirm Email:
Note: Your email is used to log back in
Password:
Must be at least 5 characters
How did you hear about us?
Please select...
Submit

Shannon and L.J.
Engaged: July 30, 2005

New Service for Married Couples!
eHarmony Marriage is an online program designed to be an alternative to marriage counseling.
LEARN MORE

About Singles Home Marriage Home Bookstore Privacy

TRUSTe site privacy statement

eHarmony.com

Quick facts:

Year Established:	2000
Number of members:	8 Million plus
Number of photos allowed:	1
Best Feature:	Scientific approach to matchmaking
Biggest Complaint:	Long (436) part profile
Cost:	$59.95 (1 month)- $251.40(1 year) for singles program, $75-$239 for married program
Services offered:	Personality profile, scientific-based matchmaking, online marriage counseling
Wikipedia reference:	http://en.wikipedia.org/wiki/Eharmony

eHarmony.com was established in 2000 by Dr. Neil Clark Warren, an evangelical Christian, and heavily promoted on James Dobson's Focus on the Family radio show. This relationship continued until 2005, when eHarmony.com sought to publicly distance itself from Dobson's group in order to increase its public appeal.

eHarmony.com is intended for the estimated 20% of online daters seeking a long term relationship. It is with this goal in mind, and based on his claims of 35 years' research into successful marriages, that Dr. Warren established his 436 part profile (plus fields for additional information if desired), which collects information on age, ethnicity, religious affiliation, previous marital status and family status.

Note: *There are several factors that will result in immediate disqualification from eHarmony, including:*

- *Still being married*
- *Being under 21*
- *Severe depression*
- *3 or more previous divorces*

Note: *According to eHarmony, they do not participate in gay or lesbian matches, claiming legal considerations.*

Unlike many other online dating services, users are not allowed to browse profiles and make their own selections. Instead, eHarmony will arrange the potential matches. This is designed to make users rely on the scientific method and eliminate elements of human error.

In early 2006, eHarmony unveiled its marriage program, designed to assist married couples in strengthening or repairing their marriage. This is similar in many ways to the singles program, except that the couple each takes a personality questionnaire covering such topics as romance, sex and communication. There is also a 12 video series available, addressing common marriage issues.

Signing up for eHarmony.com

1. At the eHarmony.com Home Page, complete the initial account creation form.

Register to Begin

First Name:
Chris
I'm a:
Man seeking a woman
Postal Code:Country:
91212 United States
Email: (Confidential)
Note: Your email is used to log back in
perfectmatch.love@hotmail.c
Confirm Email:
perfectmatch.love@hotmail.c
Password:
Must be at least 5 characters
•••••••
How did you hear about us?
Online (Search, Banner, Email)
SUBMIT

***Note:** A strong password should be at least 8 characters long, combine letters, numbers, symbols and capitals, not contain a predictable series (such as "1234" or "qwerty") and be easy to remember but hard to guess.*

2. Complete the personality profile. This profile test will ask questions about your religious preferences, self-view, qualities and feelings.

Section 3: About Your Feelings

Please use the scale below to rate how often during the past month you have felt the following ways.

		1 (rarely)	2	3	4 (occasionally)	5	6	7 (almost always)
1.	Happy	◉	○	○	○	○	○	○
2.	Sad	○	◉	○	○	○	○	○
3.	Anxious	○	○	◉	○	○	○	○
4.	Confident	○	○	○	○	○	○	○
5.	Hopeful	○	○	○	○	○	○	○
6.	Fearful about the future	○	○	○	○	○	○	○
7.	Angry	○	○	○	○	○	○	○
8.	Calm	○	○	○	○	○	○	○
9.	Fortunate	○	○	○	○	○	○	○
10.	Out of control	○	○	○	○	○	○	○
11.	Fulfilled	○	○	○	○	○	○	○
12.	Depressed	○	○	○	○	○	○	○
13.	Energetic	○	○	○	○	○	○	○
14.	Tired	○	○	○	○	○	○	○
15.	Successful	○	○	○	○	○	○	○
16.	Unable to cope	○	○	○	○	○	○	○
17.	Satisfied	○	○	○	○	○	○	○
18.	Misunderstood	○	○	○	○	○	○	○
19.	Safe	○	○	○	○	○	○	○
20.	Plotted against	○	○	○	○	○	○	○
		1 (rarely)	2	3	4 (occasionally)	5	6	7 (almost always)

Save and Exit   Save and Continue

Check it out: *In "Section 3: About your feelings", you will be asked how often you experience certain emotions. This section could disqualify you if it identifies chronic depression.*

3. (optional) Upload your photo

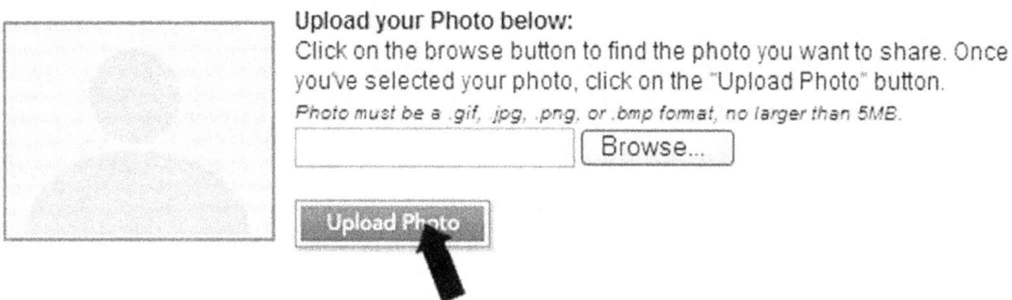
Upload Photo (Optional)
Upload your Photo below:
Click on the browse button to find the photo you want to share. Once you've selected your photo, click on the "Upload Photo" button.
Photo must be a .gif, .jpg, .png, or .bmp format, no larger than 5MB.
Browse...

Note: *Your picture should be current and accurate. Your high school football picture may look good, but your date might feel deceived! If you don't have a digital camera, don't use a webcam because the quality won't be very good. You can send in a developed picture for eHarmony to scan.*

4. Congratulations! Your profile is complete. At this point, you will have the option to subscribe, view potential matches, or view the results of your personality profile.

Congratulations!

You have completed our in depth Relationship Questionnaire. You can now read your two FREE reports: your Personality Profile and Compatibility Profile®. After learning more about yourself and who you would be best matched with, see how these compatibilities are revealed in the matches you receive.

Join eHarmony today and get to know your compatible matches. The love of your life could be just a match away.

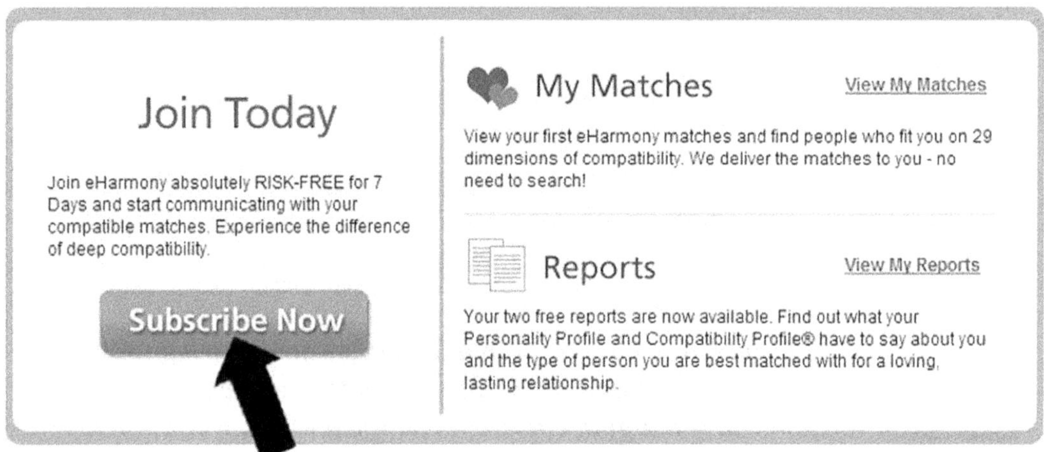

Note: *Until you subscribe, you will only have limited access to the eHarmony features. For instance, you will not be able to view pictures of prospective dates and you will only have a maximum of 10 matches.*

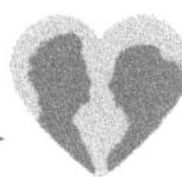

Using eHarmony.com

1. Upon logging in, you will have access to the user panel. This allows you to view matches, your reports, and change your settings or information.

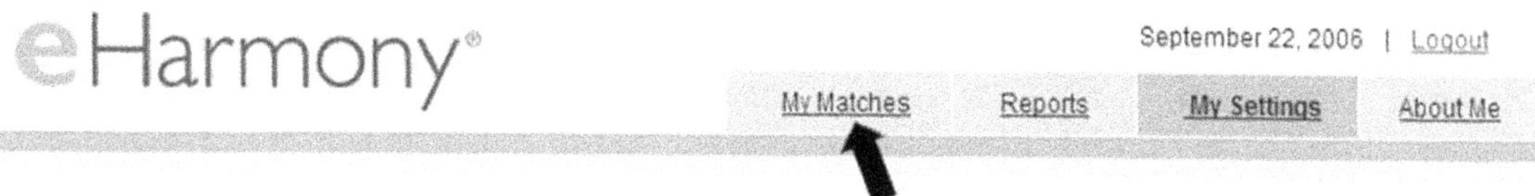

2. Under the "All Matches" tab in after logging in, you can view the matches that eHarmony has selected for you.

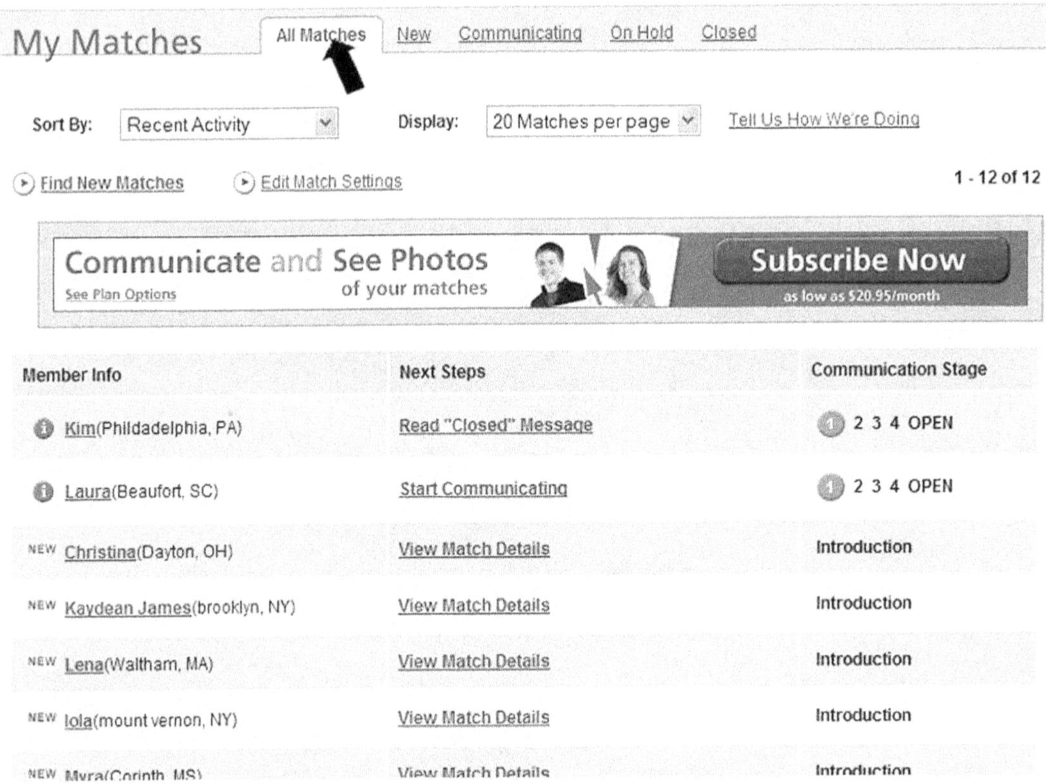

3. Click on "View Match Details" to view a user's profile.

NEW	Kaydean James(brooklyn, NY)	View Match Details	Introduction
NEW	lola(mount vernon, NY)	View Match Details	Introduction
NEW	Myra(Corinth, MS)	View Match Details	Introduction
NEW	Rachel(Cleveland, TN)	View Match Details	Introduction

4. Once in the user's profile, you can view their details and interests, as well as start communicating with him or her.

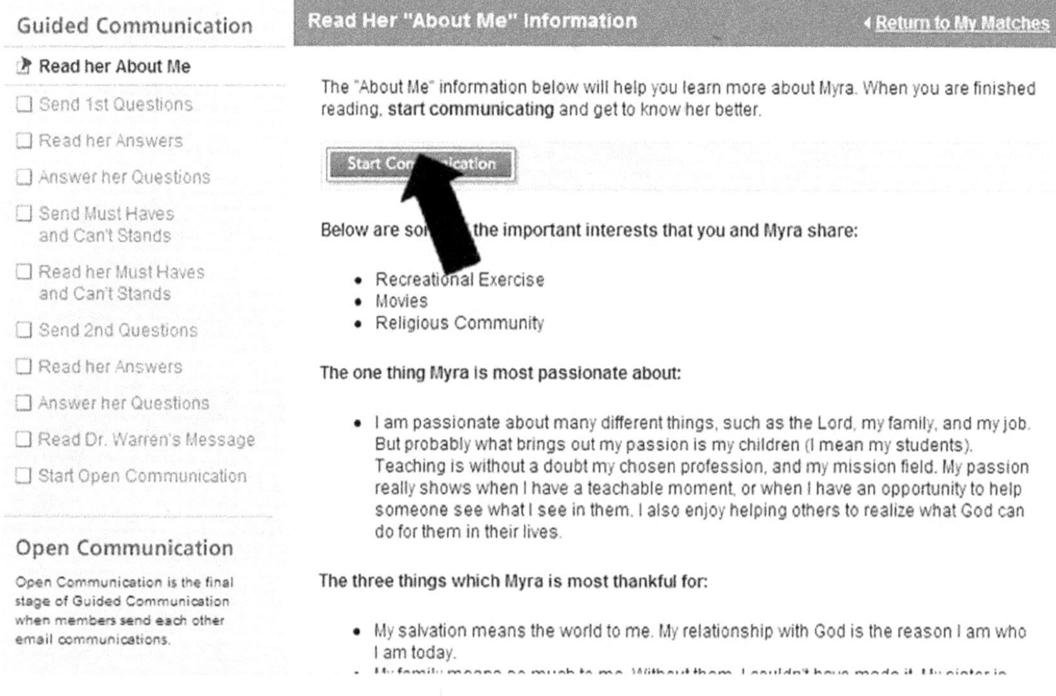

***Check it out:** When you first begin communicating with a potential match, you will be asked to answer a series of multiple choice questions. For each question, you have the option of choosing "E" to enter your own short answer. Using this option will make your answers seem more personal.*

In my opinion, online dating is one of the safest places to meet new people and make new friends. By creating a profile, I introduce myself to other people from all over the world effortlessly, which cannot be done physically unless I am a billionaire who can travel to places. Even though some of these people are not compatible with me, we can be friends and I can add them to my networking contacts that can bring other benefits in the future.

- Noradlina A.

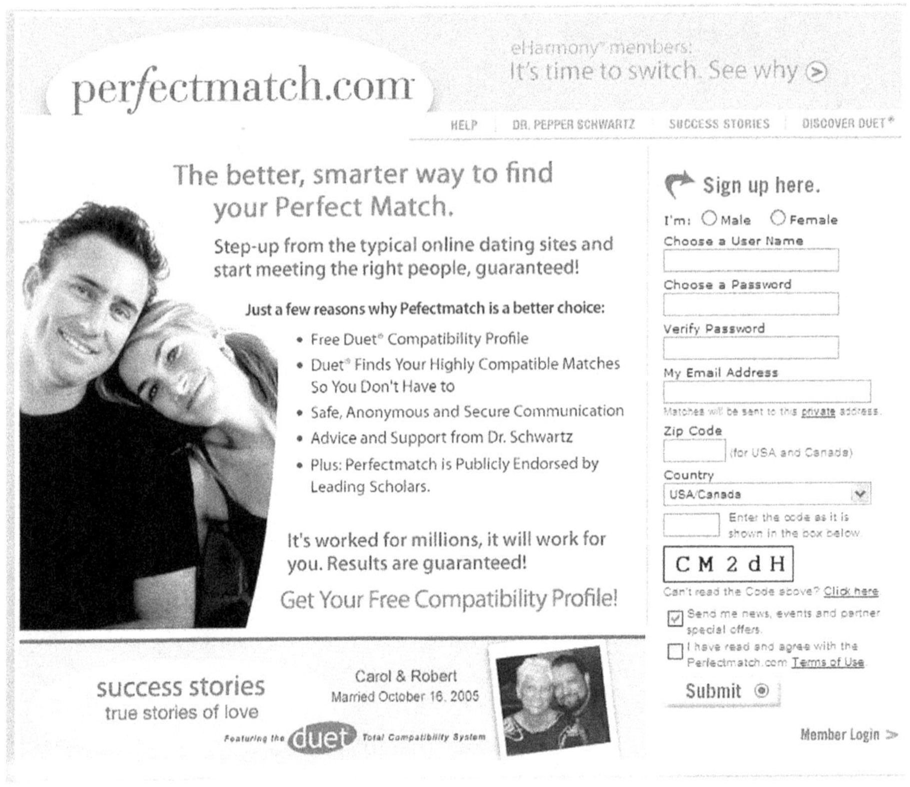

PerfectMatch.com

Quick facts:

Year Established:	2002
Number of members:	3 Million plus
Number of photos allowed:	1
Best Feature:	Highly accurate results
Biggest Complaint:	Expensive
Cost:	\$19.95 (one month)- \$119.95 (one year)
Services offered:	Personality profile, scientific-based matchmaking, dating advice
Wikipedia reference:	http://en.wikipedia.org/wiki/Pepper_Schwartz

Perfectmatch.com was designed to compete with eHarmony.com, and claims to be the fastest growing dating site on the internet. Founded in 2002 by a team of relationship experts, and with the compatibility system co-created by Dr. Pepper Schwartz, Perfectmatch.com has achieved quick fame due to appearances in films such as "Must Love Dogs" and "Superman Returns", as well as endorsements by Dr. Phil and Regis and Kelley.

Perfectmatch.com features the Duet® Total Compatibility system, which Dr. Schwartz claims to be the result of 30 years of research on relationships and compatibility. This is similar to the evaluation methods used by eHarmony, with one key difference: while eHarmony will only display users that their system feels is an appropriate match, perfectmatch.com will display the recommended matches but allow the option of browsing based on their on user-selected criteria.

Signing up for PerfectMatch.com

1. At the PerfectMatch.com Home Page, complete the initial account creation form.

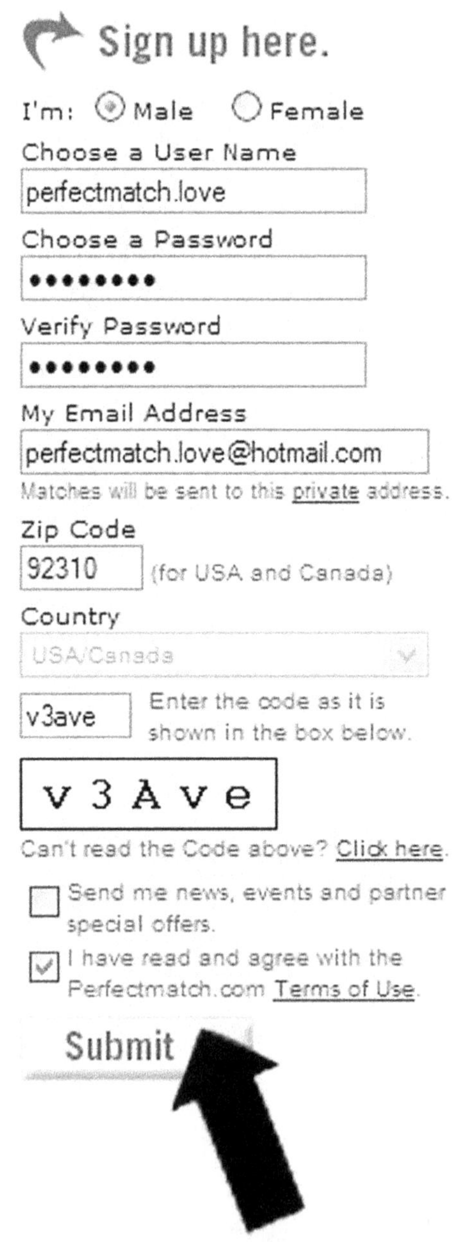

2. Complete the introductory profile.

perfectmatch.com

ESSENTIALS

It's our pleasure to help you show everyone how special you are. A welcoming profile makes you seem accessible, and having a current picture in your profile will yield the best results. Be positive! Our members appreciate honesty, so keep that in mind when you provide descriptions of yourself. Remember, your perfect matches will be suited to the real you - if you present yourself honestly. What matters most is that you and your soul mate be open with each other right away!

duet Analysis | Essentials | Values & Ideals | Deal Breakers | Life & LoveStyle

GENERAL INFORMATION

Your First Name (Up to 20 characters)

Date of Birth Month Day 1968

City Barstow Fort Irwin

Highlight your city from list above.

State California

Country United States

Click Here to change selected location

Relationship Status

Choose the relationship service that works. Guaranteed!

Chrissy & Daniel Married February 4, 2006

"I truly have found

Check it out: *Your progress can be followed by the pie chart in the upper-right hand corner.*

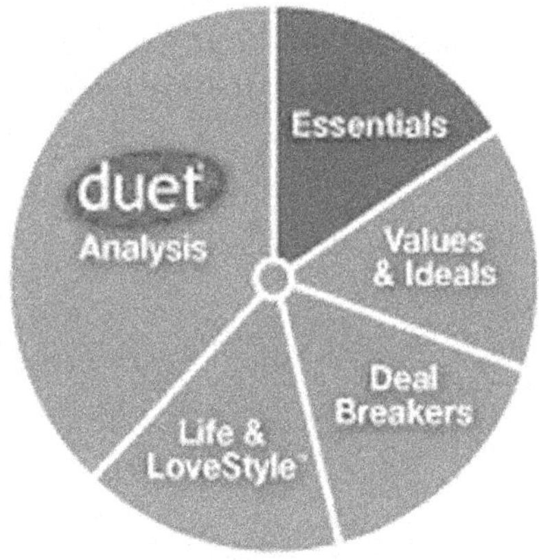

3. Stage 4 of the assessment will begin the Duet® portion of the profile. Note the addition of the Duet® test elements map, showing your progress for this portion. There will also be an explanation of each section above the questions.

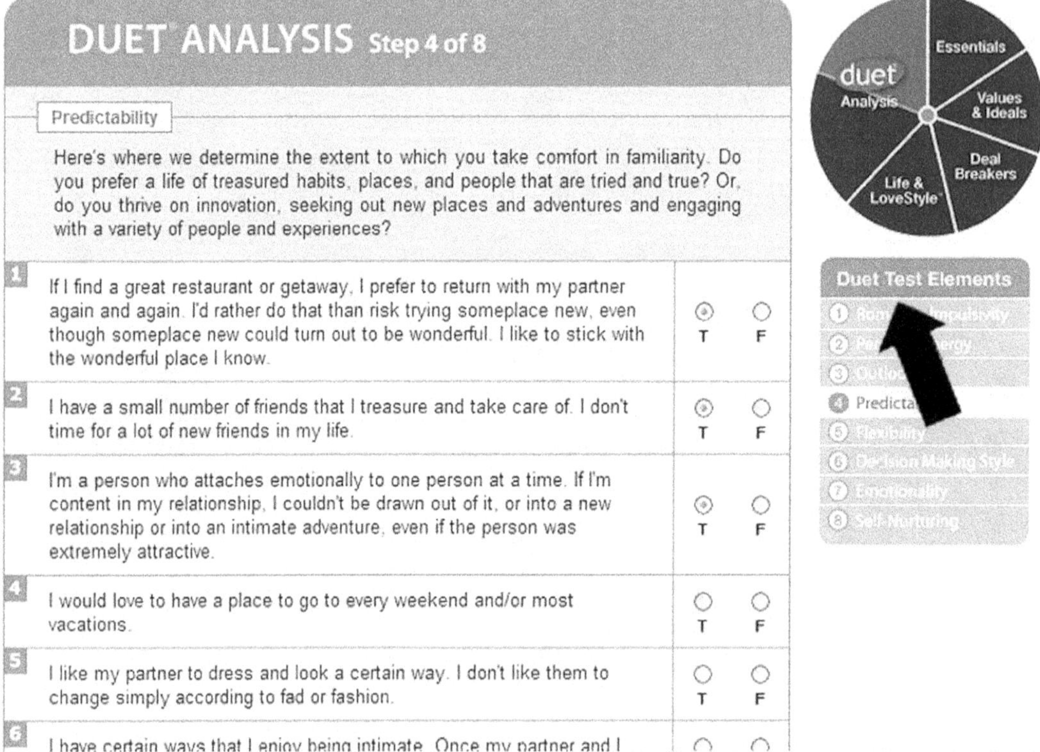

DUET ANALYSIS Step 4 of 8
Predictability
Here's where we determine the extent to which you take comfort in familiarity. Do you prefer a life of treasured habits, places, and people that are tried and true? Or, do you thrive on innovation, seeking out new places and adventures and engaging with a variety of people and experiences?
1 If I find a great restaurant or getaway, I prefer to return with my partner again and again. I'd rather do that than risk trying someplace new, even though someplace new could turn out to be wonderful. I like to stick with the wonderful place I know. T F
2 I have a small number of friends that I treasure and take care of. I don't time for a lot of new friends in my life. T F
3 I'm a person who attaches emotionally to one person at a time. If I'm content in my relationship, I couldn't be drawn out of it, or into a new relationship or into an intimate adventure, even if the person was extremely attractive. T F
4 I would love to have a place to go to every weekend and/or most vacations. T F
5 I like my partner to dress and look a certain way. I don't like them to change simply according to fad or fashion. T F
duet Analysis
Essentials
Values & Ideals
Deal Breakers
Life & LoveStyle
Duet Test Elements
Predicta

Check it out: *The Duet® Personality profile is very similar in form and function to the Myers-Briggs personality assessment.*

4. After completing the analysis, you will be shown your personality profile, along with an explanation of your personality type. Click "Next" to continue.

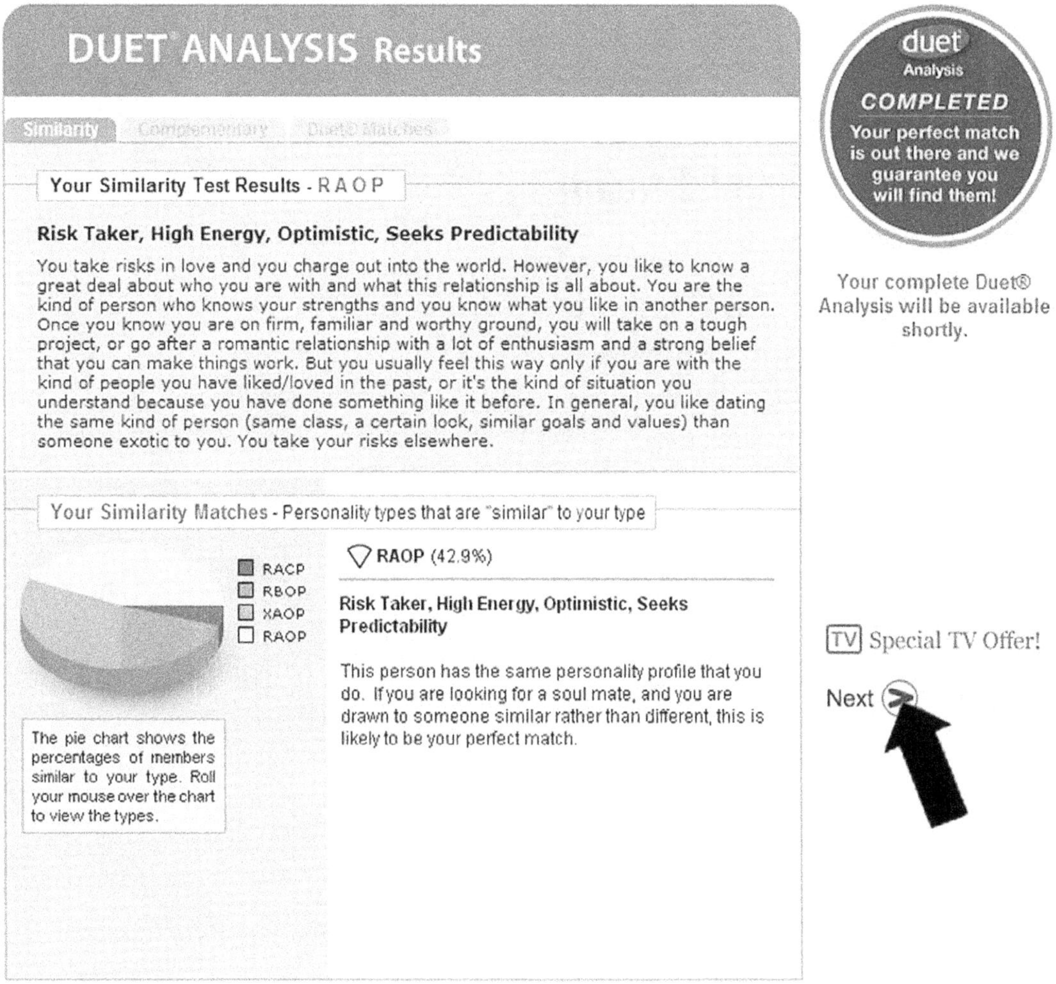

DUET ANALYSIS Results

Similarity | Complementary | Duet® Matches

Your Similarity Test Results - R A O P

Risk Taker, High Energy, Optimistic, Seeks Predictability

You take risks in love and you charge out into the world. However, you like to know a great deal about who you are with and what this relationship is all about. You are the kind of person who knows your strengths and you know what you like in another person. Once you know you are on firm, familiar and worthy ground, you will take on a tough project, or go after a romantic relationship with a lot of enthusiasm and a strong belief that you can make things work. But you usually feel this way only if you are with the kind of people you have liked/loved in the past, or it's the kind of situation you understand because you have done something like it before. In general, you like dating the same kind of person (same class, a certain look, similar goals and values) than someone exotic to you. You take your risks elsewhere.

Your Similarity Matches - Personality types that are "similar" to your type

RACP
RBOP
XAOP
RAOP

The pie chart shows the percentages of members similar to your type. Roll your mouse over the chart to view the types.

RAOP (42.9%)

Risk Taker, High Energy, Optimistic, Seeks Predictability

This person has the same personality profile that you do. If you are looking for a soul mate, and you are drawn to someone similar rather than different, this is likely to be your perfect match.

duet Analysis

COMPLETED

Your perfect match is out there and we guarantee you will find them!

Your complete Duet® Analysis will be available shortly.

TV Special TV Offer!

Next

5. If there are any current specials or offers, you will be redirected to an offers page. However, your actual results will open in a new window.

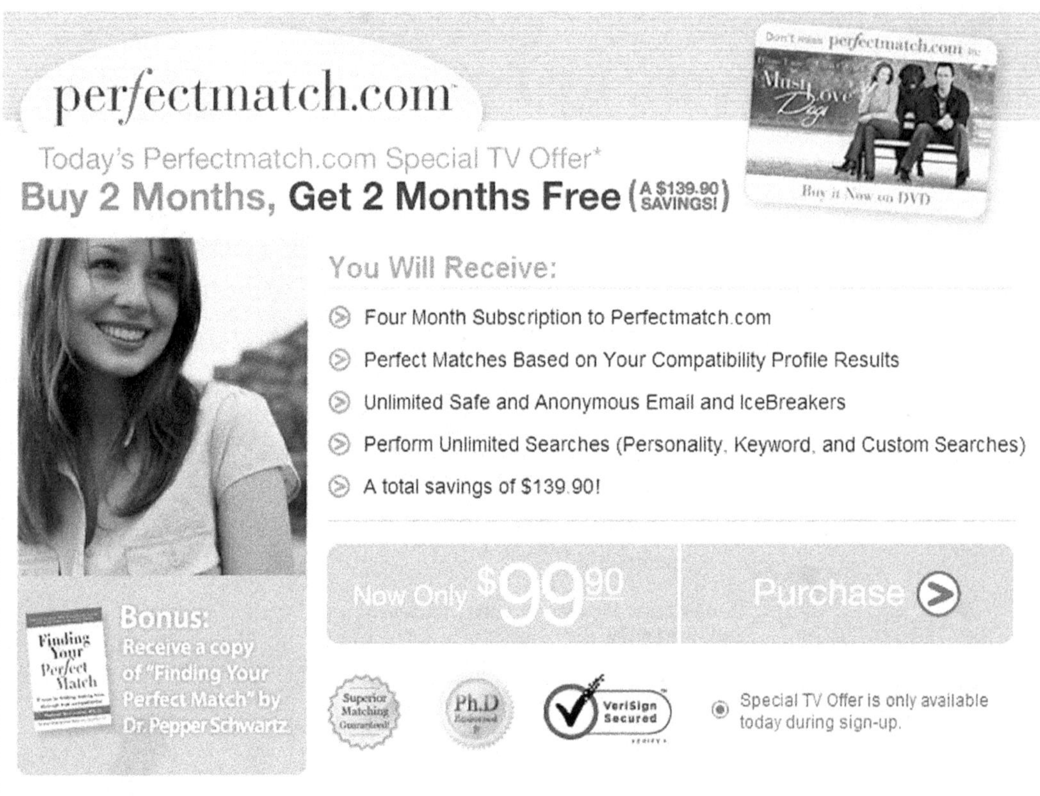

***Note:** Although it may appear to be the case, you <u>are not</u> obligated to purchase anything from this screen should it appear. The second window will contain your results*

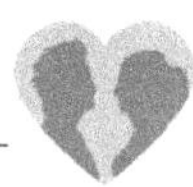

6. Congratulations! Your profile is complete. In the results screen, you will be able to view your "Perfect Matches", view your own profile, view your homepage or post your photos.

perfectmatch.com

YOUR PROFILE IS COMPLETE

Congratulations, you've done it! You are now ready to take that next important step in the journey to meet your perfect match. We encourage you to take the time to post photos of yourself, review your Compatibility Profile and take a tour of our community. No need to rush things - it's more important you become familiar with your new surroundings.

Posting photos is easy and will allow everyone to see your beautiful smile! You can even keep your photos hidden until you want to share them with someone special.

Reviewing your Compatibility Profile results are crucial, as this will give you a greater understanding of yourself, and of your perfect match. You've taken the first positive steps toward true love. Get ready to meet some exciting people.

- You already have (3) new Perfect Matches!
- View your Compatibility Profile
- Go to My Home
- Post Your Photos
- Special TV Offer

Dr. Pepper Schwartz

Dr. Pepper Schwartz, Ph.D

duet Analysis

COMPLETED

Your perfect match is out there and we guarantee you will find them!

Using PerfectMatch.com

1. Select "Go to Home" in the results screen. This will take you to your personal control panel. This is also the page that you will see when you log in.

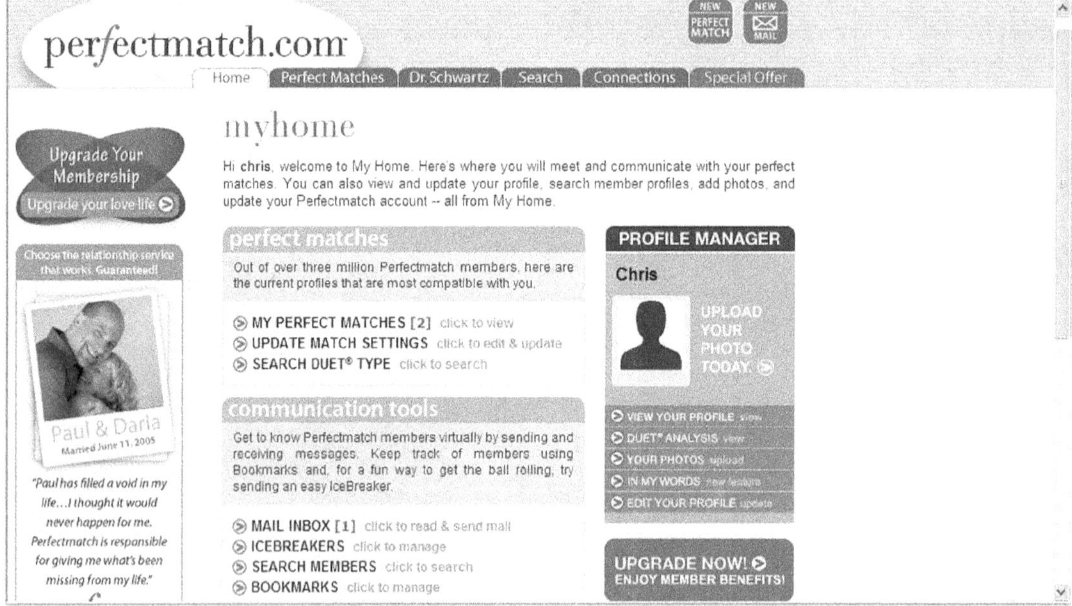

2. Review the "Profile Manager". This panel allows you to view your profile, view your analysis, upload your photos, describe yourself in your own words or edit your profile.

Check it out: *Selecting "Your Photos" allows you to add one photo to your profile. You have the option of uploading it from your computer, emailing it to PerfectMatch.com or mailing it to PerfectMatch.com*

3. Review the "perfect matches" section. This section allows you to view your current matches, edit your match settings, or browse results based on personality type.

perfect matches

Out of over three million Perfectmatch members, here are the current profiles that are most compatible with you.

MY PERFECT MATCHES [2] click to view
UPDATE MATCH SETTINGS click to edit & update
SEARCH DUET® TYPE click to search

4. Review the communication tools section. This section allows you to read and send email, send "Icebreakers" (short introductory messages), search for a member or view saved matches.

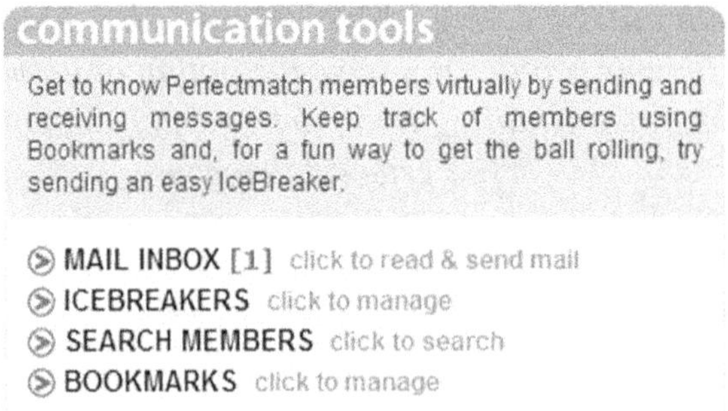

communication tools

Get to know Perfectmatch members virtually by sending and receiving messages. Keep track of members using Bookmarks and, for a fun way to get the ball rolling, try sending an easy IceBreaker.

MAIL INBOX [1] click to read & send mail
ICEBREAKERS click to manage
SEARCH MEMBERS click to search
BOOKMARKS click to manage

Check it out: *An "icebreaker" can be sent to a user when viewing your matches. An icebreaker is a series of up to four open ended questions designed to give you insight into the personality of your prospective date.*

icebreaker : level one

Select 4 questions you would like to ask Emily

- [ ] +VIEW **How would you spend a rainy afternoon?**
- [ ] +VIEW **How would you describe your best friend?**
- [ ] +VIEW **What best represents your feelings about Presidential elections?**
- [ ] +VIEW **Where would you be most likely to max out a credit card?**
- [ ] +VIEW **Where's your dream vacation?**
- [ ] +VIEW **What's your Saturday morning attire?**
- [ ] +VIEW **Do you enjoy being alone?**
- [ ] +VIEW **Which of these would you like to have the most?**
- [ ] +VIEW **Which type of restaurant would you choose for a nice dinner out?**
- [ ] +VIEW **What type of movies do you enjoy?**
- [ ] +VIEW **What do you like to do when you stay "in" for the night?**

I had gotten over a previous break-up and was ready to start looking again. Since it was buzzed about, I thought I would give online dating a try. I saw a picture of a guy I thought was really cute and set up a profile so I could talk to him.

- Lady V.

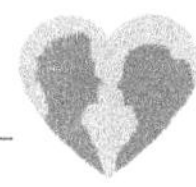

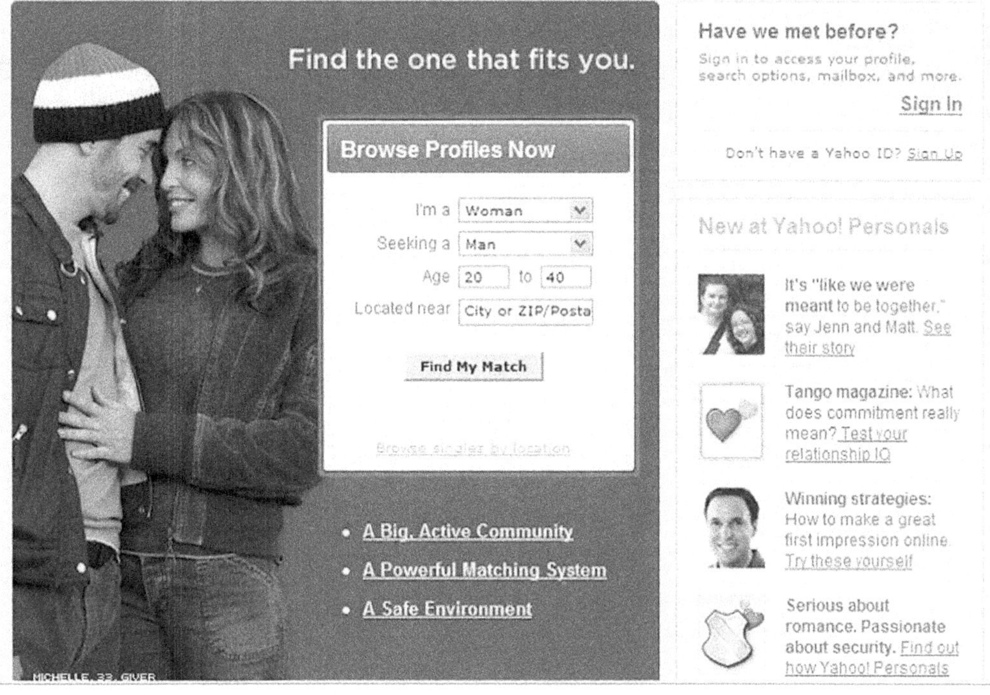

Personals.Yahoo.com

Quick facts:

Year Established:	1996
Number of members:	9 million plus
Number of photos allowed:	5
Best Feature:	Free searches
Biggest Complaint:	None identified
Cost:	Free search, free 7 day pass. $24.95- $74.95
Services offered:	Regional search, profile browsing
Wikipedia reference:	http://en.wikipedia.org/wiki/Yahoo_personals

Yahoo Personals is one of the oldest modern dating sites in existence. Until recently, it was a completely free service, but currently only the searches are free. In order to contact a member, it is necessary to create a premium account.

Unlike the previous dating services, Yahoo Personals does not offer scientific personality analysis, but instead relies on user input.

On Sep 22, 2006, Yahoo Personals teamed up with match.com to service the UK and Ireland, creating the UK's largest dating service.

Note: *Because the personals section is a part of the Yahoo community, it is compatible with existing Yahoo accounts, such as a mail account. Using a current account, it will still be necessary to create a profile, but not a Yahoo account.*

Signing up for Yahoo Personals

Check it out: *It is not necessary to create an account to browse for members, but you will not be able to send them an email without a premier account. You can, however, send them a icebreaker message.*

1. Sign in with your Yahoo username and password. If you do not have one, select "Sign Up" and you will be redirected to a Yahoo registration screen.

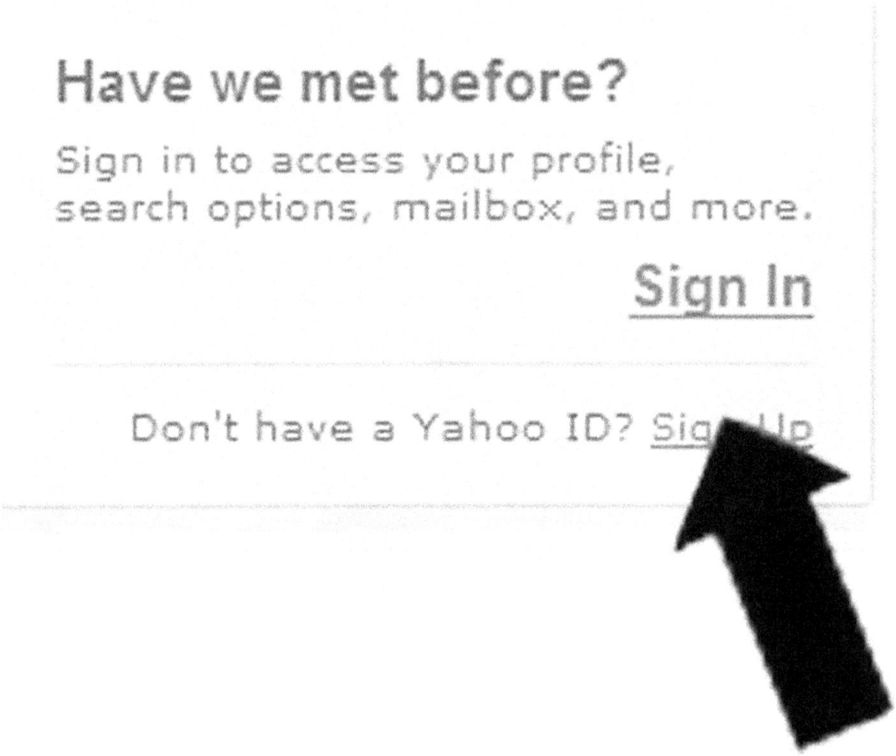

Have we met before?

Sign in to access your profile, search options, mailbox, and more.

Sign In

Don't have a Yahoo ID? Sig Up

2. After logging in, select "Create a Free Profile" at the top of the screen.

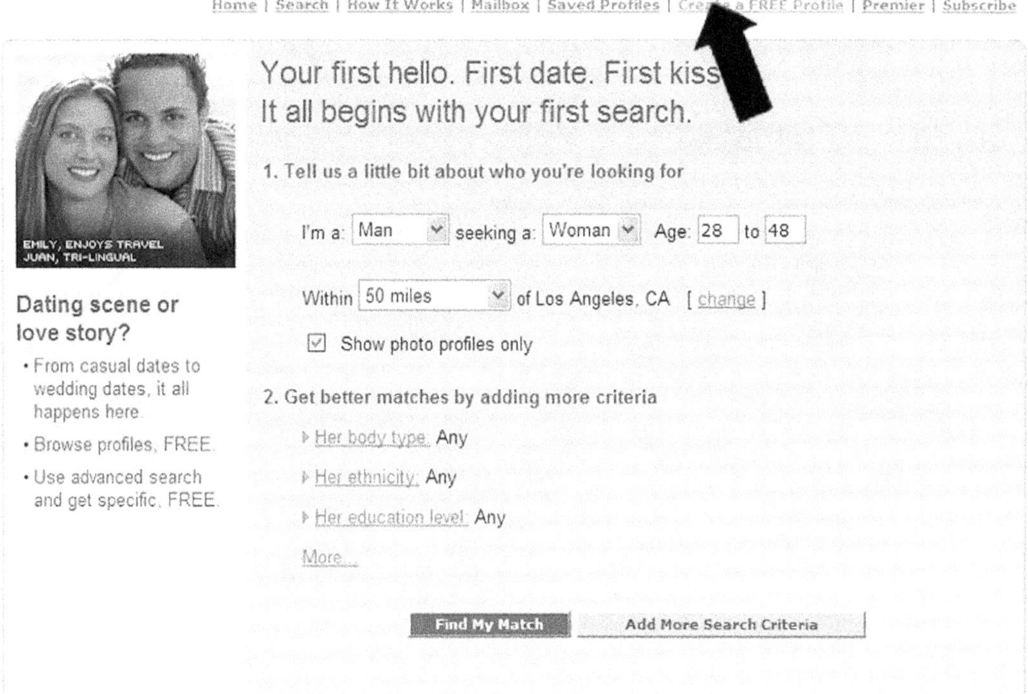

3. Complete the five part profile process.

Create A Profile

1 About Me (3 min)

Step 1: About Me

You're on your way... Creating a profile is simple!

Just five steps and you're done. Start by answering a few basic questions, and soon you'll be flirting via email. ∗ = required fields

∗ **My First Name** [Why?]

∗ **I am a** Man seeking a Woman

∗ **My ZIP/Postal Code**

∗ **My Birthdate** Month Day Year

MEGAN, 25, RUNNER
BRIAN, 26, BASEBALL PLAYER

Appearance

I consider myself Select One

I am Select One

My eyes are Select One

***Note:** Yahoo estimates 24 minutes for this process*

4. When your profile is created, you can either view matches in your area or begin a free trial. The trial will allow you to send and receive emails.

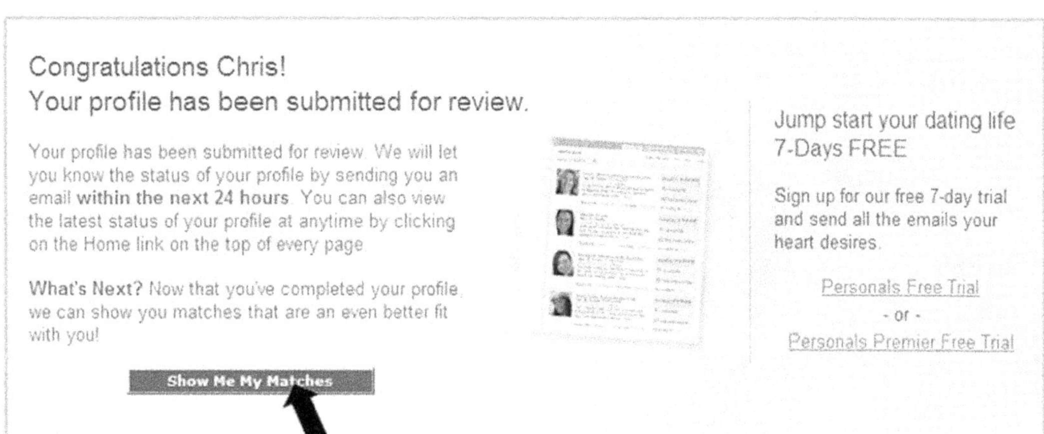

Congratulations Chris!
Your profile has been submitted for review.
Your profile has been submitted for review. We will let you know the status of your profile by sending you an email **within the next 24 hours**. You can also view the latest status of your profile at anytime by clicking on the Home link on the top of every page.
What's Next? Now that you've completed your profile, we can show you matches that are an even better fit with you!
Show Me My Matches
Jump start your dating life 7-Days FREE
Sign up for our free 7-day trial and send all the emails your heart desires.
Personals Free Trial
- or -
Personals Premier Free Trial

Using Yahoo Personals

1. The results screen will show you all of the members in the areas that you specified in the profile.

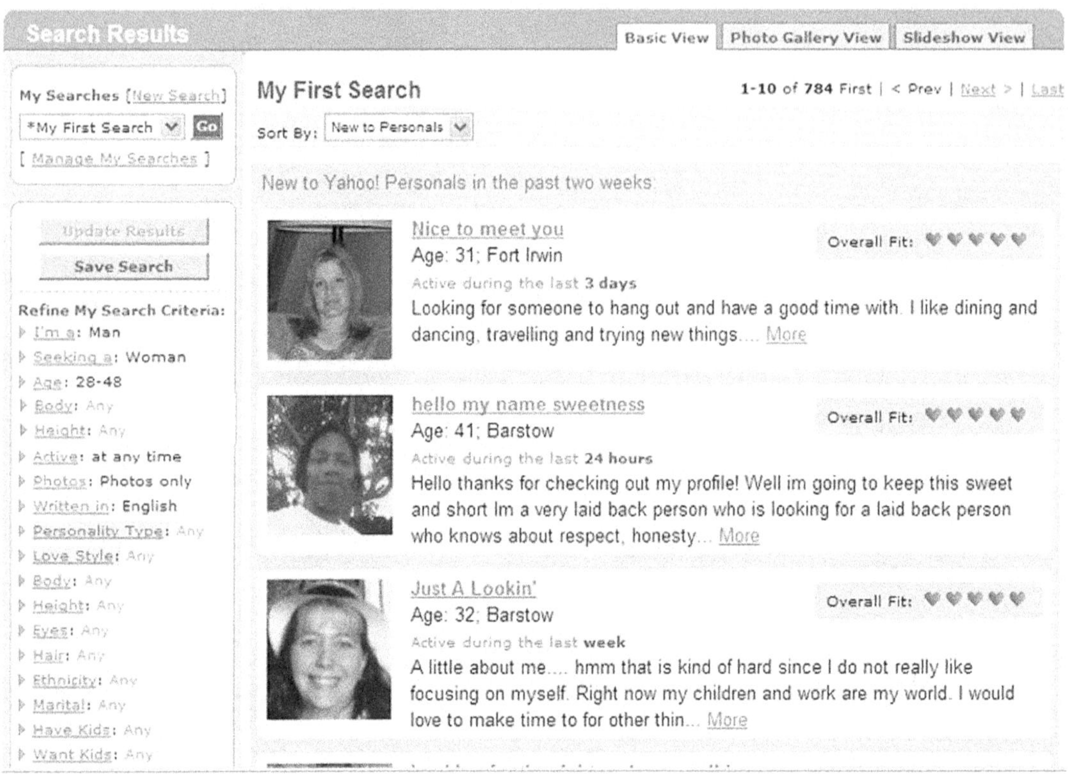

Check it out: *The panel on the left-hand side allows you to refine your search by attributes.*

Check it out: *The three tabs on the top of the screen allow you to change the views of your search results.*

2. Clicking on a user allows you to view the profile of your prospective date.

Home | Search | How It Works | Mailbox | Saved Profiles | My Profile | Premier | Subscribe

Profile Details: Back to Search Results

1 of 784 matches < Prev | Next >

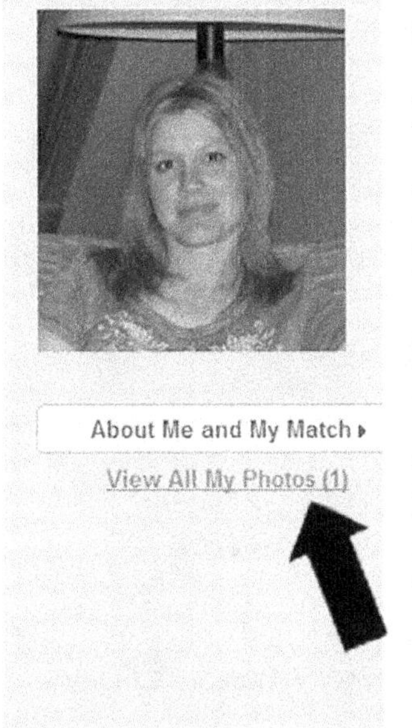

Nice to meet you

Age: 31; Fort Irwin, CA
Active during the last 3 days

About Me

First Name:	Heather
Gender:	Woman seeking a Man
Marital Status:	Divorced
Body Type:	Slender
Height:	5' 7"
Eyes:	Brown
Hair:	Light Brown
Ethnicity:	Caucasian (white)
Sense of Humor:	Clever / Quick Witted
Social Setting:	The life of the party
TV Watching:	Sitcoms, Dramas, Movies
Smoking:	Doesn't smoke
Drinking:	Drinks socially
Living Situation:	With kids
Have Kids:	Yes - at home full-time
Want (more) kids:	No
Education:	College Grad
Employment Status:	Full-time

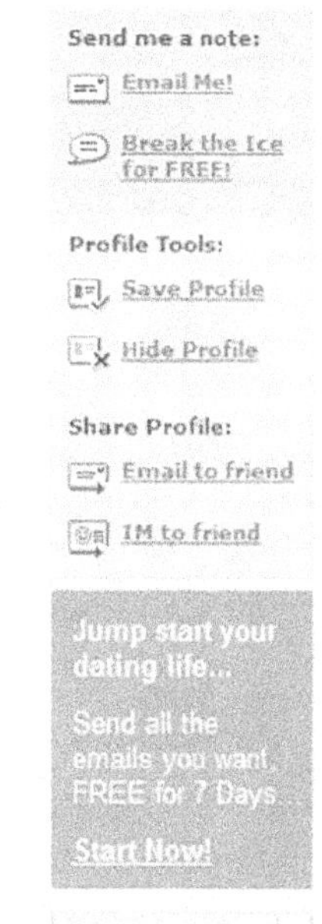

***Check it out:** The panel under the picture will allow you to view any additional photos.*

***Check it out:** The right-hand panel will allow you to email the member (if you have a premier account), send a free icebreaker, save or hide the profile or share the profile.*

3. Clicking "Home" on the upper tabs will bring you to your Yahoo Personals Home Page.

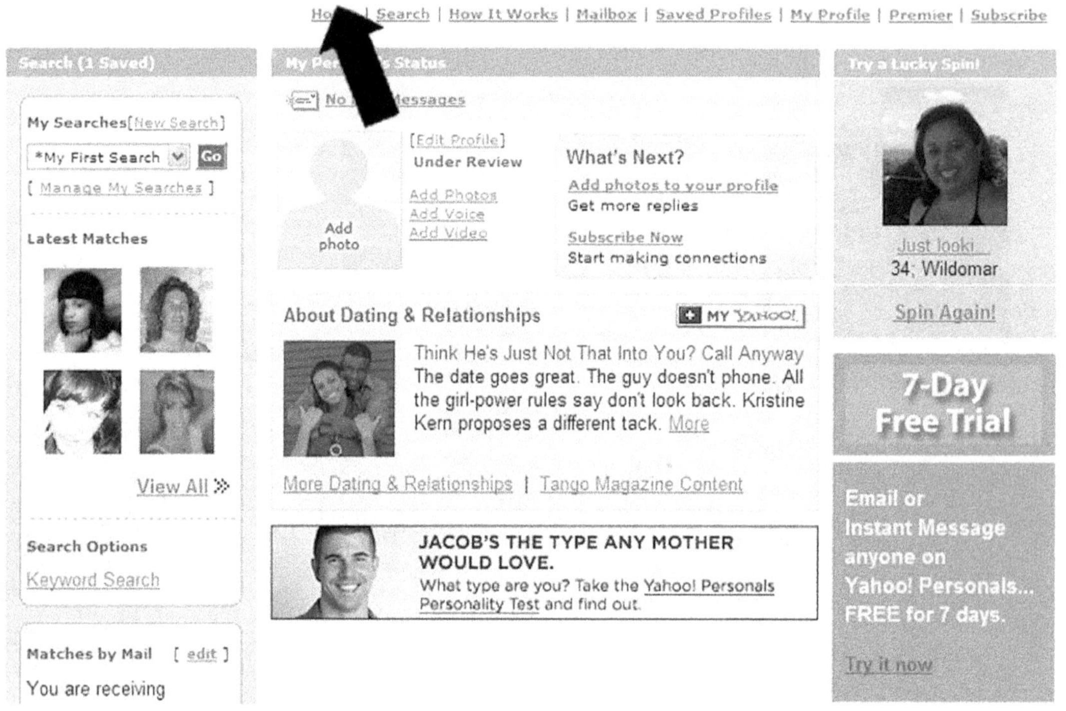

***Check it out:** Through the Home Page, you can add items, perform custom searches and access email.*

In 1998, I created a (FREE) online dating profile because online dating was very new and I was an early adopter. I thought it would be a wonderfully exciting way to meet new and interesting people - and it was indeed!

- Ashley U.

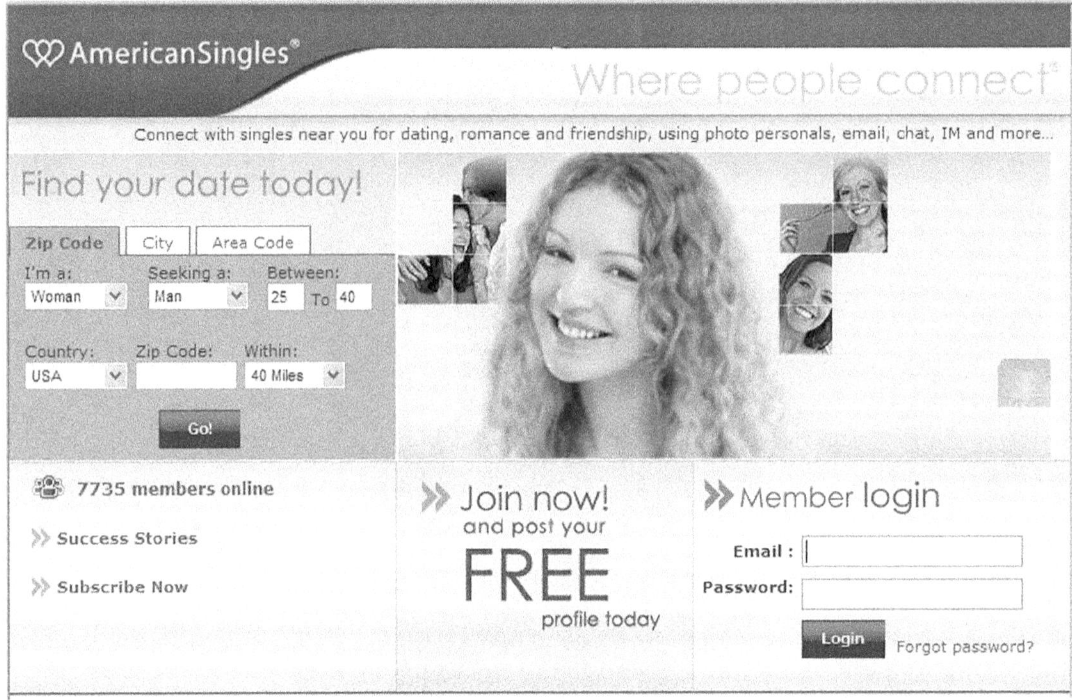

AmericanSingles.com

Quick facts:

Year Established:	1997
Number of members:	7 million
Number of photos allowed:	4
Best Feature:	"Click", which allows you to secretly find out if someone Returns your affections
Biggest Complaint:	Paid members are limited to 1500 characters in emails
Cost:	\$29.99-\$74.99
Services offered:	"Click", online personals, real-time chat and instant messaging
Wikipedia reference:	None

AmericanSingles.com has been on the scene since the inception of online dating, and boasts tens of thousands of singles online every day. Although the name would seem to imply that the site is only for Americans, there are a number of users from other countries. The majority of members, however, are American.

One of the sites greatest features is the historical information that is made available to the user. As a member, you are able to see who you have viewed in the past, who has viewed you, who has saved ("hot listed") your profile and the exchange of one line "teases".

One unique feature of AmericanSingles.com is that it allows access to the chat room to both members and non-members. You can also start your own chat room. The only major flaw in the chat room is that it is unmoderated and has a tendency to get overcrowded. To further the potential confusion, chat room users are able to highlight text and change font colors, which can make the chat difficult to read.

AmericanSingles.com seems genuinely interested in helping members find quality matches. From its easy to use interface and open ended communications system to its exhaustive advice section, AmericanSingles.com rates among the best of the net.

Signing up for AmericanSingles.com

1. To begin registration at AmericanSingles, click "Join Now". Note that you can search for free, but will not be able to communicate with other singles until you register.

2. Register on the site. This step does not create your profile, but records your basic information.

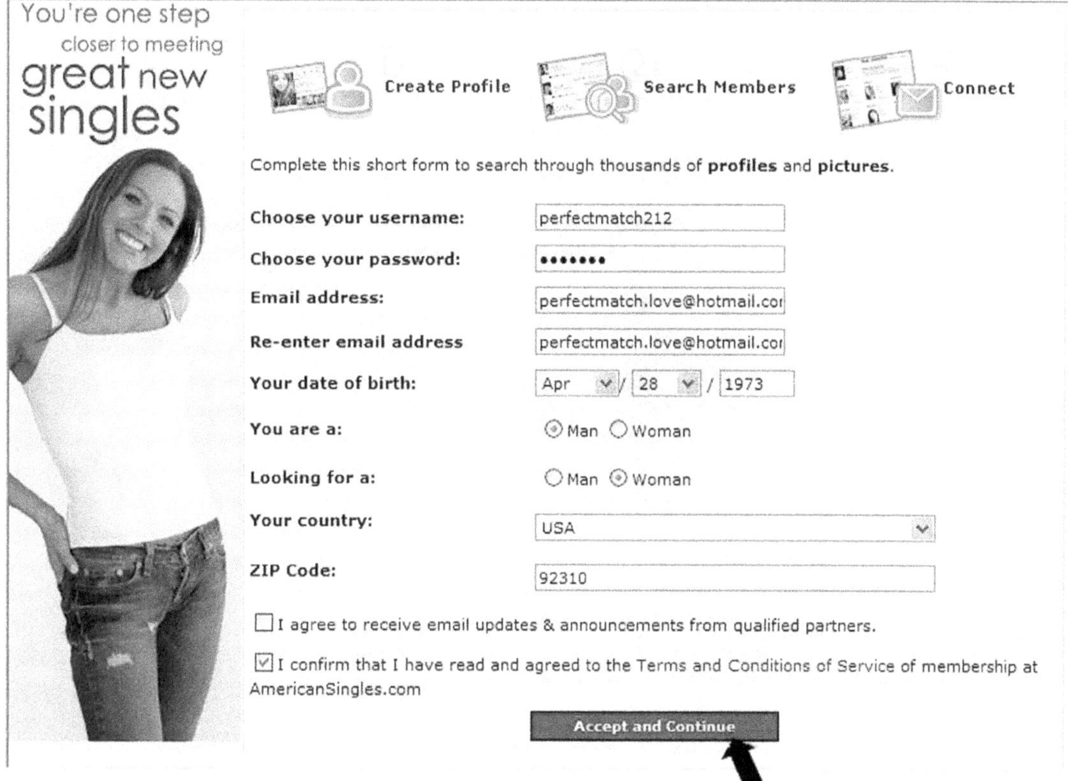

3. Now that you are registered, click "Complete Profile" to create your actual profile.

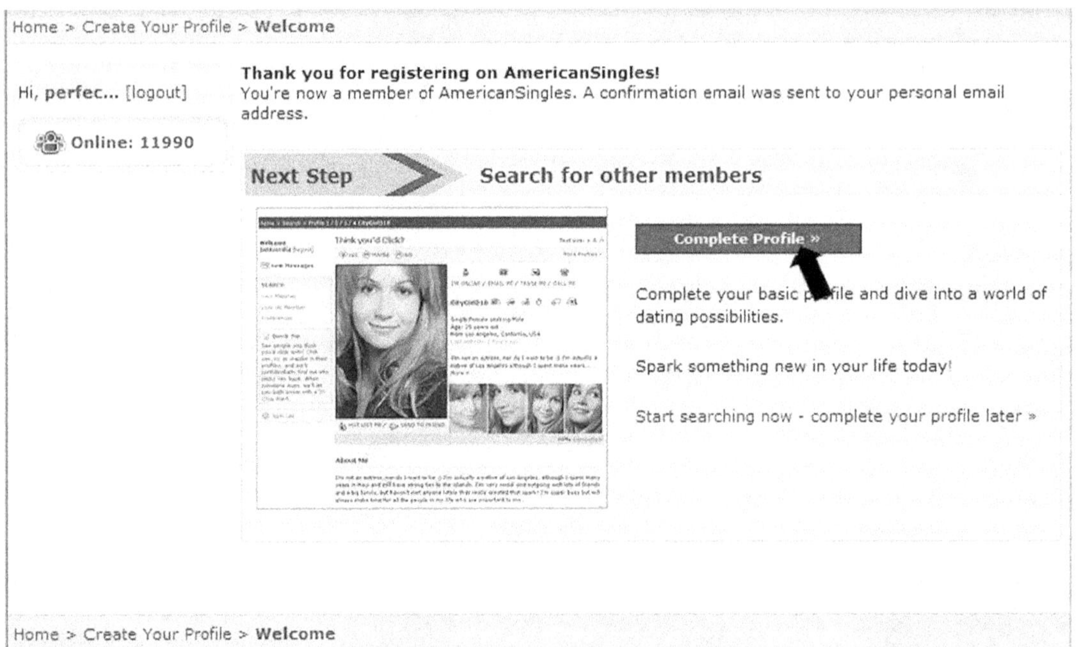

4. Complete the profile. Select which type of relationship you are seeking, such as long-term, friendship of physical.

Hi, perfec... [logout]

Online: 11803

CREATE PROFILE

Personal Info

» Basics

More About You

Interests

Your Photos

Quick Tip

Your profile tells others about you. It's only a few steps: so be sure your essay expresses the real you, and make sure every section is complete. And don't forget your photo!

Create Your Profile - Basics

LifeStyle

What type of relationship are you looking for? (check all that apply)

☐ A Date ☐ Friendship ☐ Marriage

☐ Long-term Relationship ☐ Intimacy/Physical Chemistry ☐ Marriage & Children

☐ Activity Partner ☐ Email/Chat

Would you relocate for the right person or relationship?

What is your current relationship status?

Do you have children?

Do you plan on having children? ○ Yes ○ No ○ Not sure

Your smoking habits: Your drinking habits:

People who know you would describe you as:

Physical Information

Your height: Your weight: Your body style:

***Check it out:** AmericanSingles has the distinctive feature of allowing the user to rate how important appearance and intelligence are in a potential match. If intelligence and appearance are selected as unimportant, this creates a larger pool of potential dates.*

Your height: 6'4"(193 cm)

Your weight: 134 lbs (61 kg)

Your body style:

Your hair color: Blonde

Your eye color: Blue

You think your appearance is: Most Important

Background

Where did you grow up? (optional)

Your ethnicity:

Languages you speak:

☐ Arabic	☐ Hebrew	☐ Romanian
☐ Bengali	☐ Hindi	☐ Russian
☐ Bulgarian	☐ Italian	☐ Spanish
☐ Chinese	☐ Japanese	☐ Swedish
☐ Czech	☐ Korean	☐ Tagalog
☐ Dutch	☐ Malay	☐ Thai
☑ English	☐ Norwegian	☐ Urdu
☐ Finnish	☐ Persian/Farsi	☐ Vietnamese
☐ French	☐ Polish	☐ Yiddish
☐ German	☐ Portuguese	☐ Other
☐ Greek		

Your religious background:

Your education level:

Your emphasis of studies or areas of interest: (optional)

You consider intelligence to be:

What do you do for a living?

5. Adding photos is optional, but highly recommended. To add photos at another time, select "Save" to complete the profile.

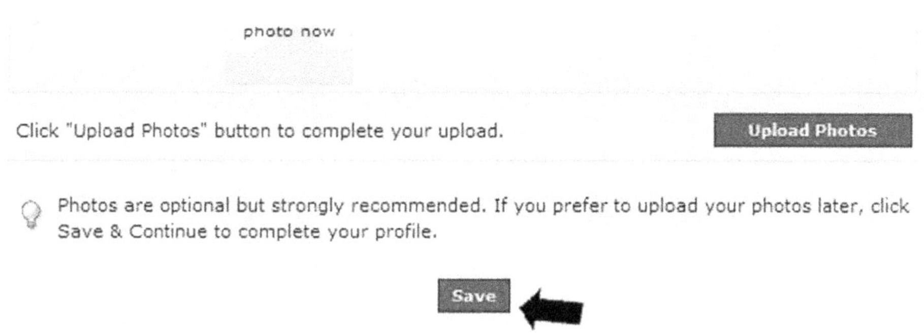

6. Once the profile is complete, you will be able to start searching right away.

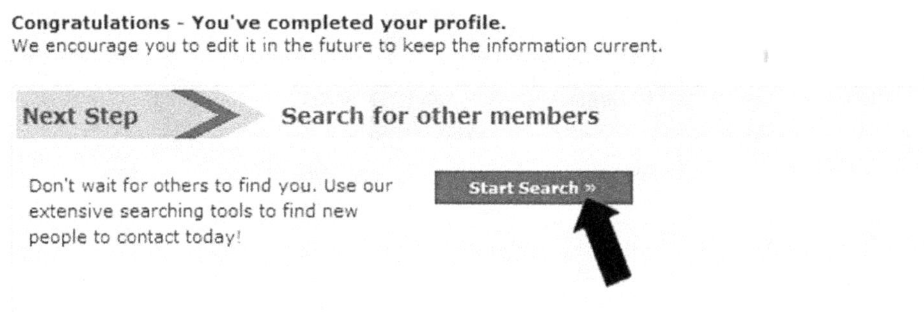

Using AmericanSingles.com

1. After completing the profile, you will be taken to your member Home Page. Your matches will be selected from members that are compatible with your profile and in your geographical region. From here, you can easily view profiles and communicate with members.

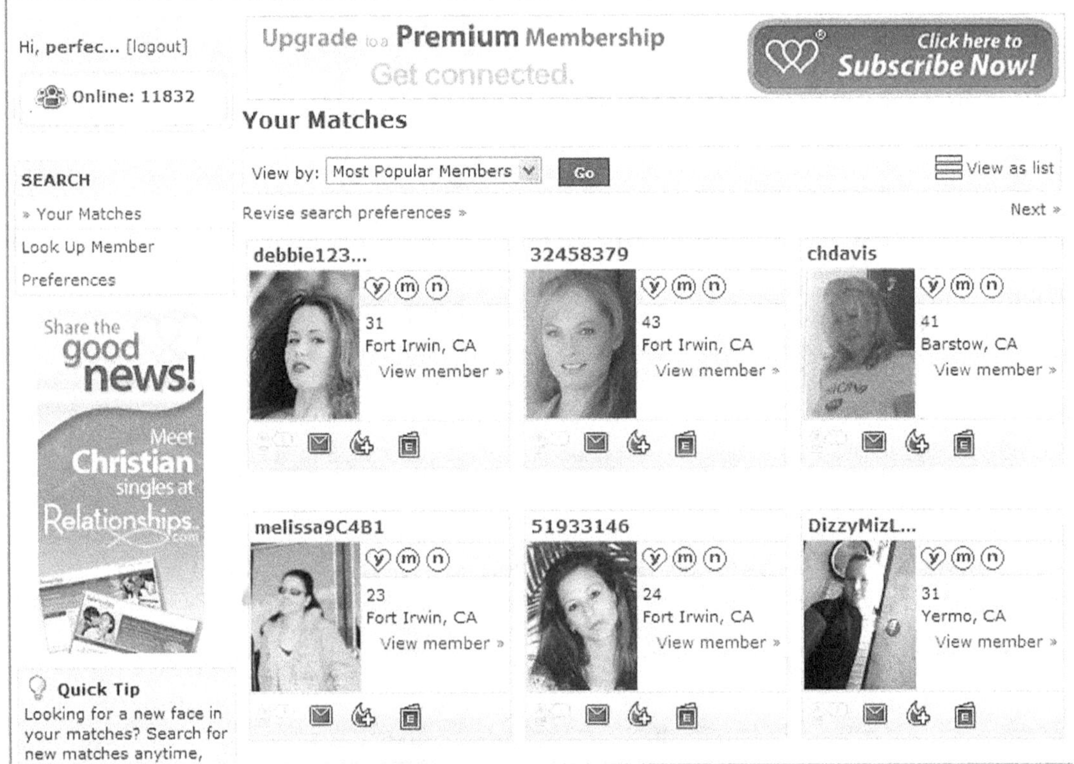

Check it out: *The envelope icon next to a match's name is a "click". When you "click" someone, your profile will be sent to them along with several randomly chosen decoy profiles. Once they receive your profile along with the others, they will be able to decide which ones they are interested in, and which ones they are not. If they choose you, you are both notified of a match.*

I wanted to give someone out there an idea of who I was, and what I believed in, hoping I'd find someone that had the same values, too.

- Debbie M.

BlackPeopleMeet®

The Black People Network

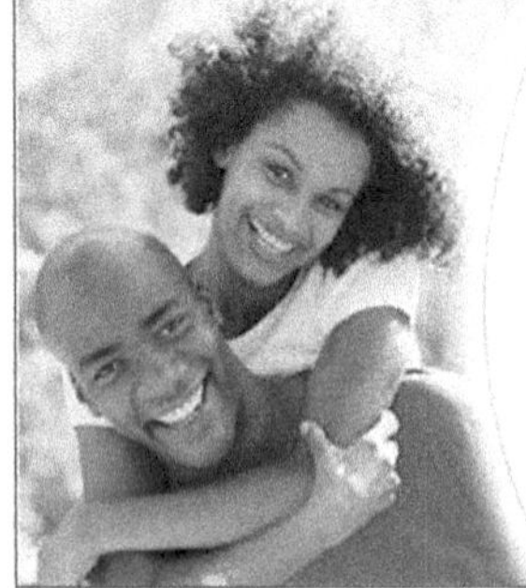

Meet Other Black Singles Today!

FREE TO BROWSE CLICK HERE »

Browse Pictures and Videos

Use Our Real Time Chat

Communicate Anonymously

Free to Initiate Contact

Sign Up Now! - Click Here!

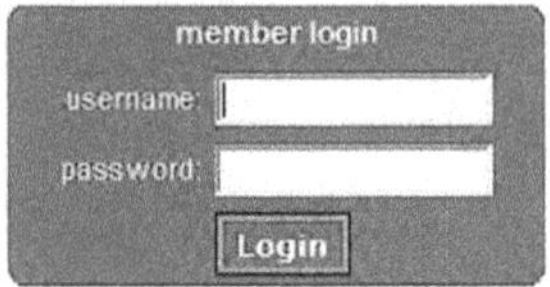

success stories!

I want to thank you all so much.I met the most beautiful woman through your service.We exchanged e-mails,talked on the phone and when I heard her,it ......

Pensacola,FL

more success stories

BlackPeopleMeet.com

Quick facts:

Year Established: 2000

Number of members: 7 million

Number of photos allowed: Does not specify. 6+ is common

Best Feature: Easy uploads of video, pictures and audio. Lots of storage space.

Biggest Complaint: Does not allow you to narrow searches past state, "buggy" interface

Cost: $9.95/month-$189.95/year

Services offered: Online personals, video and audio greetings.

Wikipedia reference: None

BlackPeopleMeet (Commonly referred to as "BPM") was founded in 2000 specifically to cater to the African American community. However, any race is able to join.

Online customer reviews range from glowing to scathing, mostly relating to the quality of matches. This is not surprising, however, given the popularity and relative low cost of the site. This means that there will be a far greater amount of high-quality and low-quality matches.

Although registration for the site is free, which allows browsing and basic searching, all other site functions can only be accessed by paid members. With this limitation, BPM can be considered a pay site.

Signing up for BlackPeopleMeet.com

1. The links on the Home Page are redundant. Clicking on "Free To Browse" and "Sign Up Now" both take you to the same registration page. You will not be prompted to upgrade until the profile is created.

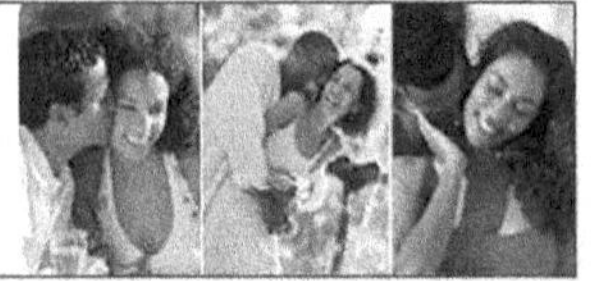

Meet Other Black Singles Today!
Browse Pictures and Videos
FREE TO BROWSE CLICK HERE
Use Our Real Time Chat
Communicate Anonymously
Free to Initiate Contact

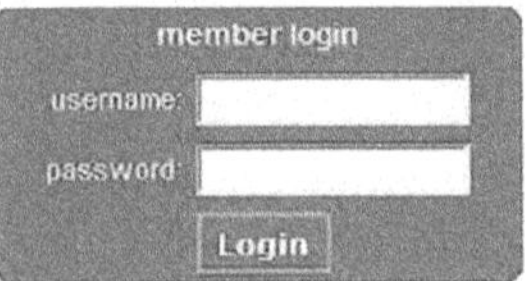

success stories!
I want to thank you all so much.I met the most beautiful woman through your service.We exchanged e-mails,talked on the phone and when I heard her,it .....
Pensacola,FL
more success stories

2. Complete the profile, beginning with site registration.

BlackPeopleMeet ® The Black People Network

Sign Up Now

Access our database of thousands of active members!

To begin choose a username and a password and then click continue.

Username:	(4-16 Characters - Letters / Numbers)
Password:	
Country:	USA

Already a Member? - Click Here

(Username and password must be between 4-16 ers in length
and should only contain letters, numbers, and not dashe ers or underscores.)

Continue >>

Tech Issues? Email us at contact@BlackPeopleMeet.com

BlackPeopleMeet.com WorldWideWeb pages are copyrighted by Zencon Technologies and may not be reproduced in any form without the expressed written consent of Zencon Technologies © 2000 - 2006.

Check it out: *After completing the profile, you will be taken to your Home Page. Notice the "Upgrade Special", counting down from ten minutes. Don't panic, it shows up every time you log in until you register.*

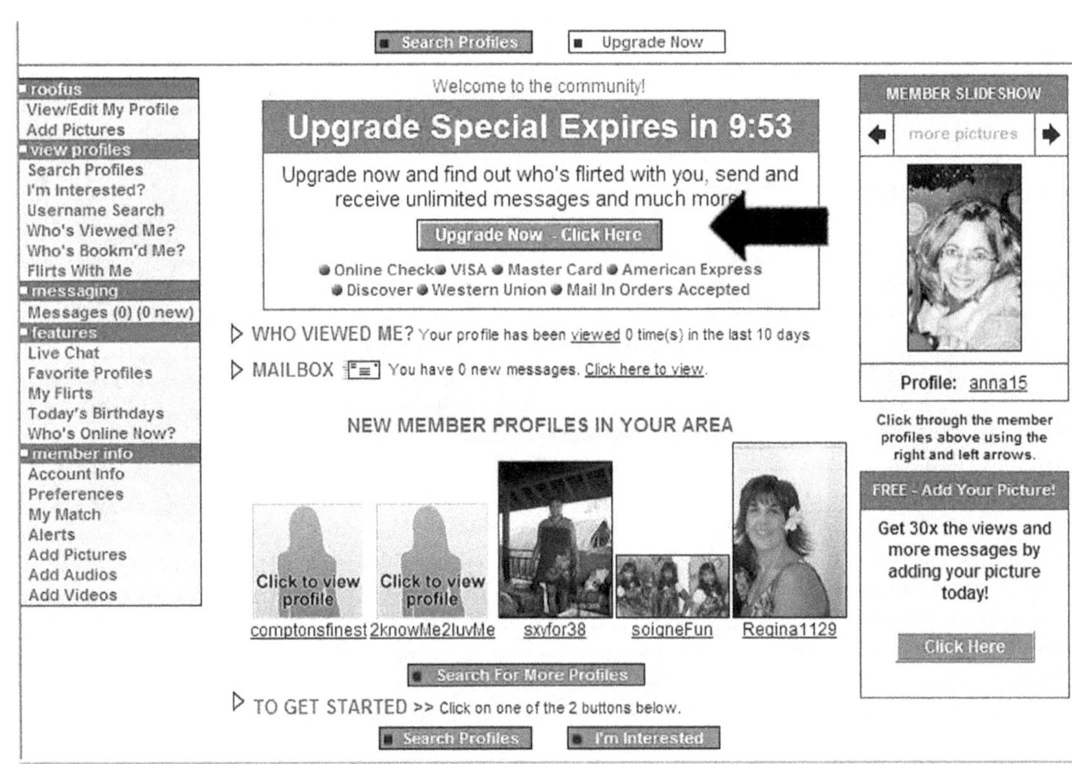

Using BlackPeopleMeet.com

Check it out: *You can view random profiles through the slide show.*

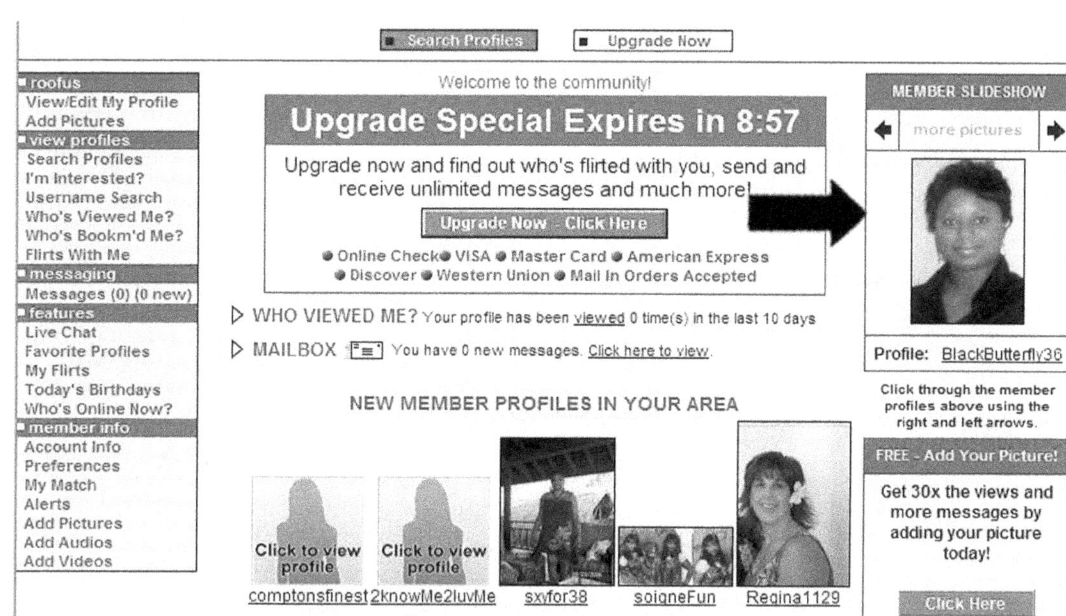

1. Clicking on a profile brings up a picture and bio of the person. Note the link for the photo album under the main image.

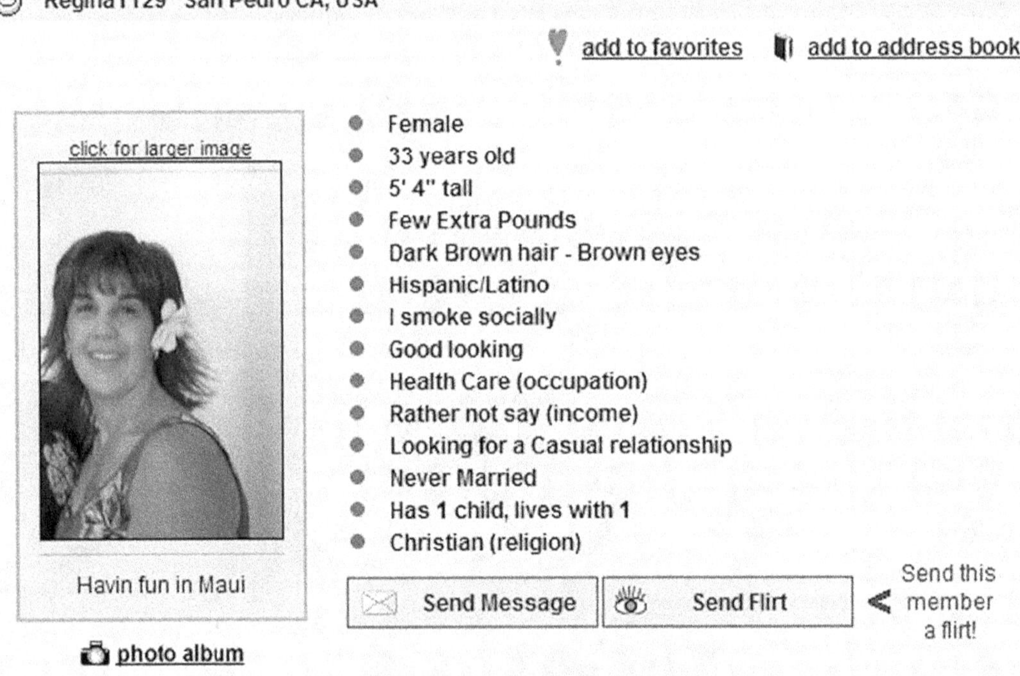

2. On the Home Page, you can search for users, or play "I'm Interested".

NEW MEMBER PROFILES IN YOUR AREA

teabuzzin reginasoul Coolblahblah ChynnaDolle Sistah05

Search For More Profiles

ARTED >> Click on one of the 2 buttons below.

Search Profiles I'm Interested

Check it out: *If you select "I'm Interested", you will be able to view random members and decide whether or not you want to view more information on them.*

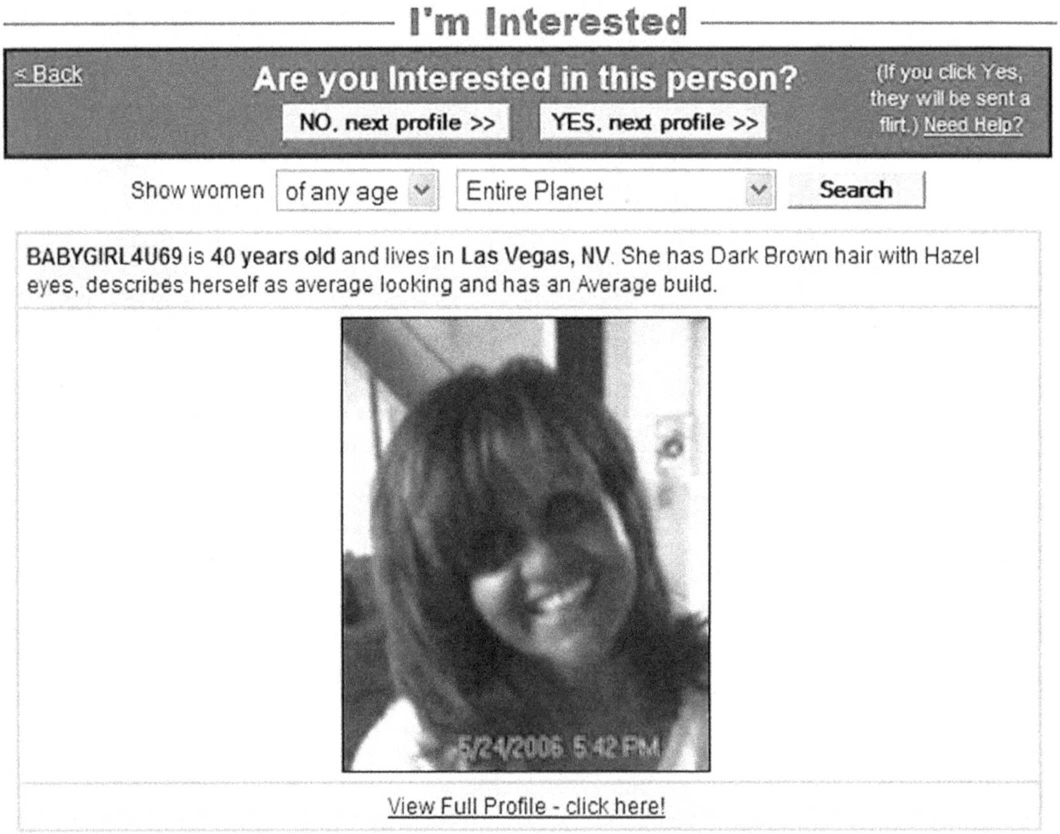

I'm Interested

< Back

Are you Interested in this person?

NO, next profile >> YES, next profile >>

(If you click Yes, they will be sent a flirt.) Need Help?

Show women | of any age | Entire Planet | Search

BABYGIRL4U69 is **40 years old** and lives in **Las Vegas, NV**. She has Dark Brown hair with Hazel eyes, describes herself as average looking and has an Average build.

5/24/2006 5:42 PM

View Full Profile - click here!

3. Also on the Home Page, you can add pictures, audio and video.

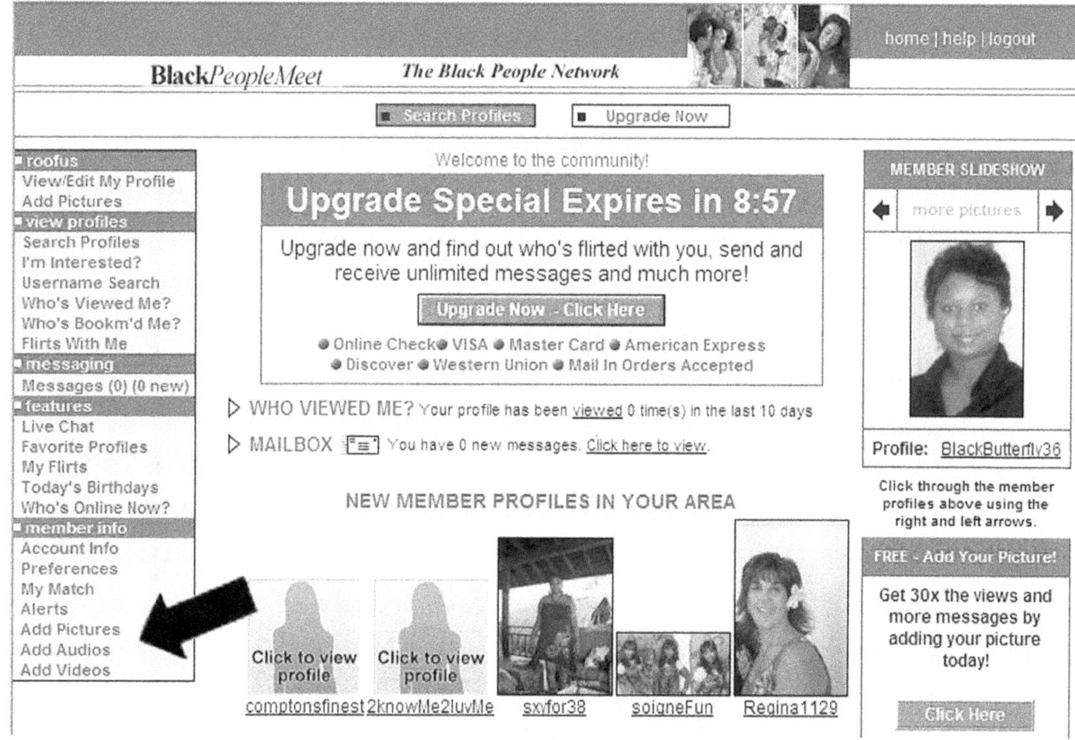

Check it out: *When uploading Audio, you can choose to do it over the phone or via computer microphone.*

Upload Your Audio

Go Back View Profile

Check it out: *Videos need to be uploaded from your hard drive*

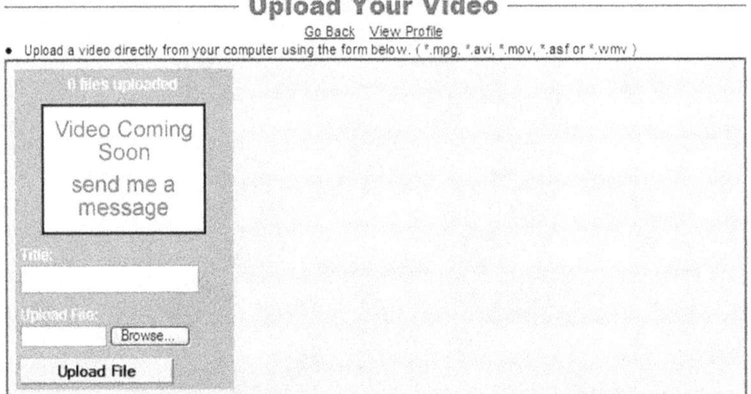

I know most people who resort to the Internet in their quest for love, especially young adults, tend to give the stock "I was tired of the local bar scene" justification. I, for one, was in no way tired of the local bar scene; I took advantage of it at every available opportunity. However, I found the selection of potential life mates at these watering holes less than appealing. Ditto for the church scene and the Young Republicans mixer scene. I thought I may as well put a little faith in technology. And besides, I thought if my story turned out to be a successful one, I might (just might) someday be able to one day submit a delightful satirization of the event to a collection of short stories on the subject.

- Will M.

Sign In | Tour | How It Works

chemistry
ONLINE

Spark something lasting.

Find someone who's looking for the **lasting relationship** you are. Our entirely new approach, based on science gets you **face-to-face**, so you can find out if that someone special has that something special.

Get Started Now

What makes Chemistry so different?

Take a closer look at how we use compatibility and science to provide you with personalized matches.

Stacie and Jay found chemistry

Married June 17th, 2006

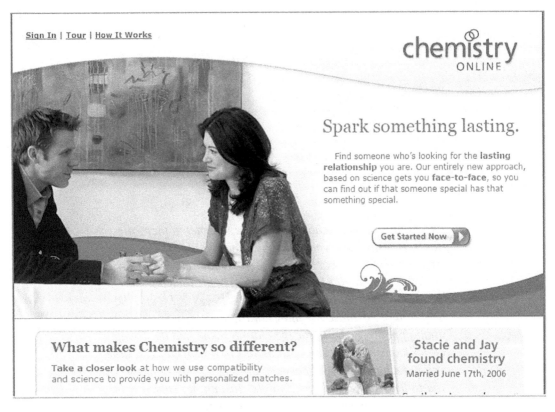

Chemistry.com

Quick facts:

Year Established:	2002
Number of members:	"Millions"
Number of photos allowed:	26 (images can be hidden until approved for a member)
Best Feature:	Extensive personality profile
Biggest Complaint:	Expensive
Cost:	$49.95/month-$26.65/month for 6 months
Services offered:	Online personals, personality profiles, guided communication process
Wikipedia reference:	None

Chemistry.com, a spin-off of Match.com, was founded with the same scientific foundation as eharmony.com. The philosophy behind chemistry.com is that, although people tend to be attracted to those with similar interests and beliefs, those connections tend to become platonic rather than romantic. Chemistry.com has pioneered a technique combining compatibility and chemistry.

To do this, Chemistry.com starts of with an in depth personality profile (called the "chemistry profile") to give you (and chemistry.com) an idea of your personality traits, what you desire in a mate and who you would likely fall in love with. You are then matched with singles who would compliment your personality traits, and with whom you would be a likely successful match.

If you agree with Chemistry.com's suggestions, and find someone that interests you, you can send out a "first-meeting" request, which relies on the site to coordinate a first date. After the date, you will be asked to provide feedback on your date. This allows chemistry.com to review their matching process and constantly improve their system.

This merging of science and compatibility has resulted in hundreds of thousands of successful matches for matches.

Signing up for Chemistry.com

1. To being, click "Get Started Now".

Sign In | Tour | How It Works

chemistry ONLINE

Spark something lasting.

Find someone who's looking for the **lasting relationship** you are. Our entirely new approach, based on science gets you **face-to-face**, so you can find out if that someone special has that something special.

Get Started Now

What makes Chemistry so different?

Take a closer look at how we use compatibility and science to provide you with personalized matches.

Stacie and Jay found chemistry

Married June 17th, 2006

2. Register for the site, then click "Begin" to start the test.

First, some basics...and then on to the test

Already a member? Sign In

First Name

Why do we ask for your first name?

Login Name

Password

Confirm Password

Email Address

Phone Number

Why do we ask for your number?

I am a — Choose

Seeking a — Choose

My Birth Date — Month — Day — Year

Country — United States

Zip/Postal Code

☐ A Chemistry Concierge may contact me.

☑ Send me special offers and partner promotions. I'd like to receive exclusive deals and timely updates from selected partners.

☐ I am at least 18 years old and have read and agree to Chemistry's Terms of Use and Privacy Policy.

Promotion Code

If you have a promotion code, enter it here.

Begin

3. The test will include many traditional questions, such as likes and dislikes, as well many unique questions, such as the relative size of your fingers.

Help Sign Out

chemistry CONCIERGE™ Questions? 866-610-MEET

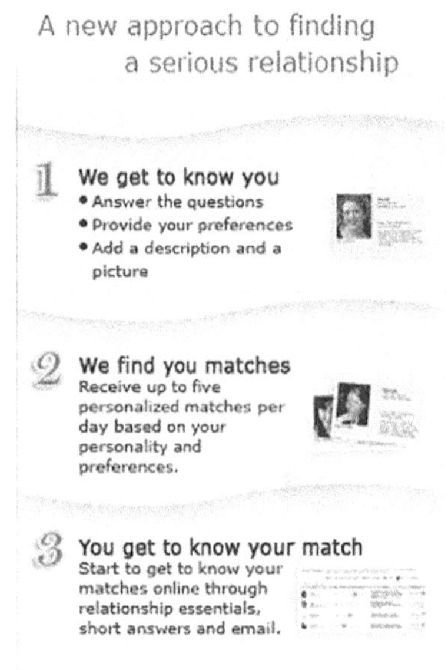

A new approach to finding a serious relationship
1 We get to know you
• Answer the questions
• Provide your preferences
• Add a description and a picture
2 We find you matches
Receive up to five personalized matches per day based on your personality and preferences.
3 You get to know your match
Start to get to know your matches online through relationship essentials, short answers and email.

Get Started by taking our fun and interactive profile. Upon completion, you'll see your first matches!

Question 1

Which one of the following images most closely resembles your left hand?

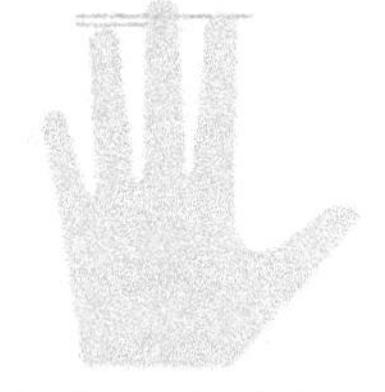

Index finger slightly longer than ring finger

○

Index finger about the same length as ring finger

○

Check it out: *The questions are interesting and distinctive. You are asked several times to pick out your interpretation of an image.*

Help Sign Out

chemistry ONLINE

chemistry CONCIERGE™ Questions? 866-610-MEET

Non-Verbal Communication: 1

9% Complete

Self Perception
Page 1 of 5

What is the relationship between these two people?

- ○ They are co-workers discussing a business issue.
- ○ They are siblings planning a family event.
- ○ They are old college friends catching up.
- ○ They are new acquaintances getting to know each other.
- ○ They are a long-married couple on vacation.

Save and Continue

4. The stage at which you describe your ideal match will introduce the significance slider. When this is present, you will be able to rate how important that question is to you. For instance, in this question, you can declare how important race is to your decision.

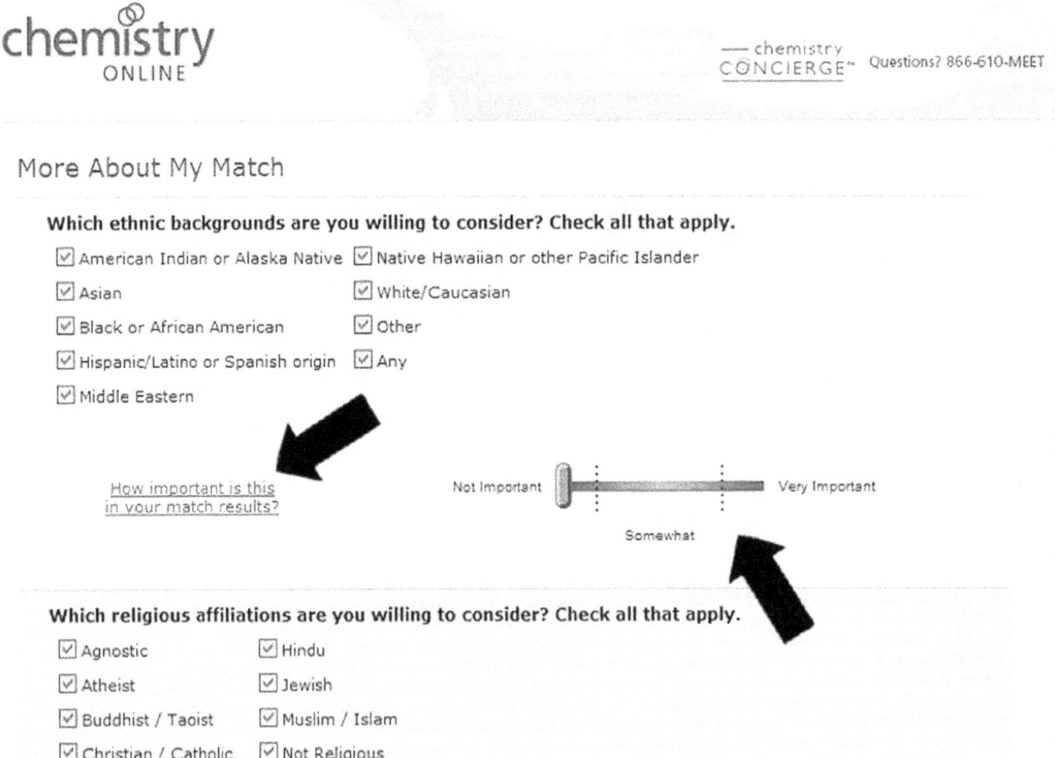

Using Chemistry.com

1. After registration, Chemistry.com will display your matches. Click "Review Profile" to get more information on a match.

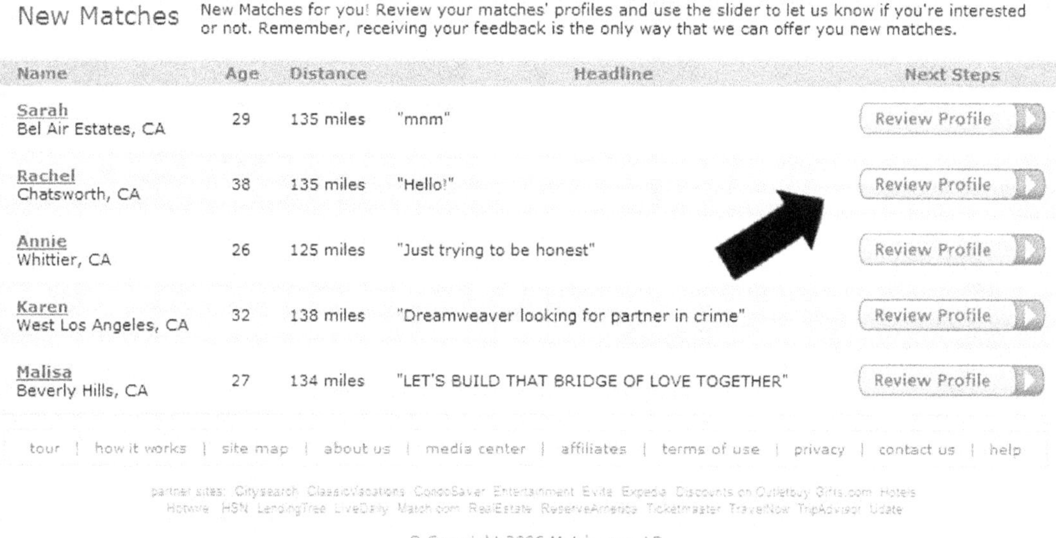

New Matches
New Matches for you! Review your matches' profiles and use the slider to let us know if you're interested or not. Remember, receiving your feedback is the only way that we can offer you new matches.
Name
Age
Distance
Headline
Next Steps
Sarah
Bel Air Estates, CA
29
135 miles
"mnm"
Review Profile
Rachel
Chatsworth, CA
38
135 miles
"Hello!"
Review Profile
Annie
Whittier, CA
26
125 miles
"Just trying to be honest"
Review Profile
Karen
West Los Angeles, CA
32
138 miles
"Dreamweaver looking for partner in crime"
Review Profile
Malisa
Beverly Hills, CA
27
134 miles
"LET'S BUILD THAT BRIDGE OF LOVE TOGETHER"
Review Profile
tour | how it works | site map | about us | media center | affiliates | terms of use | privacy | contact us | help
© Copyright 2006 Match.com, LP.

2. After viewing the photo and profile, you can rate your interest in the person. Once you have done so, click "Continue" to go to the next step.

Get to Know Sarah

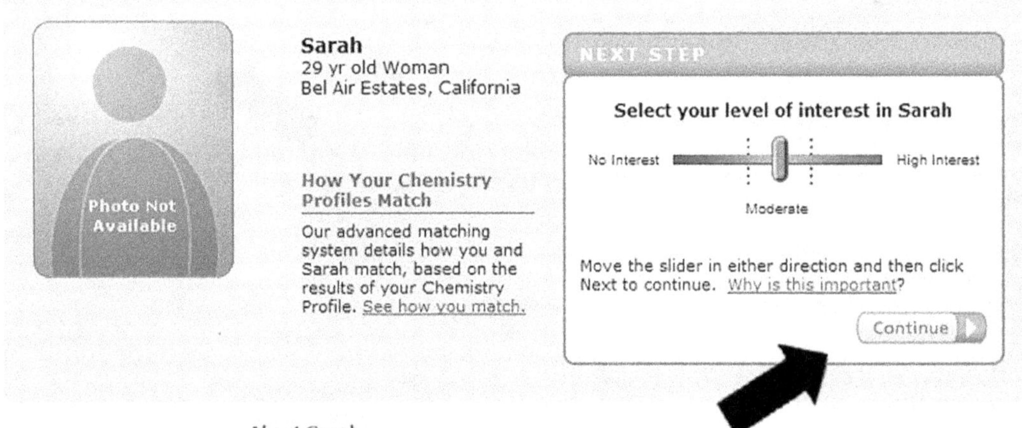
Photo Not Available
Sarah
29 yr old Woman
Bel Air Estates, California
How Your Chemistry Profiles Match
Our advanced matching system details how you and Sarah match, based on the results of your Chemistry Profile. See how you match.
NEXT STEP
Select your level of interest in Sarah
No Interest
High Interest
Moderate
Move the slider in either direction and then click Next to continue. Why is this important?
Continue

About Sarah

Profession/Occupation: Production Coordinator

Height: 5'6"

Eyes: Green

Build: Curvy

Hair Color: Light brown

Full Profile

I just wanted to see what my personality would be after hearing about it on TV, quite sad really. Interesting personality perspective, although there only seemed to be positive things to say which is why I think so many people may like it.

Looking for:	25 to 45 year old Man within 100 miles of Bel Air Estates, California
Relationship history:	Single (never been married)
Ethnic background:	White/Caucasian
Body type:	Curvy
Height:	5'6"

3. You can either archive this match to view later, or make the match active.

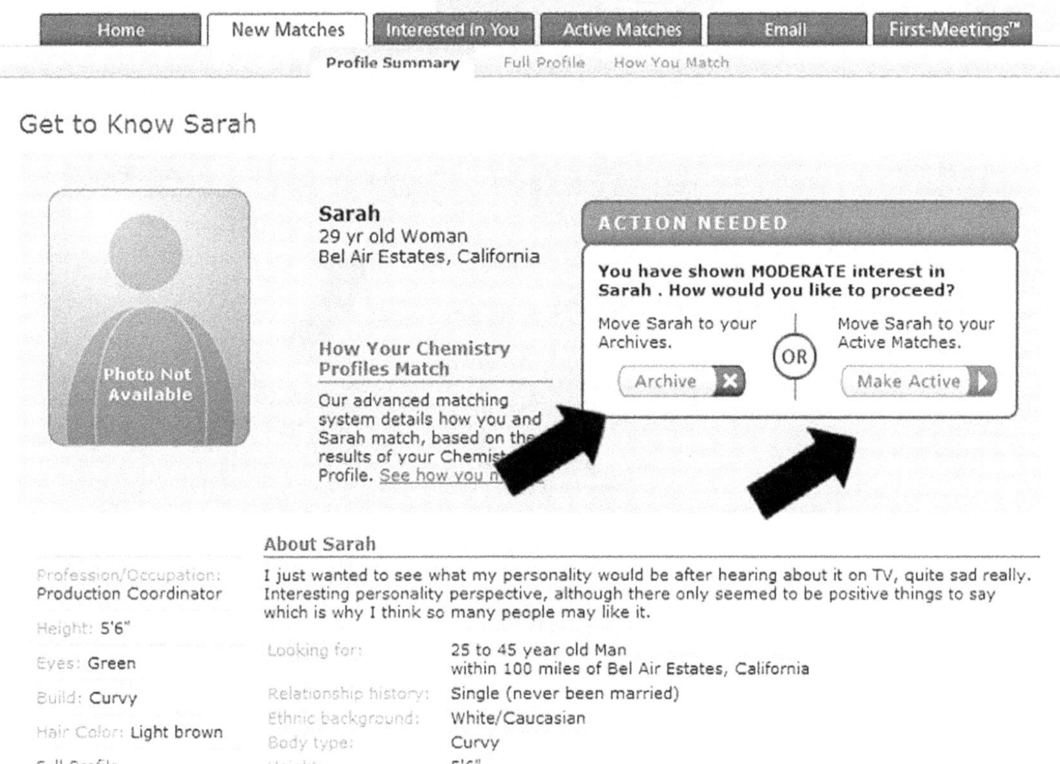
Home
New Matches
Interested in You
Active Matches
Email
First-Meetings™
Profile Summary
Full Profile
How You Match
Get to Know Sarah
Photo Not Available
Sarah
29 yr old Woman
Bel Air Estates, California
How Your Chemistry Profiles Match
ACTION NEEDED
You have shown MODERATE interest in Sarah . How would you like to proceed?
Move Sarah to your Archives.
Archive
OR
Move Sarah to your Active Matches.
Make Active
About Sarah
Profession/Occupation: Production Coordinator
Height: 5'6"
Eyes: Green
Build: Curvy
Hair Color: Light brown
Full Profile
I just wanted to see what my personality would be after hearing about it on TV, quite sad really. Interesting personality perspective, although there only seemed to be positive things to say which is why I think so many people may like it.
Looking for: 25 to 45 year old Man within 100 miles of Bel Air Estates, California
Relationship history: Single (never been married)
Ethnic background: White/Caucasian
Body type: Curvy
Height: 5'6"

4. Finally, you can view a report on why that person was selected as a potential match. You can view your personality profile, as well as theirs.

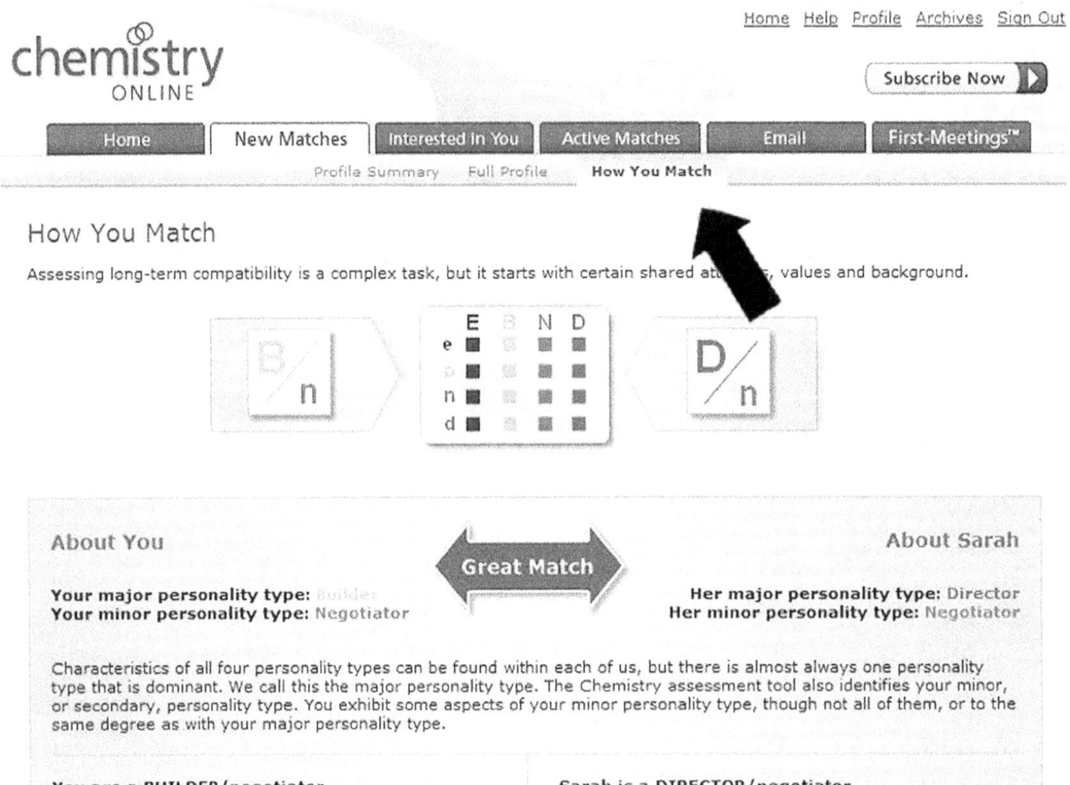

I needed the chance to show my soul and mind first. They were my best assets. The rest of me I wasn't so sure about. In person, my obsessive worries about my appearance or my awkwardness gummed up my wit and charm. Online, I was in control of all of it, and could reveal each bit when I felt comfortable.

- Therese O.

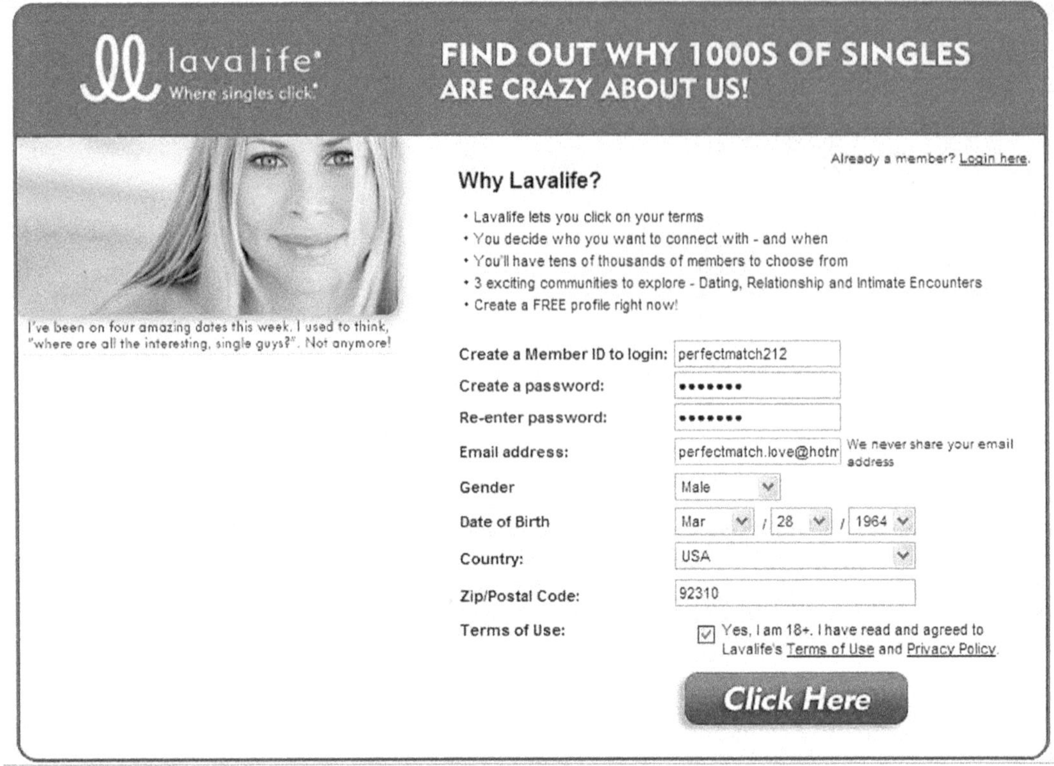

LavaLife.com

Quick facts:

Year Established:	1987 (as webpersonals until 2001)
Number of members:	Unreported
Number of photos allowed:	10
Best Feature:	Many Free features with "pay for play" plans.
Biggest Complaint:	Site can be slow
Cost:	$14.99/50 credits - $39.99/200 credits
Services offered:	Online personals, compatibility reports, casual encounter search
Wikipedia reference:	http://en.wikipedia.org/wiki/Lavalife

Lavalife (or Webpersonals until 2001) stands alone among online dating sites. The most notable feature of Lavalife is the fact that registration is free and there are no monthly fees. This is because most contact with other members of the site requires the use of credits. As a free member, you can reply to messages and view videos, but sending emails or instant messages require expending credits.

The credits do allow substantial time for communications, however. The first email message is six credits, and all subsequent messages to the same recipient are free. Six credits buy a twenty minute instant messaging session, and twelve credits buy an hour. Two credits will extend your chat time by five minutes.

Lavalife allows great flexibility in match searches. There is no compatibility profile, as is in many online dating sites, so the user is forced to use their own judgment to make a match. Users can search for friendships, long-term relationships or casual encounters. When coordinating a casual encounter, there are several options to narrow the search, including blindfolds, spankings and aggressiveness.

Again, unique to Lavalife, is the ability to hide or change your profile name. You can also log in without an active profile name, allowing you to chat in a hidden mode. This would allow the user to "start over" after meeting an undesirable match.

Signing up for Lavalife

1. To begin, enter your basic information, and select "Click Here"

2. Most successful matches require some communication, so it will be necessary to purchase credits to begin.

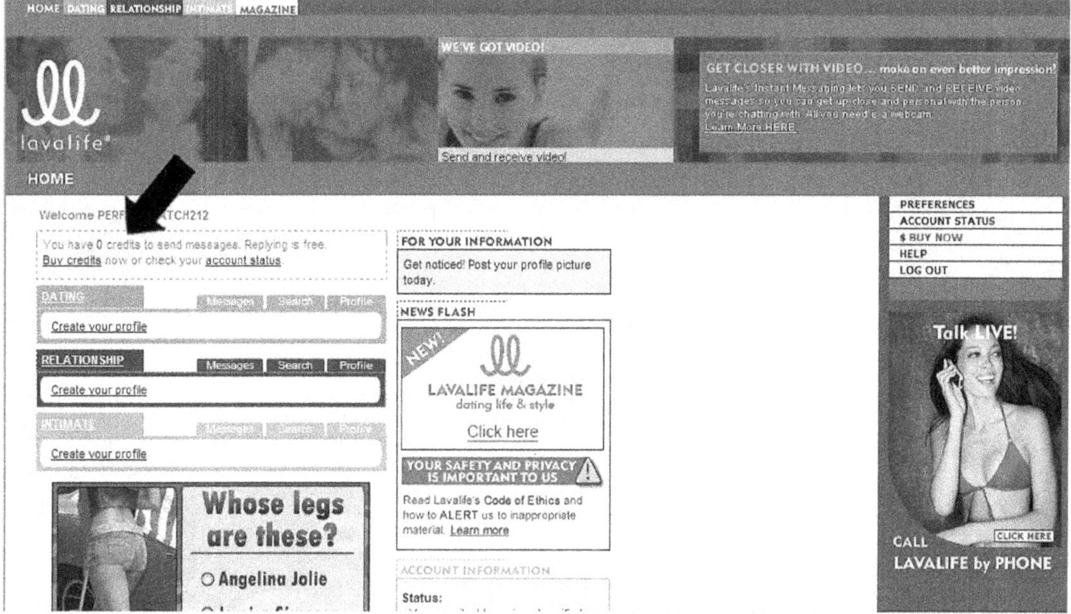

3. At the credit purchase screen, select the amount of credits desired and the payment option.

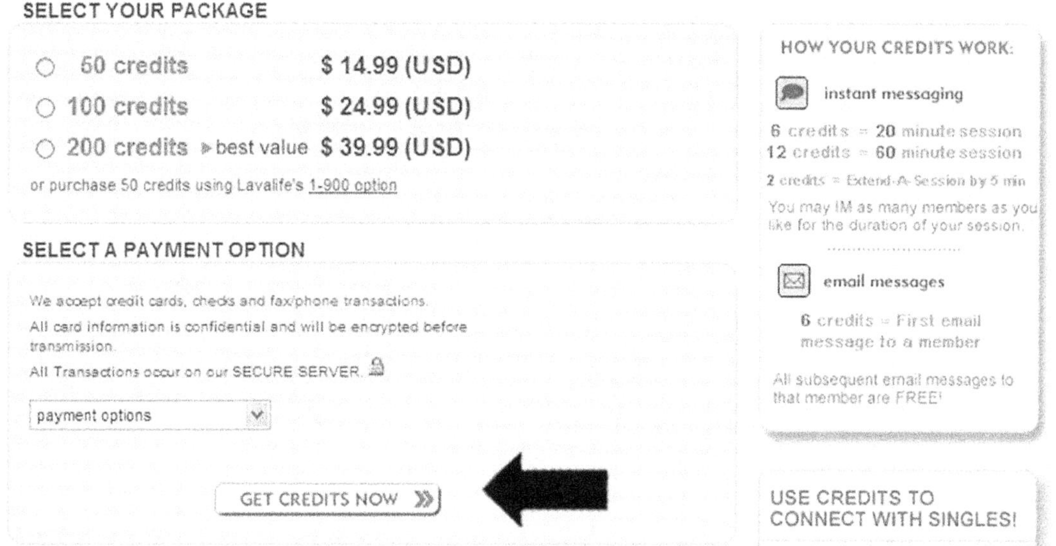

4. With credits, and back at the Home Page, let's look at the profiles. You can create a profile in any of the three categories. Once you create a profile, you will be able to receive matches in that category.

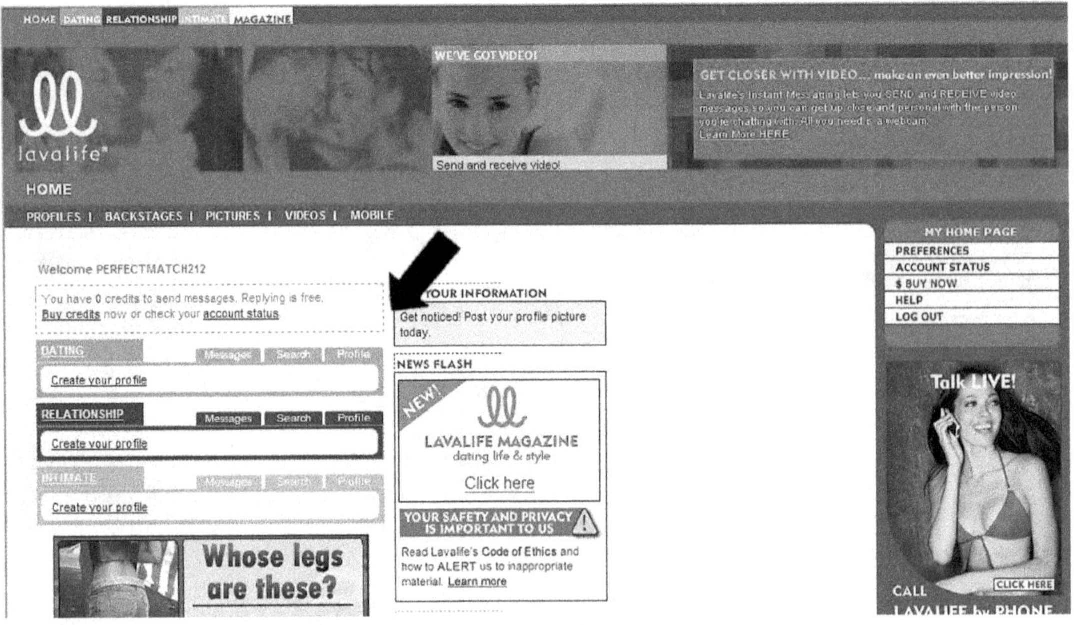

5. When creating a profile, each category will ask similar questions. However, it is necessary to create a profile in each category that you would like to become involved in.

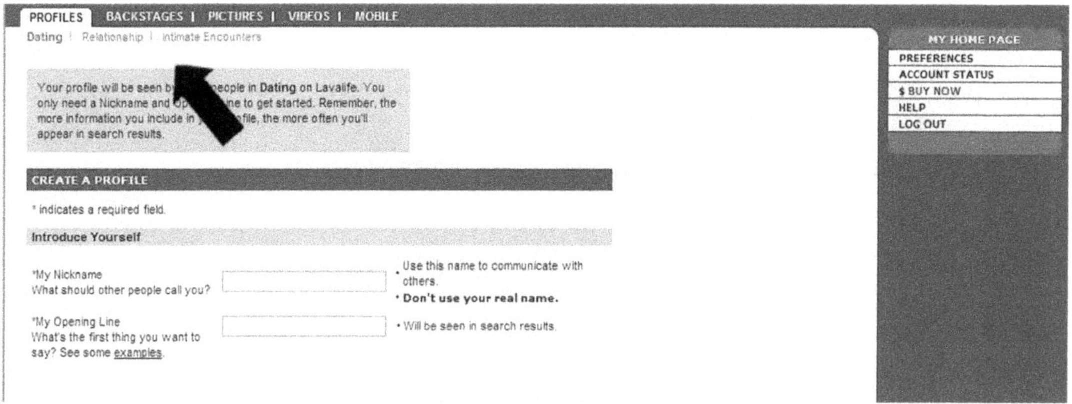

Check it out: *After the profile is created, you can choose whether or not your profile is visible to other users.*

Profile Preferences

Choose whether or not to display your profile to others. The more members who see you, the more messages you'll get! Selecting **Hide Always** means your profile will only be shown to those you communicate with.

- Show always
- Show only when online
- Hide always

Using Lavalife

1. Once the profile is created, continue on to the main category. In this case, click "Dating now".

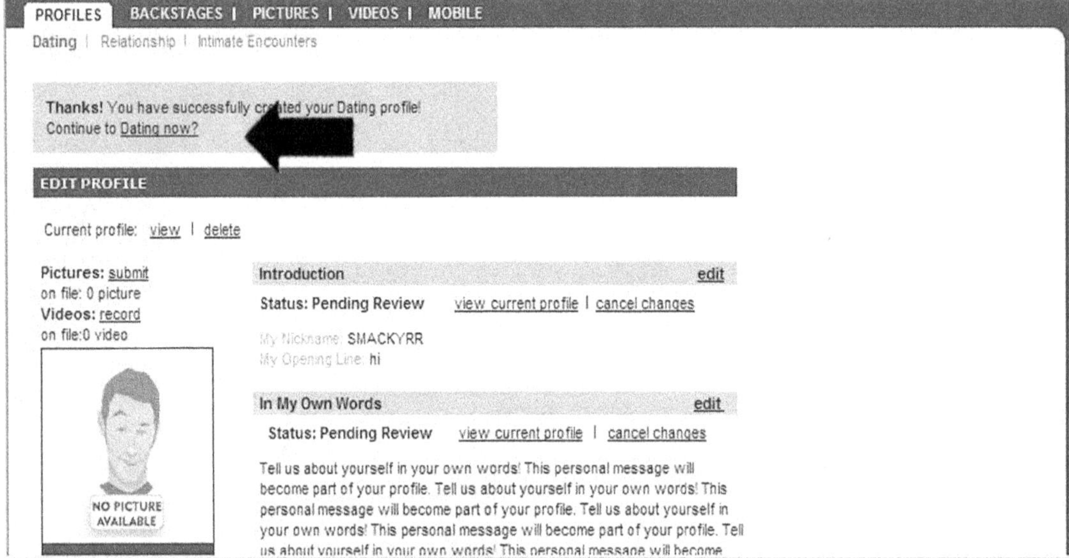

2. On the profile Home Page, you can quickly view profiles using the slide show.

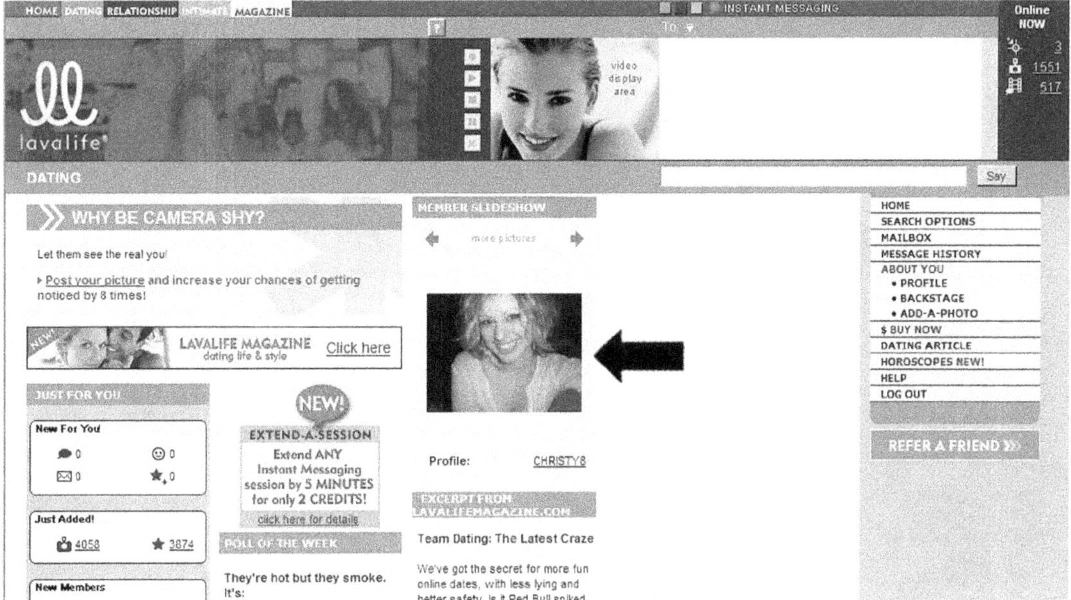

3. Back at your Home Page, select "Browse" to browse a list of members.

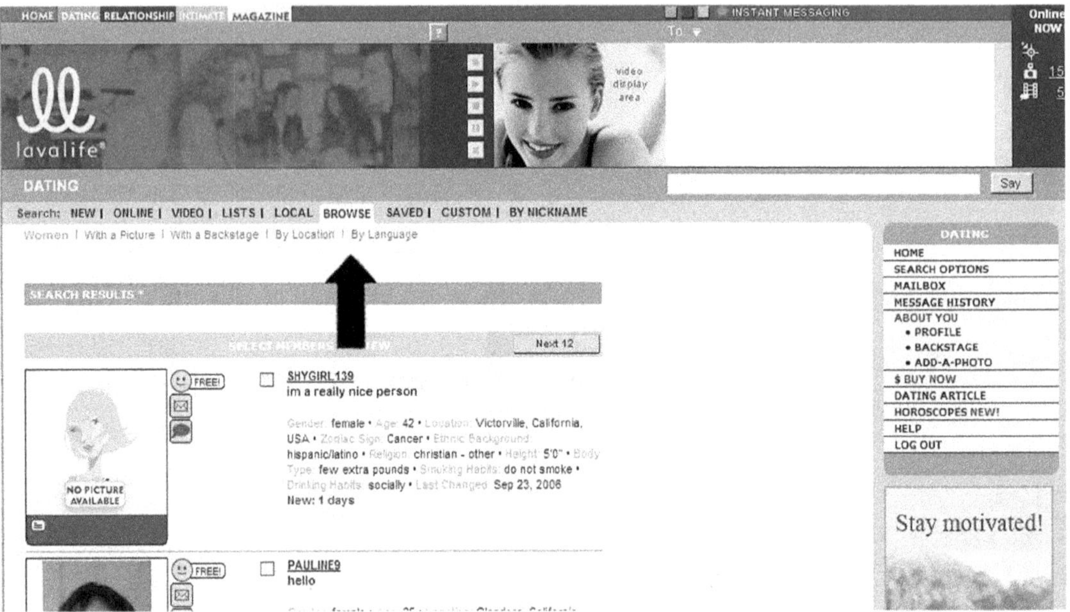

4. Chat is always active in the title bar. This allow you to chat with other singles in the chat room

Check it out: *Text "join" to 25425 will sign you up for Lavalife mobile, allowing you to browse singles and send text messages from your cell phone.*

I live in a remote small town. I got tired of spending time getting all dolled up only to spend more time driving a far distances to get to "meeting places" where I would talk to maybe two guys a night. Rather than a lot of wasted time hoping I would meet someone, I could sit with a mud mask on my face, my hair in curlers, and in my pajamas while I set up several "meet and greets" in the same day. Online dating is more of a practical resource in time management.

- Gesyka R.

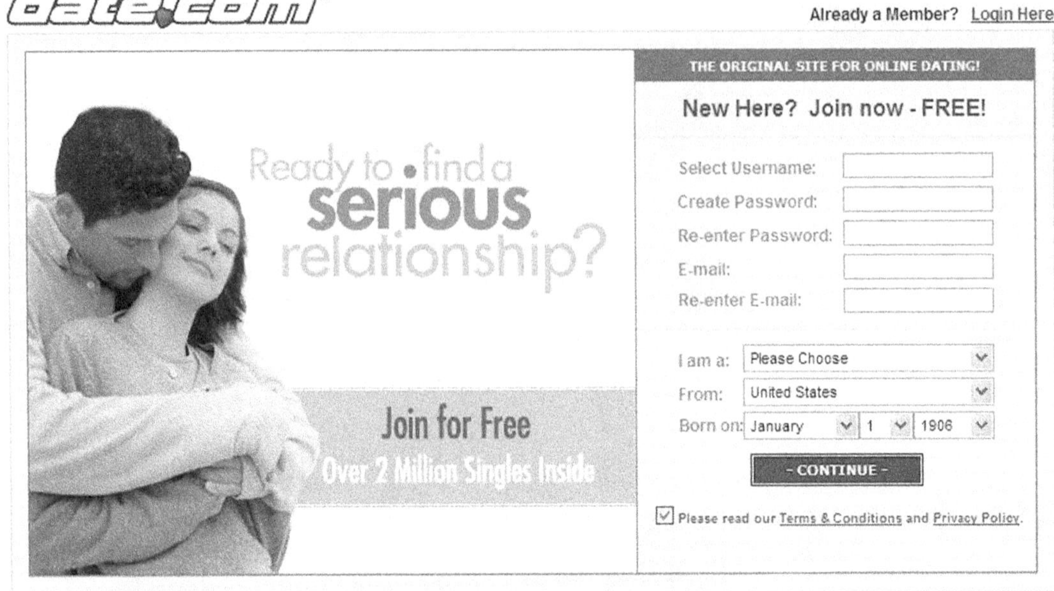

Date.com

Quick facts:

Year Established:	1997
Number of members:	2 Million +, reportedly adding 250,000 members a month
Number of photos allowed:	4
Best Feature:	Large article database, strong search features
Biggest Complaint:	Few compatibility analysis categories
Cost:	$24.95/30 days- $99.95/1 year
Services offered:	DatingMobile, optional computerized auto matching
Wikipedia reference:	None

Date.com was founded on Valentines Day of 1997 and has proven to be very successful, with 50 marriages last year alone, and 250,000 members added every month. Perhaps accounting for this popularity is the wide range of search options: you can search for matches using over 100 optional search criteria.

The only major flaw in the Date.com system is the relative few compatibility analysis categories. Whereas many sites allow you to specify hobbies, interests, religion, etc, Date.com only collects the most basic information. However, there are several text fields which allow users to answer open ended questions about their personality.

Another strength for Date.com is the user friendly navigation. All of the user controls are placed right on the user Home Page, allowing easy navigation for searches and account administration. Also, customer support is among the best with a substantial FAQ and fast email responses.

Signing up for Date.com

1. To begin, complete the registration form and click "Continue"

2. Complete the profile, including geographical information, as well as open ended questions about yourself.

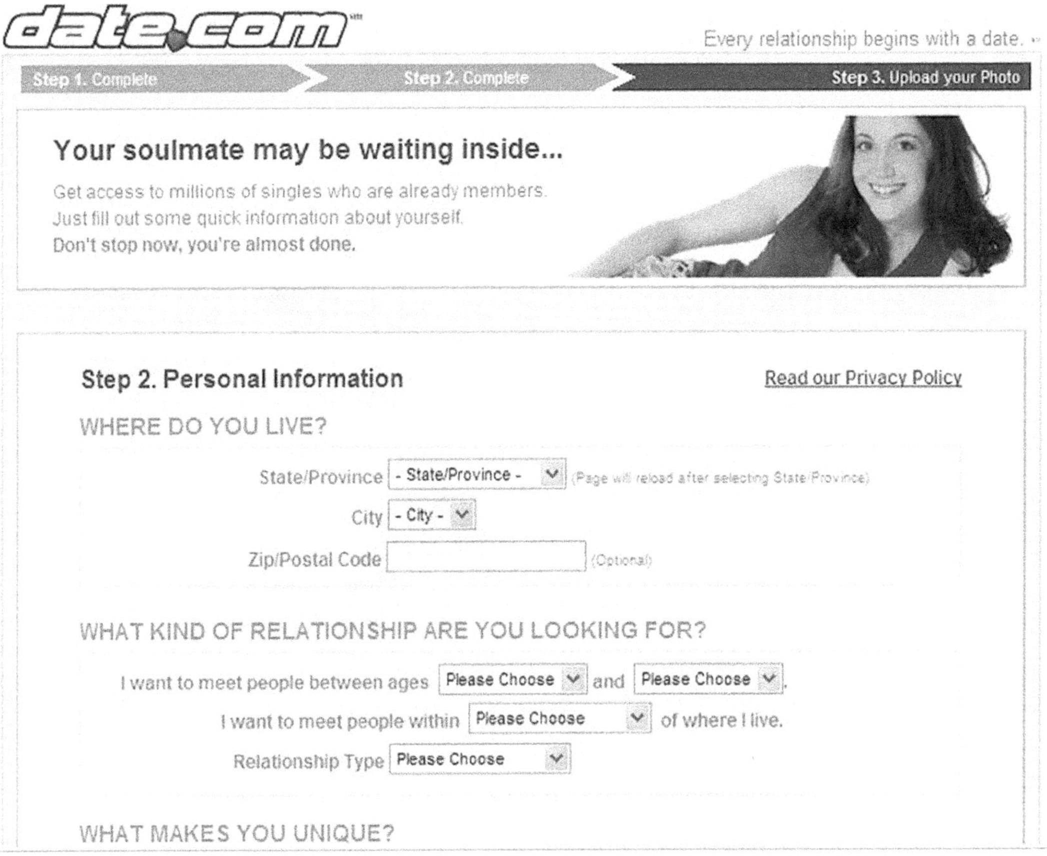

date.com

Every relationship begins with a date.

Step 1. Complete | Step 2. Complete | Step 3. Upload your Photo

Your soulmate may be waiting inside...

Get access to millions of singles who are already members.
Just fill out some quick information about yourself.
Don't stop now, you're almost done.

Step 2. Personal Information

Read our Privacy Policy

WHERE DO YOU LIVE?

State/Province [- State/Province -] (Page will reload after selecting State/Province)

City [- City -]

Zip/Postal Code [ ] (Optional)

WHAT KIND OF RELATIONSHIP ARE YOU LOOKING FOR?

I want to meet people between ages [Please Choose] and [Please Choose].

I want to meet people within [Please Choose] of where I live.

Relationship Type [Please Choose]

WHAT MAKES YOU UNIQUE?

Check it out: *Date.com features DateMobile, a service which allows you to browse singles and chat on your cell phone.*

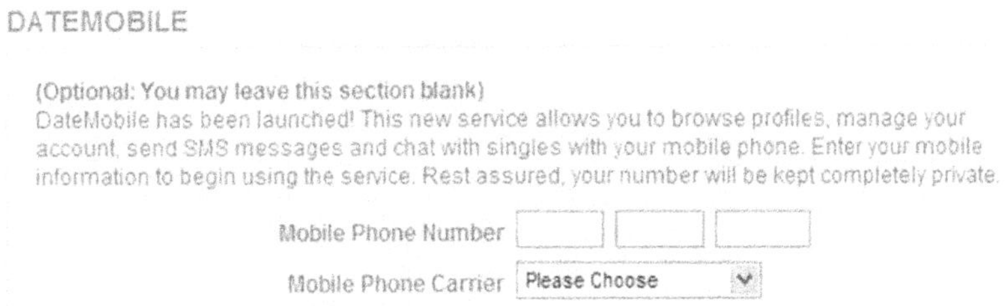

DATEMOBILE

(Optional: You may leave this section blank)
DateMobile has been launched! This new service allows you to browse profiles, manage your account, send SMS messages and chat with singles with your mobile phone. Enter your mobile information to begin using the service. Rest assured, your number will be kept completely private.

Mobile Phone Number [ ] [ ] [ ]

Mobile Phone Carrier [Please Choose]

Using Date.com

1. After registration is complete, you will be brought to your user Home Page. Click "Search" to find matches.

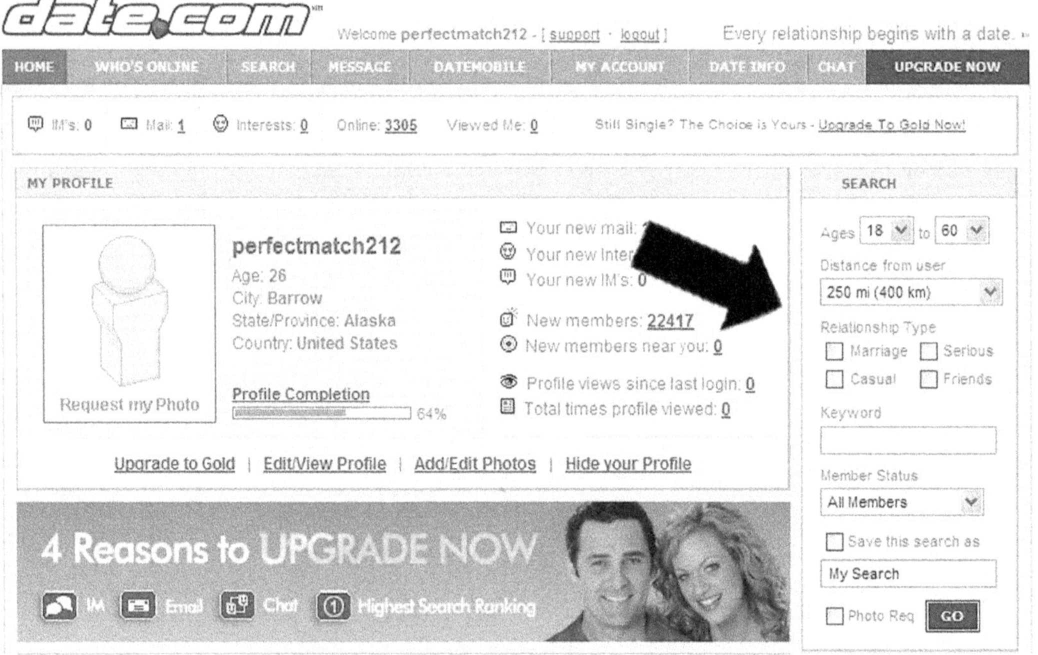

Check it out: *Also on your Home Page, you have easy access to your statistics. For instance, you can see how many times your profile has been viewed since the last login and since joining.*

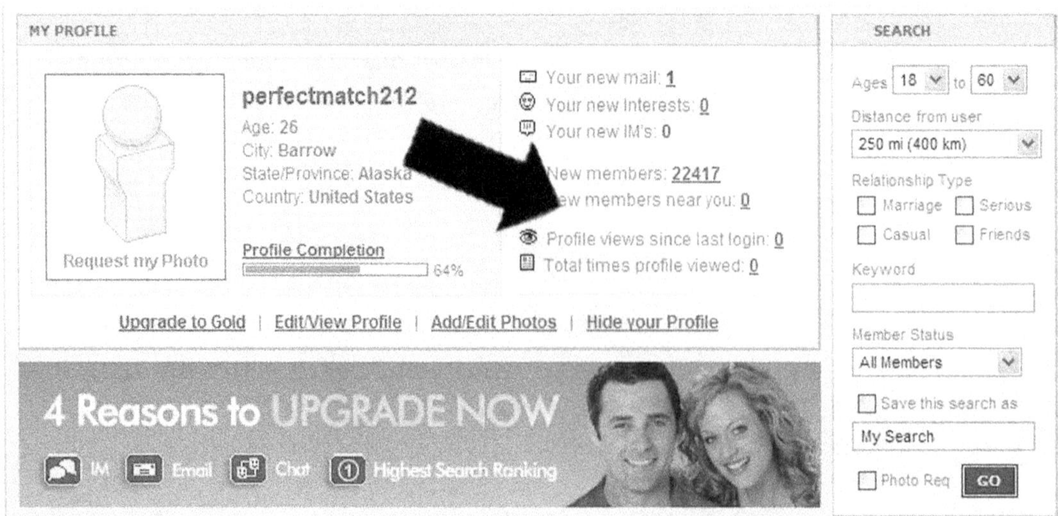

Check it out: *You can perform most functions with the free membership, but registration gives you access to IM, chat and improves your page ranking.*

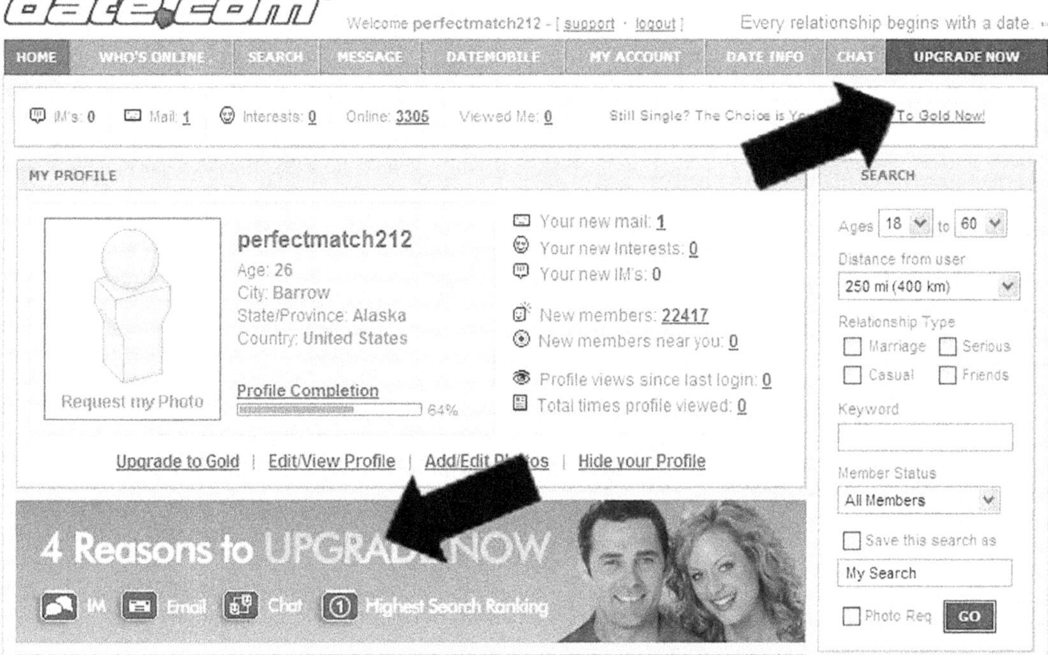

The great thing with Craig's List is that there's really no "profile" to fill out so it doesn't send you just what "matches" your interests and likes and dislikes. You can really dig into who's real and out there.

- Stephanie S.

CraigsList.org

Quick facts:

Year Established:	1995
Number of members:	Varies
Number of photos allowed:	4
Best Feature:	Free browsing, free personals posting.
Biggest Complaint:	No “dating” services, just personal ads
Cost:	Free for personal ads
Services offered:	Online personals ads
Wikipedia reference:	http://en.wikipedia.org/wiki/Craigslist

Unlike the other sites reviewed here, Craigslist.org is not specifically a dating site. Instead, it is a fully-featured online personals section run as a non-profit organization.

Craigslist.com was initially created to list events local to San Francisco, but quickly expanded to include such categories as personals ads and auto sales. This was the extent of Craigslist.org until January 2000, when current CEO Jim Buckmaster was hired as lead programmer and CTO. Under his leadership, the site layout was redone, self-posting was added, and the site expanded to a multi-city architecture.

Craigslist.org has insisted on remaining banner free (Aside from an April fools joke in 2002) and free for use, only charging employers to post help wanted ads.

Despite its many benefits and devotees, Craigslist.org has not avoided all controversies. In 2005, Craigslist.org was accused of encouraging overbreeding and irresponsible sales of pit-bulls for allowing breeders to post ads on the site. Also, Craigslist.org was sued in February 2006 by the Chicago Lawyers' Committee for Civil Rights Under Law for allegedly allowing users to post ads for homes that allegedly violate the fair housing act. The outcome has not yet been announced.

Craigslist.org cooperated with police in matters stemming from the casual encounters section. There have been several stings and arrests for prostitution charges. While Craigslist.org states that they can not and will not police the site, but they allow users to flag offending posts for administrative review.

Signing up for Craigslist.org

1. To create your own post, click "Post to Classifieds". To view posts, select the appropriate section under "Personals"

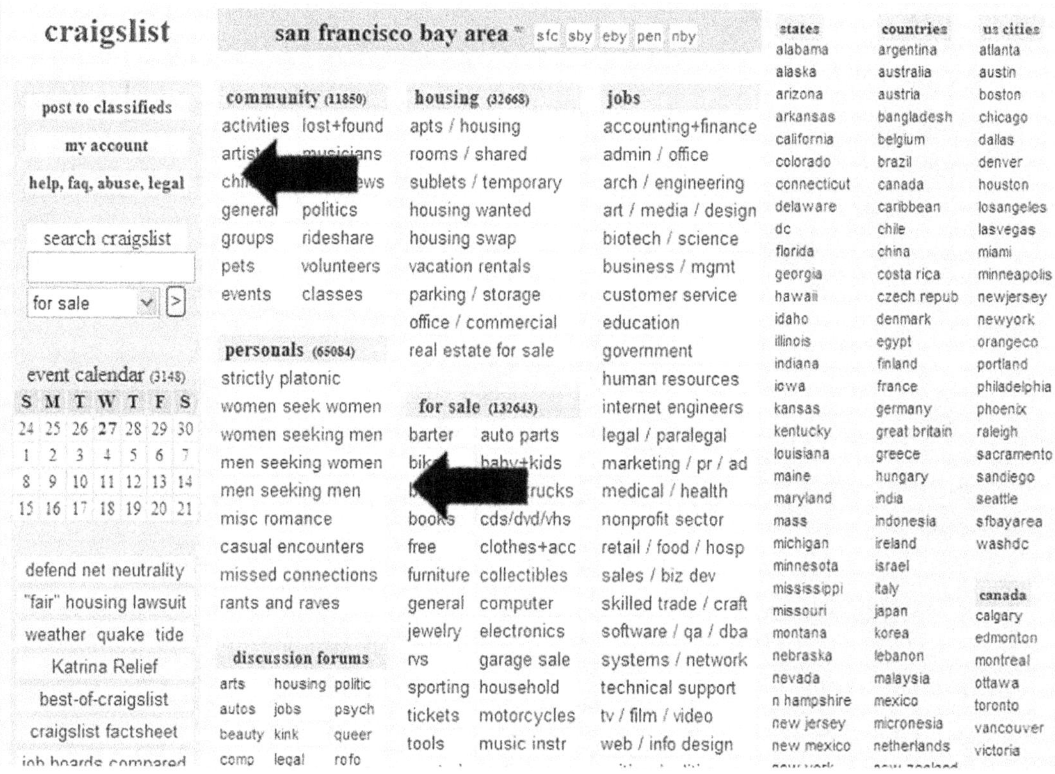

2. When creating a posting, select "personal/romance".

s.f. bayarea craigslist > > **create posting**

log in to your account
(Apply for Account)

What type of posting is this:

- job
- gigs
- housing
- for sale / wanted
- resume
- services offered
- personal / romance
- community
- event

3. Select which type of relationship you are looking for.

s.f. bayarea craigslist > personals > **create posting**

log in to your account
(Apply for Account)

if you are not at least 18 years of age, you may not post in this section!

NOTICE:
If you continue with this posting, you understand and agree that:

1. if craigslist believes that you impersonated someone by posting an ad in their name, or with their contact information, without their explicit consent, you authorize craigslist to release any and all information about you to the victim, and
2. if craigslist's actual damages cannot be reasonably determined in a court of law, you agree that you will pay craigslist liquidated damages of $1,000 for each such violation of our Terms of Use.

Which of these most closely matches what you have in mind?

- missed connection rant & rave
- strictly platonic (friends only)
- dating, romance, long term relationship (ltr)

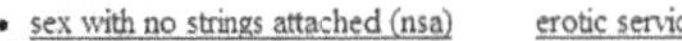

- sex with no strings attached (nsa) erotic services

4. Select the relationship makeup that you are looking for.

s.f. bayarea craigslist > **personals** > **create posting** — **log in to your account** (Apply for Account)

These 4 categories work for a lot of folks:

- i am a man seeking a woman
- i am a woman seeking a man
- i am a man seeking a man
- i am a woman seeking a woman

for something less deterministic (but still traditional dating/LTR oriented, NO hookup ads):

- miscellaneous romance

5. Choose your location. Note that the geographical area is automatically selected based on your location. For instance, if you are accessing the site from Los Angeles, you will see locations in that area.

s.f. bayarea craigslist > **men seeking women** > **create posting** — **log in to your account** (Apply for Account)

Your ad will expire in 7 days

choose the area nearest you (or suggest a new one):

please note: your posting will also appear on the main **san francisco bay area** site.

there is no need to cross-post to more than one area - doing so may get you flagged &/or blocked - thanks!

- city of san francisco
- south bay area
- east bay area
- peninsula
- north bay / marin

6. At this stage, you can pinpoint the location within the region, or skip with step and widen the search area.

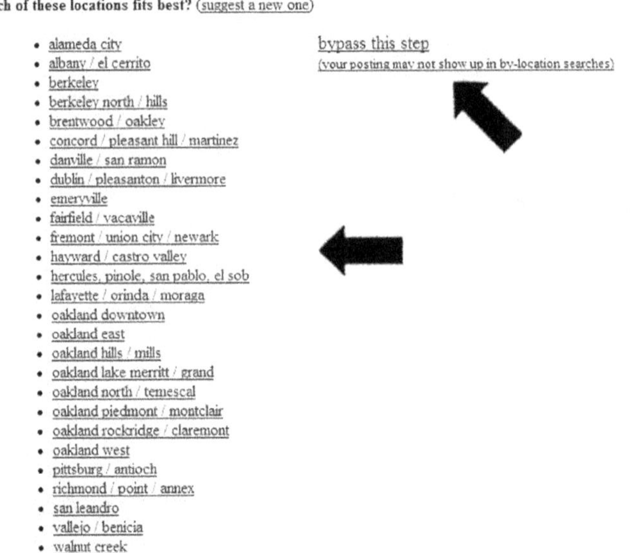
Which of these locations fits best? (suggest a new one)

- alameda city
- albany / el cerrito
- berkeley
- berkeley north / hills
- brentwood / oakley
- concord / pleasant hill / martinez
- danville / san ramon
- dublin / pleasanton / livermore
- emeryville
- fairfield / vacaville
- fremont / union city / newark
- hayward / castro valley
- hercules, pinole, san pablo, el sob
- lafayette / orinda / moraga
- oakland downtown
- oakland east
- oakland hills / mills
- oakland lake merritt / grand
- oakland north / temescal
- oakland piedmont / montclair
- oakland rockridge / claremont
- oakland west
- pittsburg / antioch
- richmond / point / annex
- san leandro
- vallejo / benicia
- walnut creek

bypass this step
(your posting may not show up in by-location searches)

7. Create your post and upload images.

Please do **not** post phone numbers, email addresses, or URLs in personals ads!

Required fields are in green.

Posting Title:

Your Age: **(hayward / castro valley)**

Posting Description:

Your Email address: (We need this to send you the self publishing kit.) (this address will NOT be visible on the website)

Add / Edit Images

Permissions:

☐ ok for others to contact you about other services, products or commercial interests

Continue

I do not really know why I filled out an online profile. If I have to think real hard about it, I guess I would say I filled one out because the bar and club scene was getting to be a bit of a bore to me. Online dating was a new way to finding that perfect Mr. Right.

- Kareem S.

FriendFinder.com

Quick facts:

Year Established:	1995
Number of members:	3.5 Million (25 million on all affiliate sites)
Number of photos allowed:	20
Best Feature:	Optional identity confirmation
Biggest Complaint:	Small thumbnail photographs. Cannot view larger unless you upgrade.
Cost:	\$22.95-\$139.94 depending on features and plan
Services offered:	Friend network/social site, chat/IM, online dating, voice introductions
Wikipedia reference:	http://en.wikipedia.org/wiki/FriendFinder

FriendFinder.com is the top level site of a group of specialized FriendFinder sites. The FriendFinder community includes AdultFriendFinder.com, GayFriendFinder.com, JewishFriendFinder.com, BigChurch.com and more.

FriendFinder encourages participation in its site and community activities by awarding points for referring friends, voting on articles (in the member-written FriendFinder online magazine), signing up for affiliate sites and more. These points can be used to upgrade your account, highlight your listing and more.

FriendFinder also maintains a social networking element. Similar to MySpace, users are able to map their friendships and relationships, as well as network with other members with similar interests.

Before purchasing an upgrade plan, it is important to decide what you require as far as service and searching options. For instance, the gold plan is more expensive than the silver plan, but includes faster customer service and improved searching options.

Signing up for FriendFinder.com

1. To begin, click "Go" to join for free.

2. Complete the basic profile. Unlike some other sites, there is no personality assessment

Join FriendFinder for FREE below!
(Login if you are already a member)

FriendFinder is designed around those seeking friends and serious relationships; more casual encounters can be found at Passion.com, the world's largest site for intimate connections.

1,937 Members online NOW!

rushprincess
24/F

SumChikUDontNo
32/F

spencer1974
31/F

Triina
32/F

Create Your Account

I am a ○ Man ○ Woman

Interested in meeting a ☐ Man ☐ Woman

For ☐ pen pals ☐ friends/activity partners ☐ dating ☐ marriage

I wish to use this site ☐ For Dating ☐ For Connecting with Friends

Birthdate January 1, 1976

Country United States

Zip/Postal code (US only) Find your zip code

Email Address

Enter a valid email address to sign up.
Your password will be sent to the address.
FriendFinder does not share your email address with other members.
See our "Privacy Policy" below for more information.

Need a spam free email account? Try BreakThru.com!

Handle

4 - 16 characters long, no spaces or special characters.
Handle uniquely identifies the member on FriendFinder.
(It is not recommended to use your real name as your handle.)

Click Here and Have Fun

Home | Join Now! | Member Login | Browse | Chat | Affiliates | Magazine | Blogs | Help

3. FriendFinder will email your password, and prompt you to login and confirm your account.

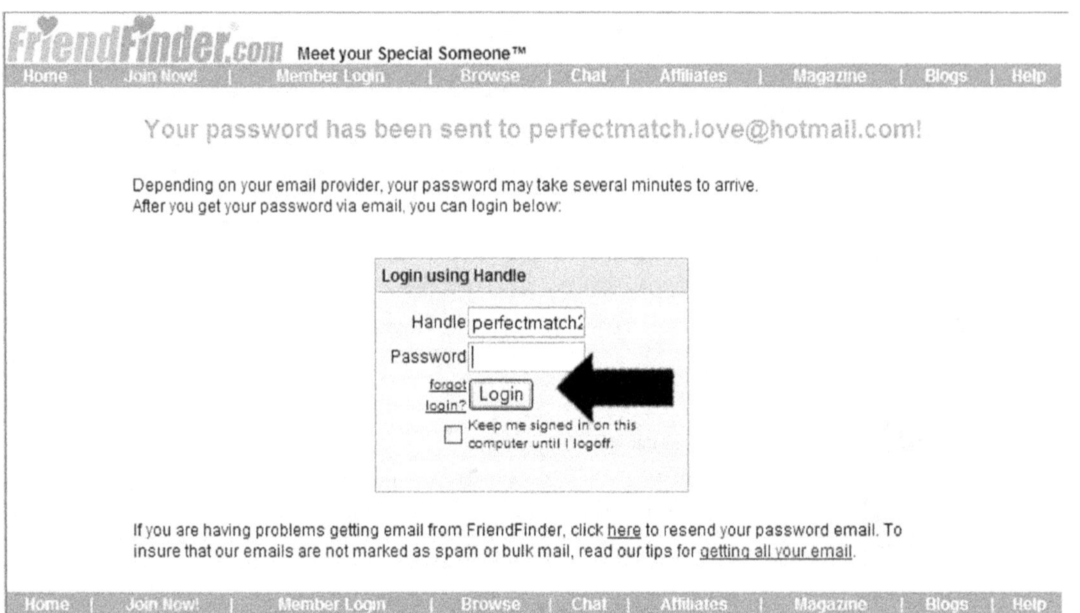

4. Once your account is confirmed, you can either upgrade to a silver or gold account, or click on "My Account" to continue setup.

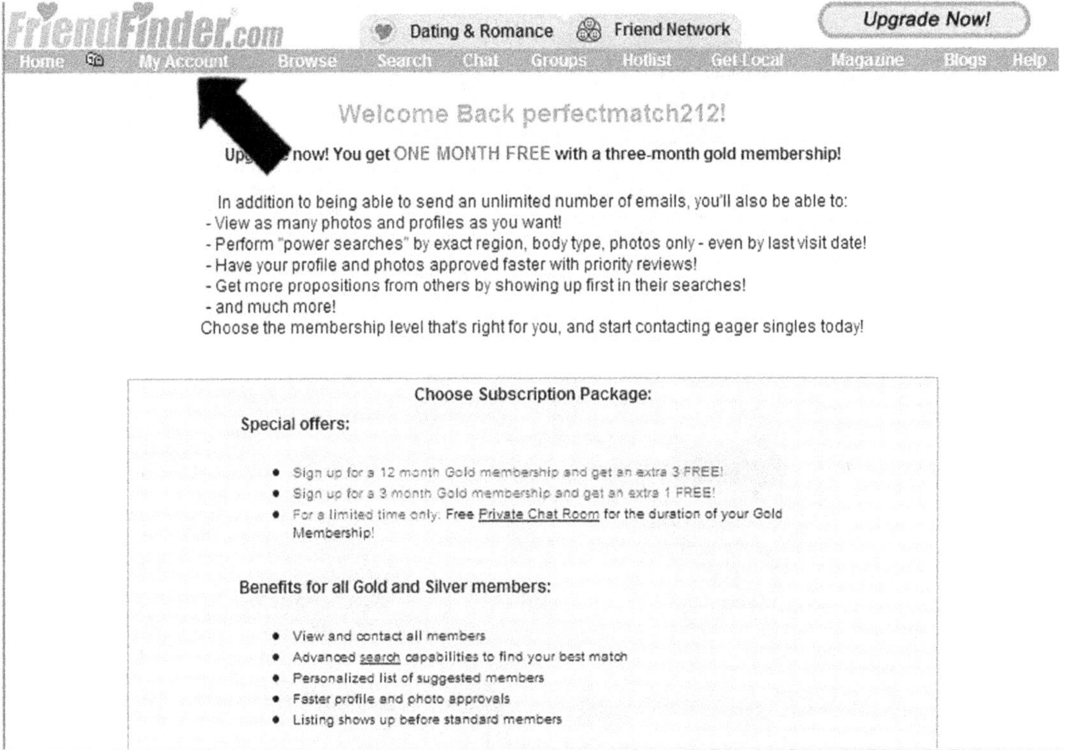

Using FriendFinder.com

1. Under "My Account", you will see the new account checklist. Although most of the categories are optional, each one increases your chances to attract a match.

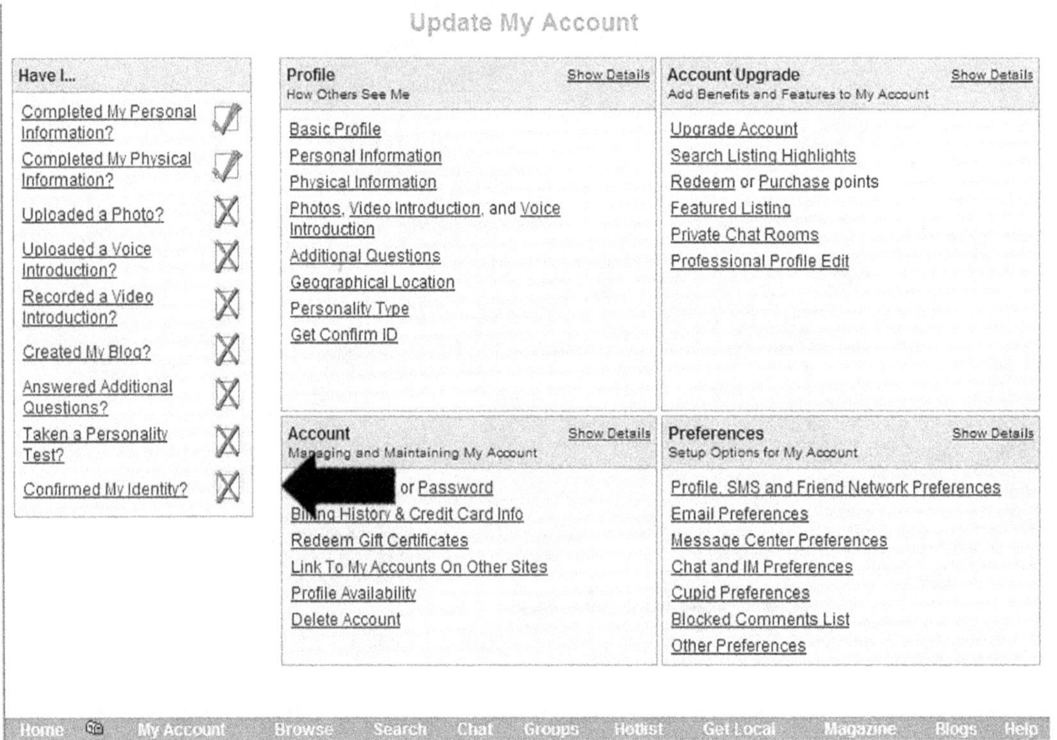

Check it out: *Confirming your identity is simple, and gives you points. Merely mailing a copy of a valid picture ID will confirm your identity and vital statistics.*

Mail completed form to: **ConfirmID, 445 Sherman Ave, Suite C, Palo Alto, CA 94306**
(we only verify by mail)

Please include a readable copy of one of these IDs that includes your photo: Your valid Driver's License*, State ID card*, or Passport. If we can't read it, we can't verify you. * U.S. and Canadian residents only. Feel free to photocopy your ID on a separate page if more space is needed. Internal Tracking ID: 13243124_24998/ff perfectmatch.love@hotmail.com	Attach ID Here (Your name and street address are never publically displayed)
Updates/Corrections (e.g. address, height, weight changes):	
Optional (Check to verify information entered above):	☐ Verify Height ☐ Verify Weight

I declare under the penalty of perjury under the law of the state, province and/or country where I reside that all the information contained herein is true and correct to the best of my knowledge.

Signature:______________________________ Date:__________

2. In the user bar, click browse.

3. You will be prompted to browse by category, such as men seeking women, pen pals, activity partners, etc.

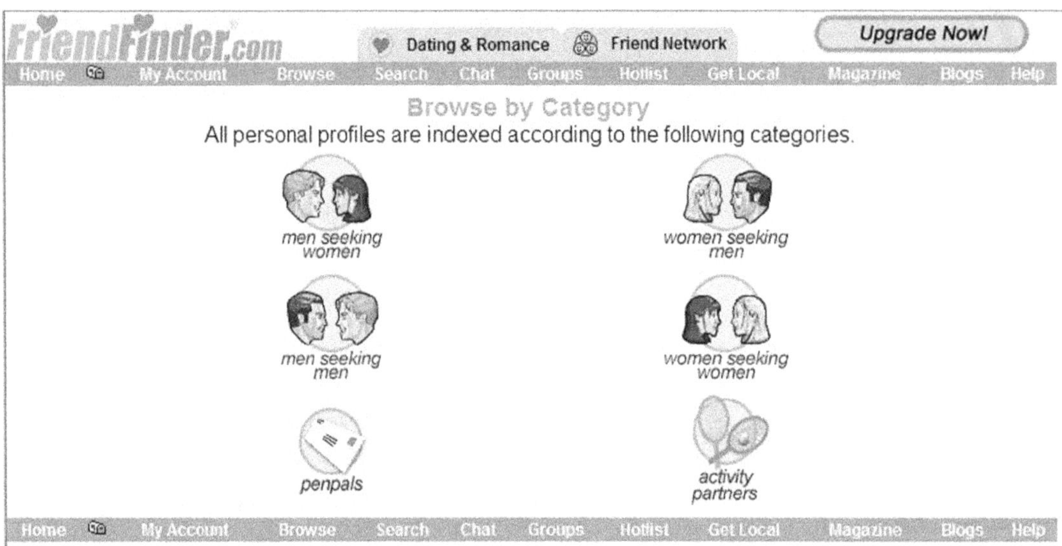

4. Selecting a category brings you to the state browser, allowing you choose a date in your region.

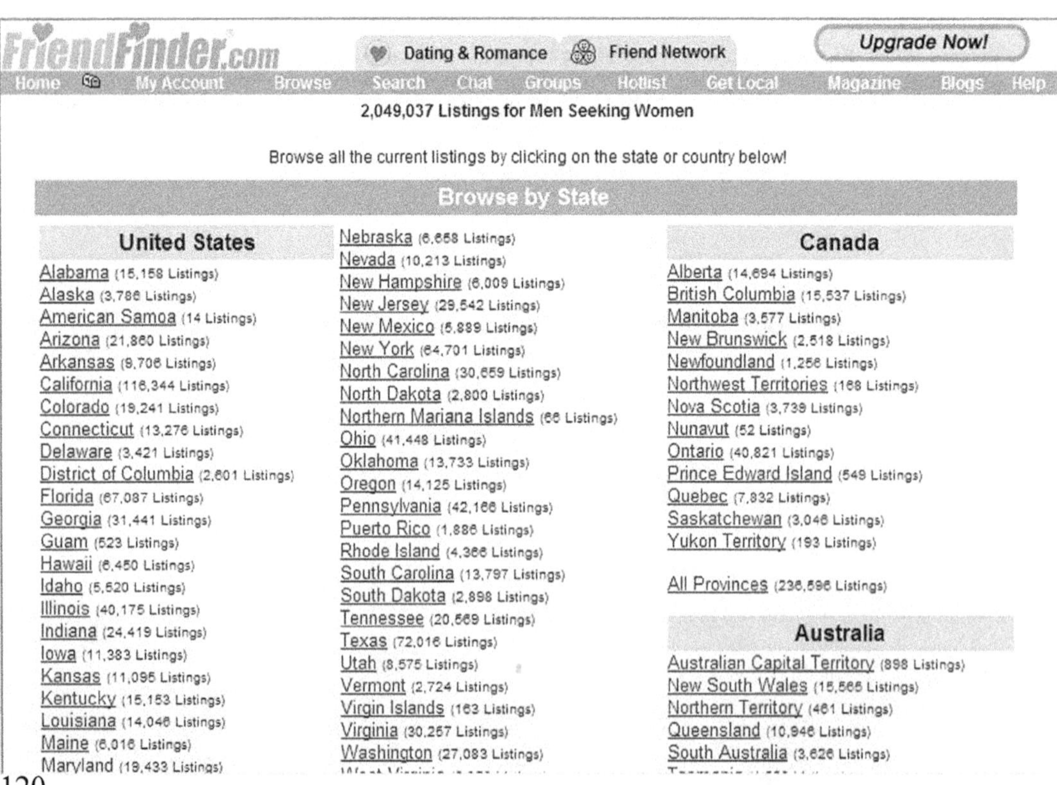

5. After selecting a state, you can either browse all profiles or browse by age range.

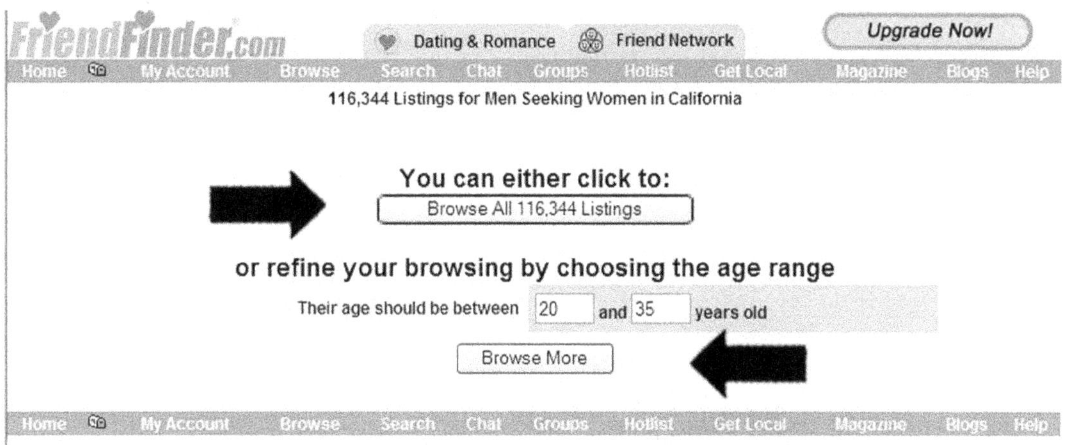

6. To get to know other users a little bit better, you can view their blogs though the user bar.

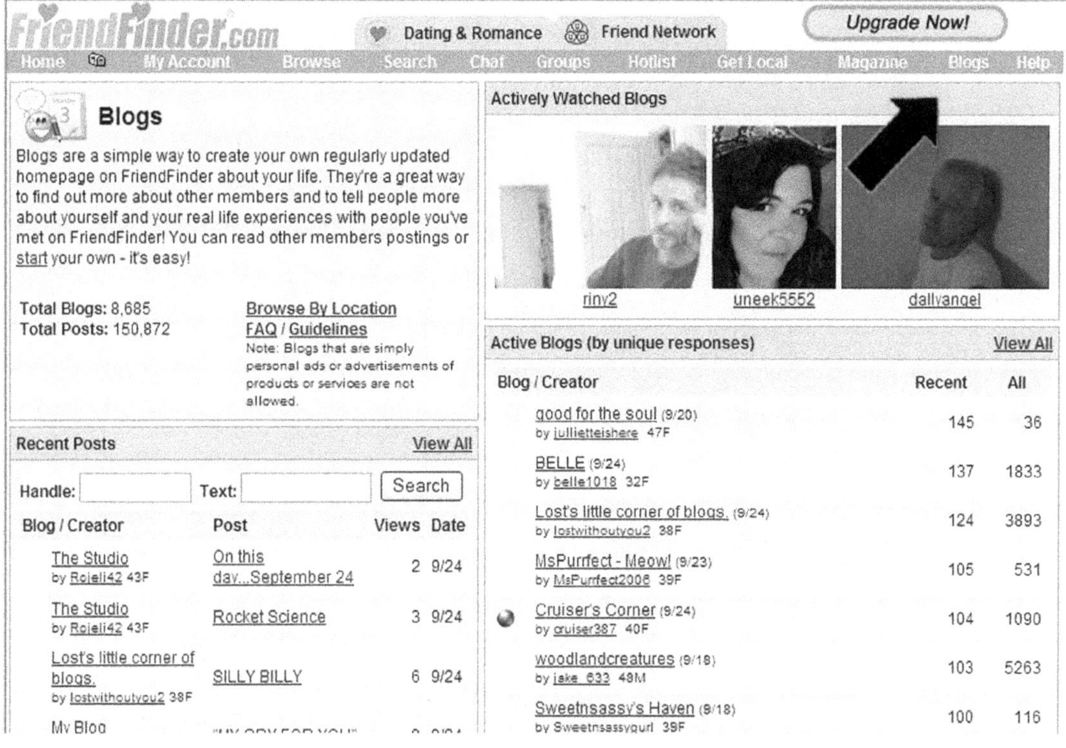

I filled out a profile on myspace rather reluctantly, actually. a friend of mine had met his girlfriend on the site and I didn't have a good answer when I asked myself 'why not?'. It's easy to do almost anything if you don't over-think it. I am very glad that I didn't listen to that little voice that says 'this is stupid/embarassing/a waste of time.' Filling out that profile changed my whole life.

- Maureen Q.

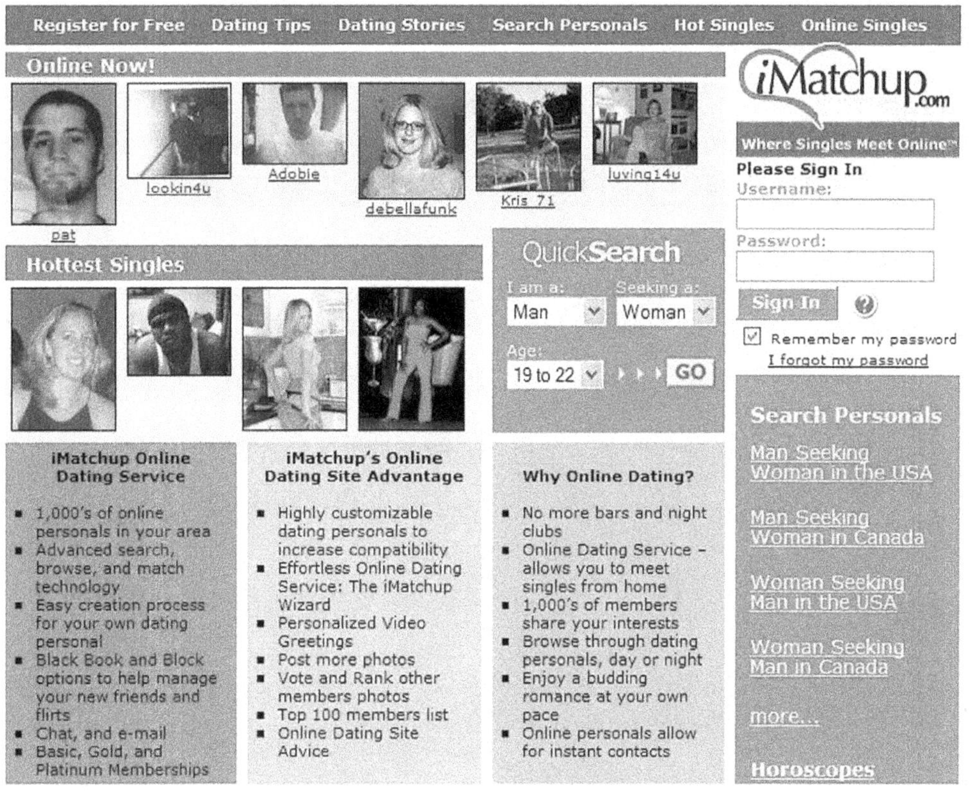

iMatchup.com

Quick facts:

Year Established: 1993

Number of members: 3 Million

Number of photos allowed: 5

Best Feature: Frequent contests and games

Biggest Complaint: Need expensive platinum membership to allow non-paying members to read your messages.

Cost: $24.95- $64.95

Services offered: Mobile phone chat with members, live chats, online personals

Wikipedia reference: None

Although the site is relatively successful with 3 million members, there is little that is unique about the site. The main draw seems to be the number of users, which in itself is not extraordinary.

The site itself is relatively easy to navigate, and the matches seem to be of a slightly higher quality than other sites, so it is worth checking out.

Signing up for iMatchup.com

1. To begin, click "Register for Free"

Register for Free Dating Tips Dating Stories Search Personals Hot Singles Online Singles

Online Now!

pat lookin4u Adobie debellafunk Kris_71 luving14u

iMatchup.com

Where Singles Meet Online™

Please Sign In

Username:

Password:

Sign In

Remember my password

I forgot my password

Hottest Singles

QuickSearch

I am a: Man Seeking a: Woman

Age: 19 to 22 GO

Search Personals

Man Seeking Woman in the USA

Man Seeking Woman in Canada

Woman Seeking Man in the USA

Woman Seeking Man in Canada

more...

Horoscopes

iMatchup Online Dating Service

- 1,000's of online personals in your area
- Advanced search, browse, and match technology
- Easy creation process for your own dating personal
- Black Book and Block options to help manage your new friends and flirts
- Chat, and e-mail
- Basic, Gold, and Platinum Memberships

iMatchup's Online Dating Site Advantage

- Highly customizable dating personals to increase compatibility
- Effortless Online Dating Service: The iMatchup Wizard
- Personalized Video Greetings
- Post more photos
- Vote and Rank other members photos
- Top 100 members list
- Online Dating Site Advice

Why Online Dating?

- No more bars and night clubs
- Online Dating Service - allows you to meet singles from home
- 1,000's of members share your interests
- Browse through dating personals, day or night
- Enjoy a budding romance at your own pace
- Online personals allow for instant contacts

2. Complete the simple profile.

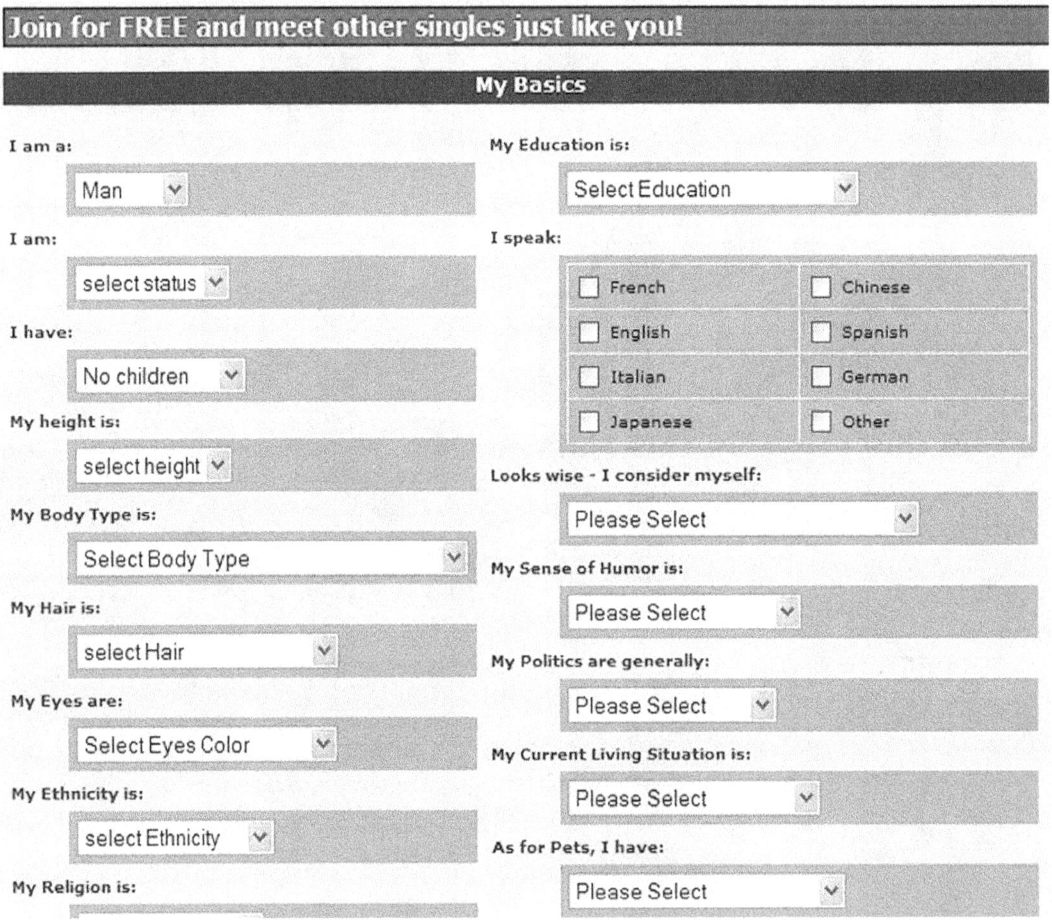

Join for FREE and meet other singles just like you!

My Basics

I am a: Man

I am: select status

I have: No children

My height is: select height

My Body Type is: Select Body Type

My Hair is: select Hair

My Eyes are: Select Eyes Color

My Ethnicity is: select Ethnicity

My Religion is:

My Education is: Select Education

I speak:

☐ French	☐ Chinese
☐ English	☐ Spanish
☐ Italian	☐ German
☐ Japanese	☐ Other

Looks wise - I consider myself: Please Select

My Sense of Humor is: Please Select

My Politics are generally: Please Select

My Current Living Situation is: Please Select

As for Pets, I have: Please Select

3. (Optional) Sign up for mobile communication or offline dating services.

Would you like to enable text messaging to you cell phone?
Enter your cell phone number here:

[ ] - [ ] - [ ]

Are you interested in trying dating options that are off line? IMatchup has p[illegible]ed with the world's largest, personal matchmaking services - Together Dating [illegible]e Right One. To learn more about these services continue with the registration page. If you qualify a dating advisor will contact you by phone.

◉ YES ○ NO

First Name	
Last Name	
Street	
City	Fort Irwin
State	CA
Zip	92310
Home Phone	- -
Occupation Phone	- -
Date of Birth	------- / --- / ---
Occupation	
My Income	- Select -
Marital Status	- Select -

4. At this point, registration is complete, and you are taken to your iMatchup Homepage.

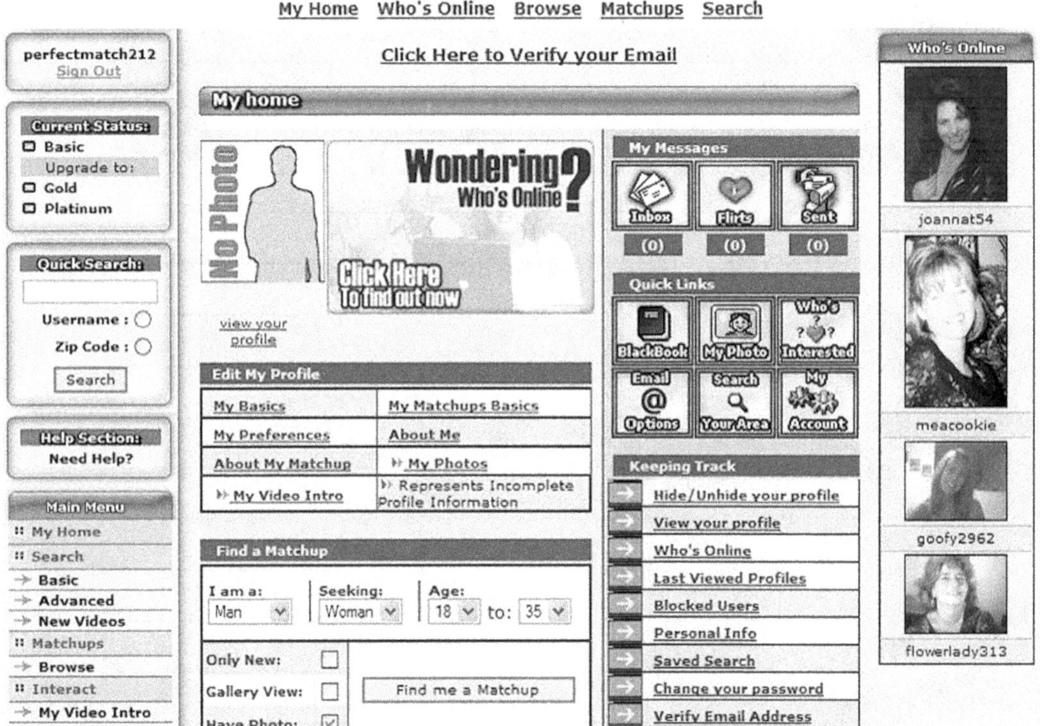

Using iMatchup.com

1. Click "Browse" to begin looking for a match.

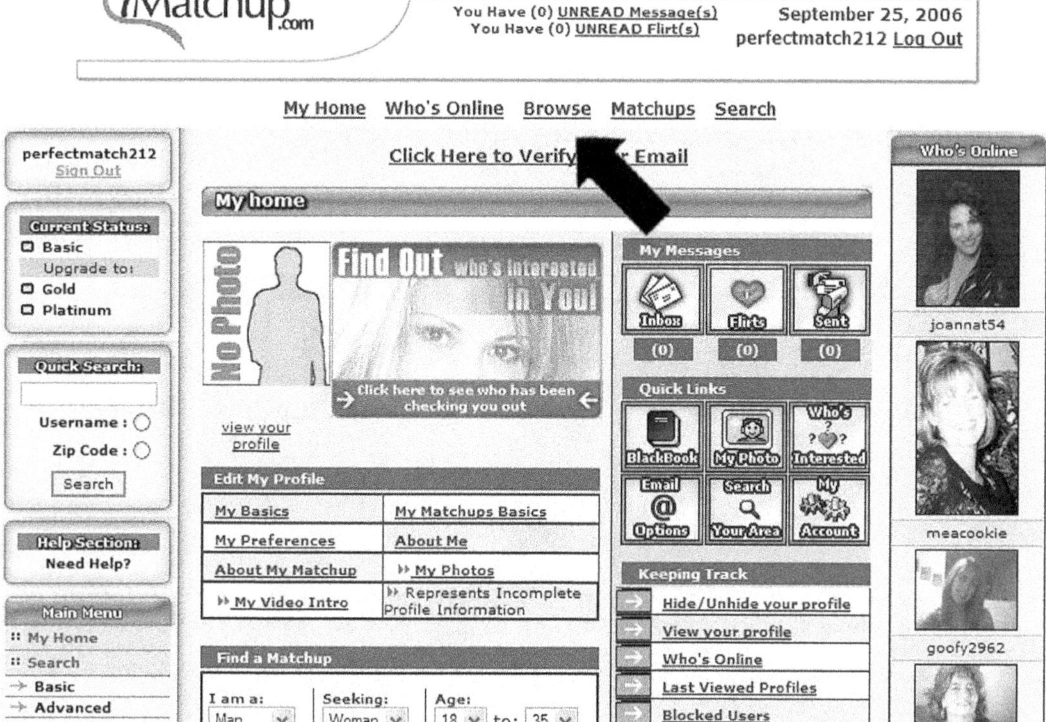

2. Select your browsing options. You are able to specify if you are a man or woman, seeking a man, woman or both. You can also limit the results to those with profiles.

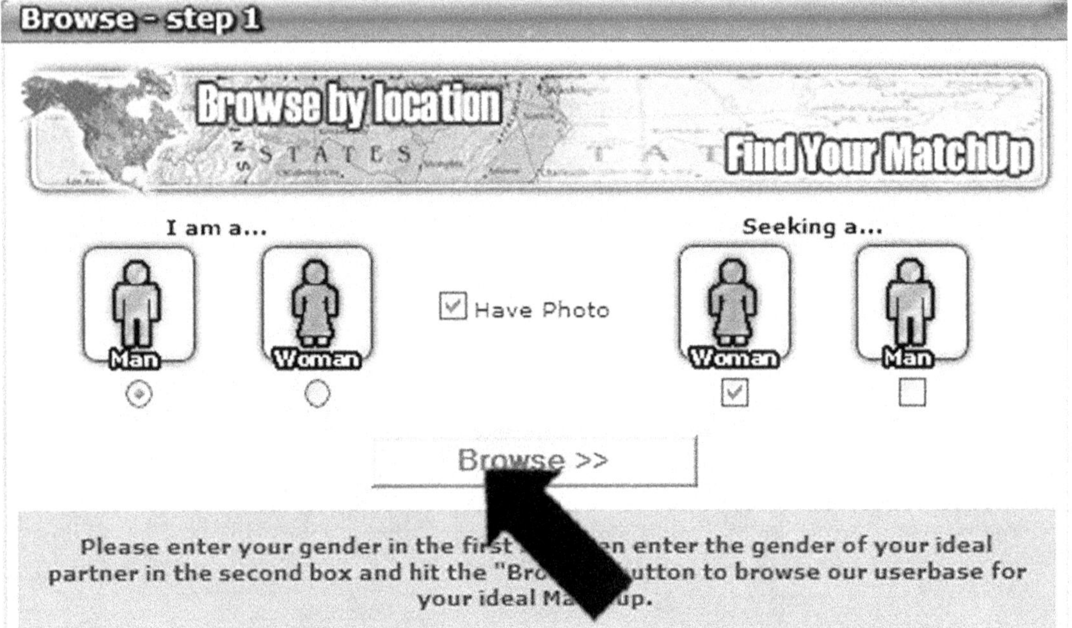

3. In addition to browsing, you can also perform searches from your user Home Page.

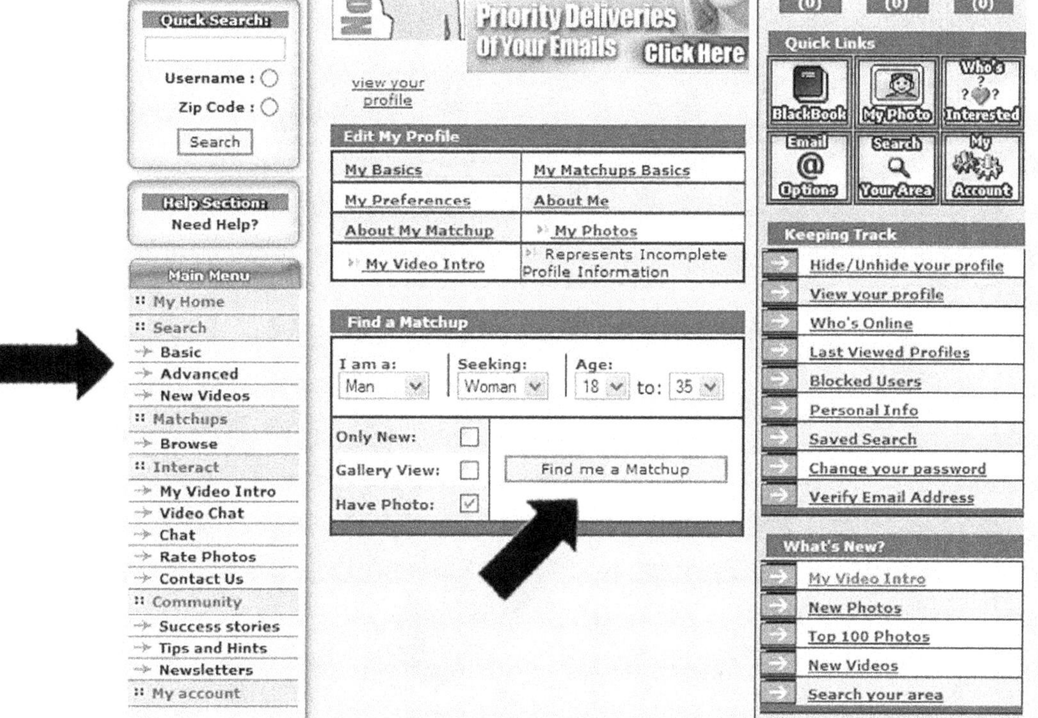

4. On your Home Page, under your profile options, you can edit the profile. This is where you can add video to your profile, which really makes it stand out!

Edit My Profile

My Basics	My Matchups Basics
My Preferences	About Me
About My Matchup	▸▸ My Photos
▸▸ My Video Intro	▸▸ Represents Incomplete Profile Information

Find a Matchup

I am a: Man | Seeking: Woman | Age: 18 to: 35

Only New: ☐
Gallery View: ☐
Have Photo: ☑

Find me a Matchup

5. Recording video is simple. With your webcam attached and powered on, click "Record Video" to begin recording.

My Intro Video

This is your main video others will see when they do searches or look at your profile.

It's easy to record a 90-second video greeting for other iMatchup members to see. You only need the following:

--A webcam attached to your computer

--A microphone attached to your computer (optional - you can record a video without sound just to give people a better idea of what you look like)

Record Video

Notes on your video:

1) Your video will be recorded live, s… e recommend that you take a few minutes in advance to compose some "talking points" to guide

I created an online dating profile to meet new people and to jump-start my dating life. I moved to a new city after college and prior to posting online, I struggled to find men that I was interested in dating. As is the case for many young professionals, there's scant opportunity to meet the right person unless you have a vast social network, so my profile was meant to expand my search wider and include people I wouldn't meet in my everyday travels between work at a very small company, the gym, and my grad school classes. The internet provided an efficient, convenient way to up the numbers. And in that sense, it worked;
I met tons of new men.

- Elaine K.

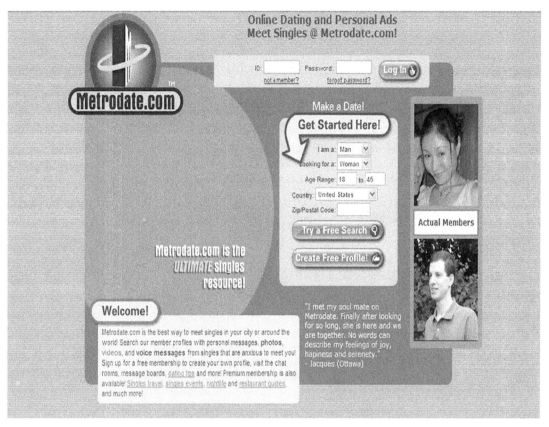

MetroDate.com

Quick facts:

Year Established:	1998
Number of members:	3.5 Million
Number of photos allowed:	5
Best Feature:	User friendly, great features
Biggest Complaint:	Some questionable profiles, including requests for illicit affairs
Cost:	$14.95/month
Services offered:	Chat rooms, online personals, city information
Wikipedia reference:	None

MetroDate.com is among the most user friendly online dating sites in existence. However, perhaps the most striking (and certainly the most unique) feature is the integrating nightlife assistance. This allows users to look up events, restaurants and travel in an area, as well as view current weather reports.

The site is also well laid out, with a well designed and intuitive layout, it is easy to understand and navigate. The secondary features of the site also function flawlessly, to include the chat and message boards.

Overall, there is a definite feeling of "fun" about the site, which permeates not only the layout, but the profiles as well.

Signing up for MetroDate.com

1. To create your profile, click "Create Free Profile" on the start page.

2. Complete the initial registration, with the basic vital statistics.

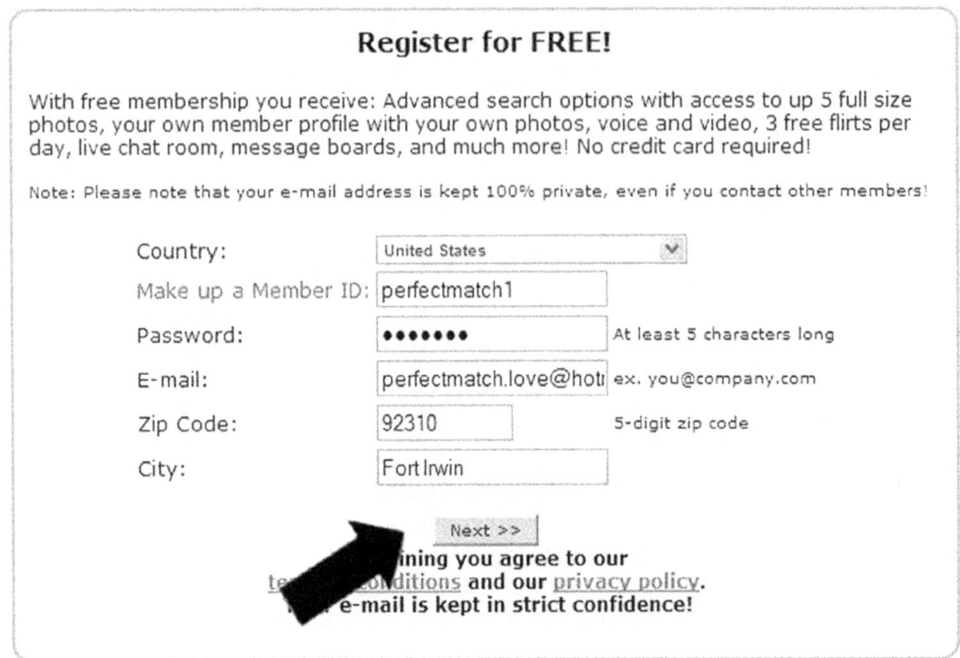

Register for FREE!

With free membership you receive: Advanced search options with access to up 5 full size photos, your own member profile with your own photos, voice and video, 3 free flirts per day, live chat room, message boards, and much more! No credit card required!

Note: Please note that your e-mail address is kept 100% private, even if you contact other members!

Country: United States

Make up a Member ID: perfectmatch1

Password: ••••••• At least 5 characters long

E-mail: perfectmatch.love@hotı ex. you@company.com

Zip Code: 92310 5-digit zip code

City: Fort Irwin

Next >>

...ining you agree to our
...ditions and our privacy policy.
... e-mail is kept in strict confidence!

3. Complete the free profile.

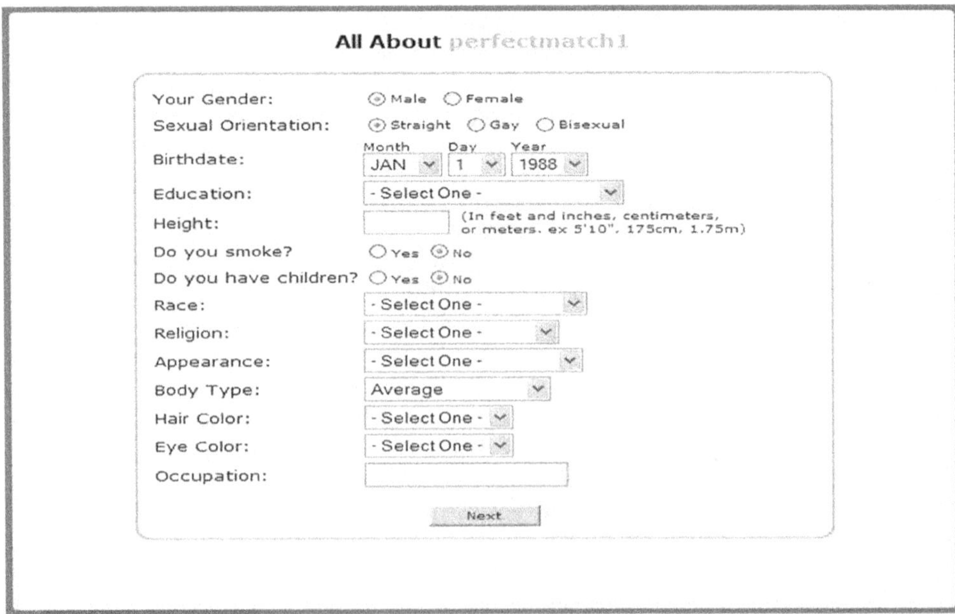

All About perfectmatch1

Your Gender: Male Female

Sexual Orientation: Straight Gay Bisexual

Birthdate: Month JAN Day 1 Year 1988

Education: - Select One -

Height: (In feet and inches, centimeters, or meters. ex 5'10", 175cm, 1.75m)

Do you smoke? Yes No

Do you have children? Yes No

Race: - Select One -

Religion: - Select One -

Appearance: - Select One -

Body Type: Average

Hair Color: - Select One -

Eye Color: - Select One -

Occupation:

Next

4. After completing the profile, select between a free or basic account. If you start with a free account, you can always upgrade later if you need to.

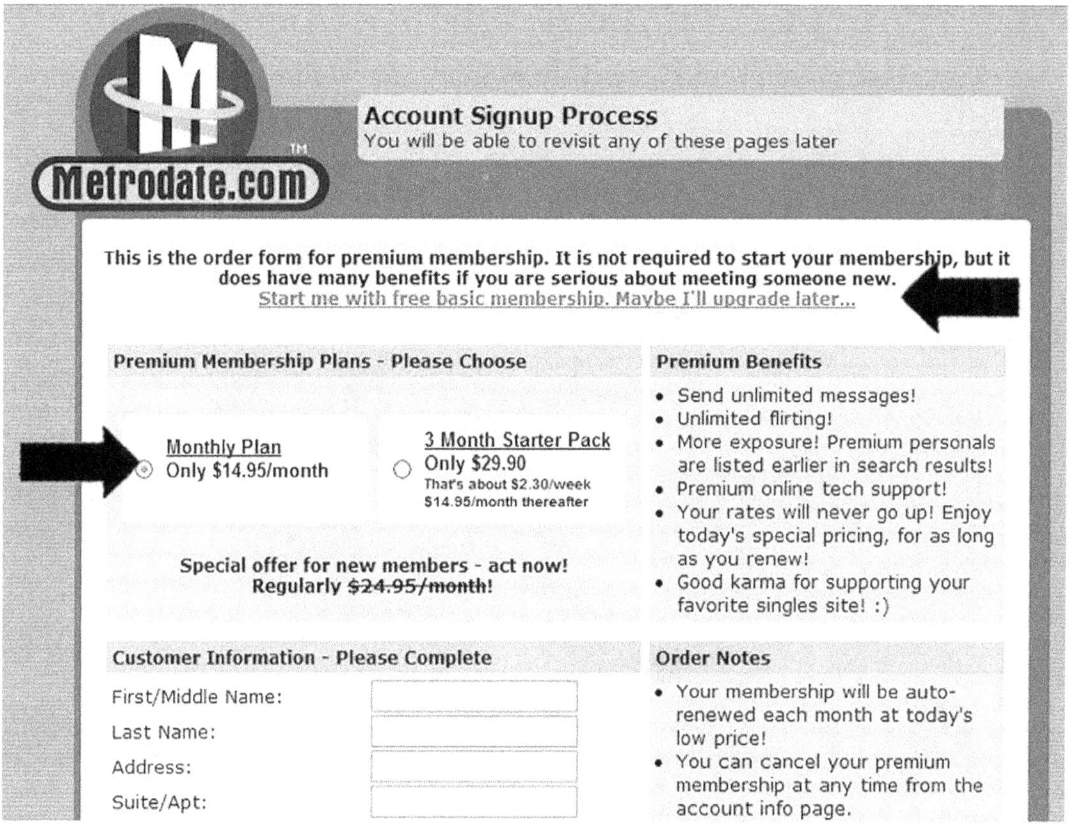

Metrodate.com™

Account Signup Process
You will be able to revisit any of these pages later

This is the order form for premium membership. It is not required to start your membership, but it does have many benefits if you are serious about meeting someone new.
Start me with free basic membership. Maybe I'll upgrade later...

Premium Membership Plans - Please Choose

Monthly Plan
Only $14.95/month

3 Month Starter Pack
Only $29.90
That's about $2.30/week
$14.95/month thereafter

Special offer for new members - act now!
Regularly ~~$24.95/month~~!

Premium Benefits

- Send unlimited messages!
- Unlimited flirting!
- More exposure! Premium personals are listed earlier in search results!
- Premium online tech support!
- Your rates will never go up! Enjoy today's special pricing, for as long as you renew!
- Good karma for supporting your favorite singles site! :)

Customer Information - Please Complete

First/Middle Name:
Last Name:
Address:
Suite/Apt:

Order Notes

- Your membership will be auto-renewed each month at today's low price!
- You can cancel your premium membership at any time from the account info page.

5. Once the profile is completed, you will be taken to your user Home Page. On this page, you will always have access to the profile checklist, listing any elements of a profile that may help you in gaining a successful match.

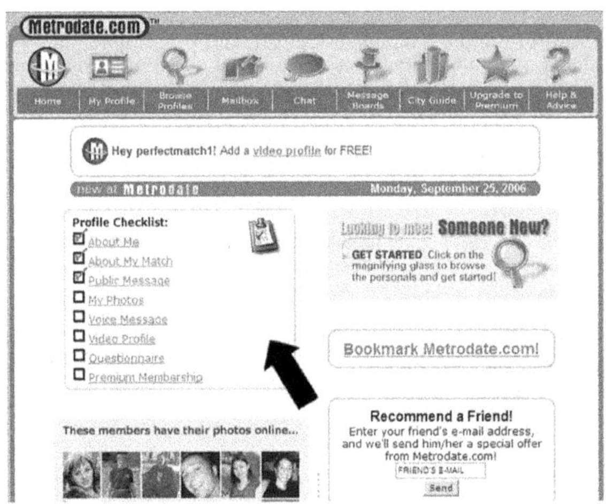

Using MetroDate.com

1. Selecting "Browse Profiles" from the user bar gives you access to a huge database of singles in your geographical area.

Check it out: *The city life tab will give you access to information on weather, restaurants, local events and travel*

Metrodate.com™

Home | My Profile | Browse Profiles | Mailbox | Chat | Message Boards | City Guide | Upgrade to Premium | Help & Advice

North Las Vegas City Guide
Events
NightLife
Restaurants
Travel

Hey perfectmatch1! Add a video profile for FRE

new at Metrodate

Profile Checklist:
About Me
About My Match
Public Message
My Photos
Voice Message
Video Profile
Questionnaire
Premium Membership

Looking to meet Someone New?
GET STARTED Click on the magnifying glass to browse the personals and get started!

Bookmark Metrodate.com!

These members have their photos online...

Recommend a Friend!
Enter your friend's e-mail address, and we'll send him/her a special offer from Metrodate.com!
FRIEND'S E-MAIL
Send

2. In the user bar are the three main methods of communication on Metrodate. From here, you have access to the mailbox, chat and message boards.

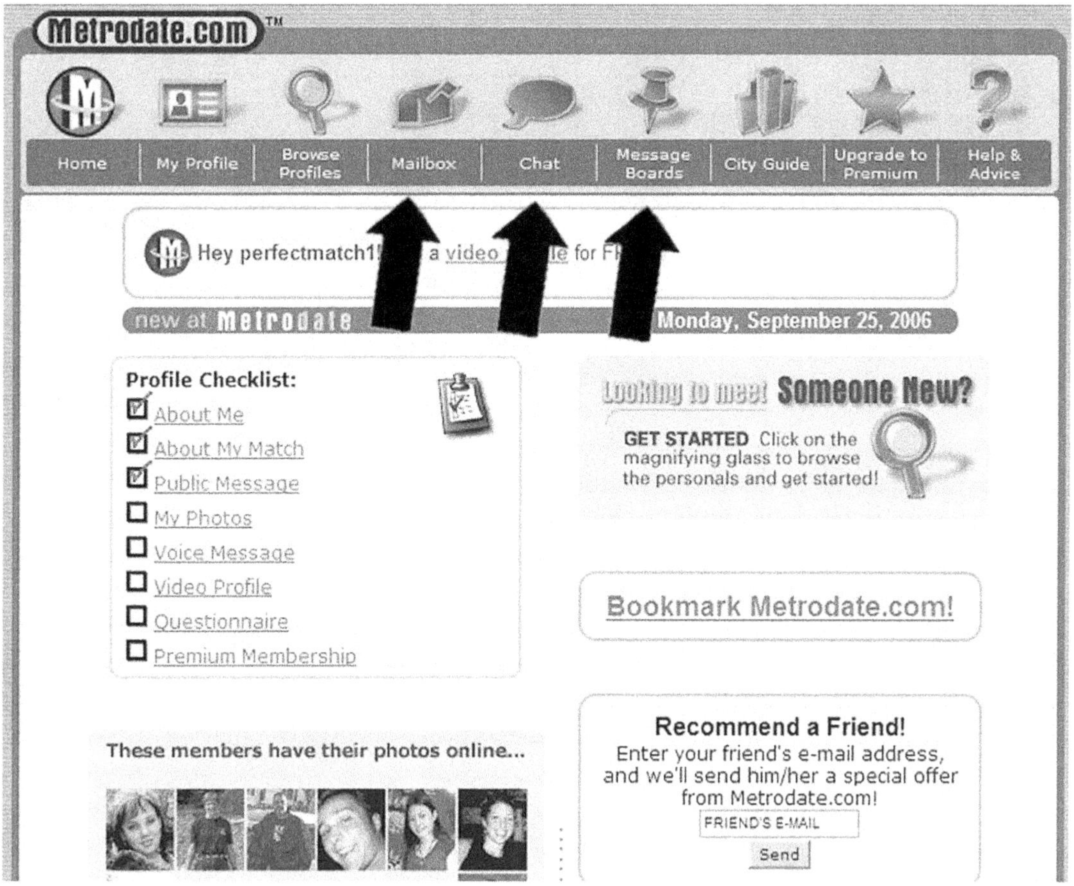

3. When you find a user that you are interested in, clicking their name will bring up their full profile, and allow you to chat with them, access their video and voice recordings, save their profile or send flirts.

blondetransy
Female / Straight
White/Caucasian / Christian
Age: 48
Occupation: beauty industry
Blonde hair and Blue eyes
Appearance: Attractive
Body Type: Average
Location: Greer, SC, US
Education: Some College
Height: 5'6" (168 cm)
Smoker
Doesn't have children
Astrological Sign: Leo
Last login: **Yesterday!**

Ideal Match
Age: 25 - 50
Education: Doesn't matter
Height: Doesn't matter
Smokers: Doesn't matter
Race: Doesn't matter
Religion: Doesn't matter

Living in New York City makes it difficult to meet anybody. Mostly, people do not move to this city to find love. People move to this city to pursue a career. They are always going, which makes it hard to stop and ask, "Hey, how about we have some coffee?" However, in NYC, if someone you don't know asks you for coffee, chances are you'd think they were going to rob you. You need every bit of help in order to meet datable single men, especially when you're in your 30s and most of the men your age are married with kids, living in New Jersey and commuting in to the city for work.

- Cara W.

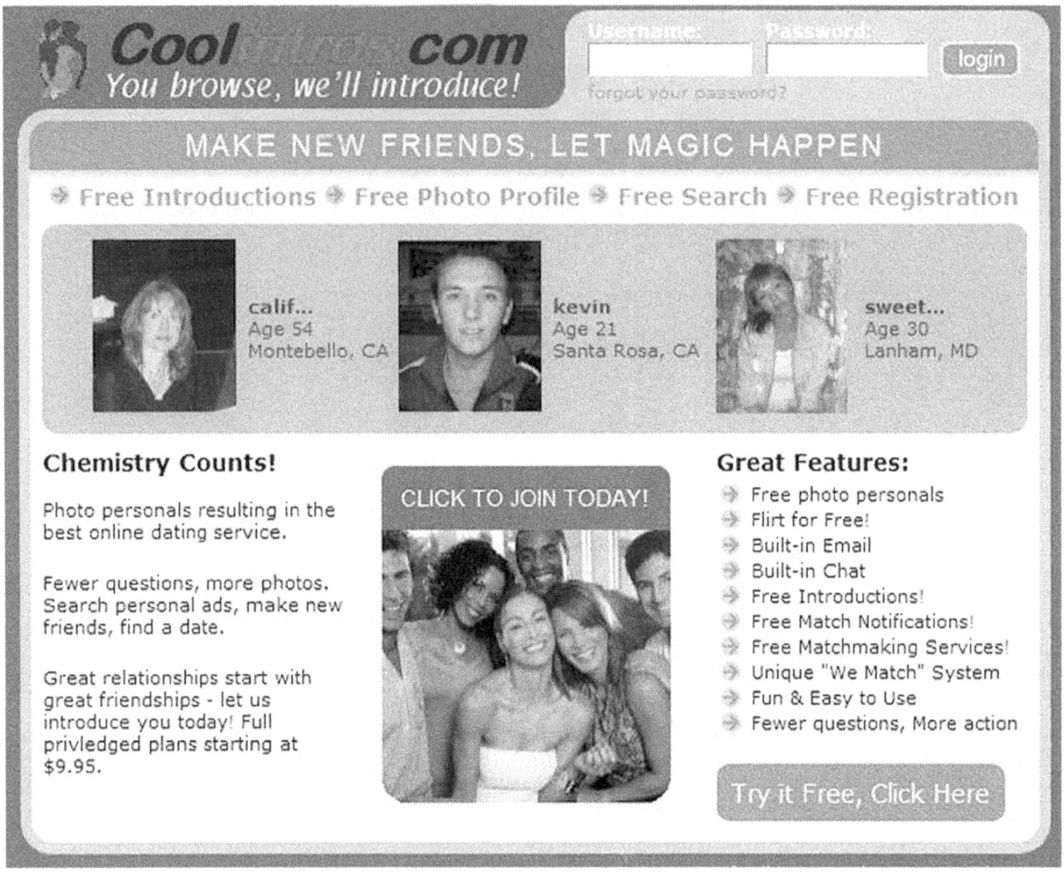

Cool .com
You browse, we'll introduce!
Username: Password: login
forgot your password?
MAKE NEW FRIENDS, LET MAGIC HAPPEN
Free Introductions Free Photo Profile Free Search Free Registration
calif... Age 54 Montebello, CA
kevin Age 21 Santa Rosa, CA
sweet... Age 30 Lanham, MD
Chemistry Counts!
Photo personals resulting in the best online dating service.
Fewer questions, more photos. Search personal ads, make new friends, find a date.
Great relationships start with great friendships - let us introduce you today! Full privledged plans starting at $9.95.
CLICK TO JOIN TODAY!
Great Features:
Free photo personals
Flirt for Free!
Built-in Email
Built-in Chat
Free Introductions!
Free Match Notifications!
Free Matchmaking Services!
Unique "We Match" System
Fun & Easy to Use
Fewer questions, More action
Try it Free, Click Here

CoolIntros.com

Quick facts:

Year Established: Unknown

Number of members: Unknown

Number of photos allowed: 4

Best Feature: Cheap and quick

Biggest Complaint: Few features without paying

Cost: $9.99/month

Services offered: Online personals ads, matching service

Wikipedia reference: None

The philosophy behind CoolIntros.com is that they will do the introduction, then you will do the rest. There are few questions during the profile setup, instead CoolIntros relies on twenty questions that they call "Deal Breakers", factors that will cause two people to be incompatible. For instance, the site will not match someone that wants a family with someone who does not.

After setting your preferences, all searches will be filtered by your preferences. This is designed to get rid of all the "clutter", and only show you matches that are compatible.

Signing up for CoolIntros.com

1. On the homepage, click "Try It Free"

CoolIntros.com
You browse, we'll introduce!
Username: Password: login
forgot your password?

MAKE NEW FRIENDS, LET MAGIC HAPPEN

Free Introductions Free Photo Profile Free Search Free Registration

calif...
Age 54
Montebello, CA

kevin
Age 21
Santa Rosa, CA

sweet...
Age 30
Lanham, MD

Chemistry Counts!

Photo personals resulting in the best online dating service.

Fewer questions, more photos. Search personal ads, make new friends, find a date.

Great relationships start with great friendships - let us introduce you today! Full privledged plans starting at $9.95.

CLICK TO JOIN TODAY!

Great Features:

- Free photo personals
- Flirt for Free!
- Built-in Email
- Built-in Chat
- Free Introductions!
- Free Match Notifications!
- Free Matchmaking Services!
- Unique "We Match" System
- Fun & Easy to Use
- Fewer questions, More action

Try it Free, Click Here

2. (Optional) CoolIntros.com partners with radio stations all over the country. If you heard about CoolIntros.com through a radio station, enter the coupon code for a discount.

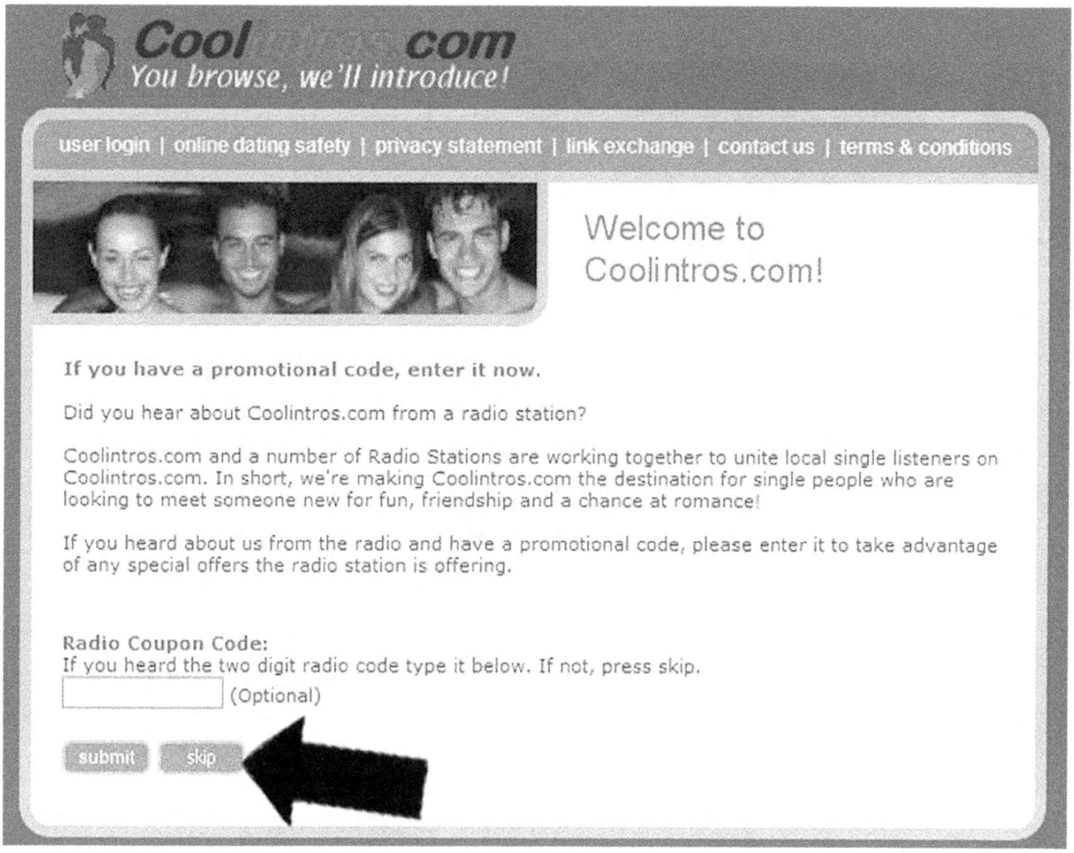

CoolIntros.com
You browse, we'll introduce!

user login | online dating safety | privacy statement | link exchange | contact us | terms & conditions

Welcome to Coolintros.com!

If you have a promotional code, enter it now.

Did you hear about Coolintros.com from a radio station?

Coolintros.com and a number of Radio Stations are working together to unite local single listeners on Coolintros.com. In short, we're making Coolintros.com the destination for single people who are looking to meet someone new for fun, friendship and a chance at romance!

If you heard about us from the radio and have a promotional code, please enter it to take advantage of any special offers the radio station is offering.

Radio Coupon Code:
If you heard the two digit radio code type it below. If not, press skip.
(Optional)

submit skip

3. Click "Continue to profile activation". Optionally, select the checkbox to be partnered with singles in your age group.

user login | online dating safety | privacy statement | link to us | contact us | terms & conditions

Profile Introductions

WELCOME TO COOLINTROS.COM - INTRODUCTIONS

At Coolintros.com, we'll get to work immediately to help you find a new friend. The first step is to introduce you to our members who live in your area and same age bracket. This is by far the fastest way to meet other singles in your area!

In just a second you'll be prompted to complete your essay answers. You must complete these essay answers in order for us to make the proper introduction. It's free, you have nothing to lose and you'll probably be exchanging emails with a new friend from Coolintros.com in the next few hours!

This is just another reason why Coolintros.com really does work! Remember, you must fill out your essay answers for us to go to work making introductions. And remember, at Coolintros.com we believe in physical chemistry, so add your photo to your profile today! This is the best way to maximize your chance for success on Coolintros.com!

☑ YES! Introduce me to nearby members in my age group!

Also now that you're a member of Coolintros.com you'll receive introductions from other new members who live near and around you as well. Get busy and have fun!

Continue to profile activation

4. Within a few minutes, you will receive an email prompting you to confirm your account. Following the URL in the message will confirm your account.

Dear perfectmatch212,

Thank you for registering with Coolintros.com. We are now ready for you to activate your account by confirming your email address. Your activation code will work for the next seven days only.

To keep your profile and activate your membership at Coolintros.com, please visit the link:
http://www.coolintros.com/activate.aspx?ac=AFHD2H3D2ZZC

Until you activate your account, you will only be able to use the basic features of the site, and no other members will be able to view your profile or communicate with you.

If you have problems navigating to the confirmation page, please log on to your account at Coolintros.com, and enter the following activation code when prompted:

AFHD2H3D2ZZC

If we do not hear from you within seven days, your account will be deleted, and your profile and email will be delete

If you have difficulty, you can our Customer Service department toll free at 866-622-8514. You can also reach us online, during normal business hours at:

AIM: SpecialtyMatch
MSN: support@specialtymatch.com
Yahoo: SpecialtyMatch

5. On your user Home Page, click "myProfile" to complete your profile.

Cool com
You browse, we'll introduce!
Yahoo! Personals
Help | Logoff
myHome | myMailbox | myProfile | Chit Chat | Search | myFriends | Who's On

perfectmatch212's H
1 new message(s)
New Members:
View All
preiss
25-year old woman
Cullman, AL
temitopewilli...
30-year old woman
Buena Park, CA
Barbi30
30-year old woman
Russian Federation
treehuggergal
50-year old woman
Albuquerque, NM
sweetladyglen...
24-year old woman
Philippines
MARINALOVES
29-year old woman
Windsor, OH

Welcome, perfectmatch212
Members Online Now: 4
To view your profile as others view it click here!
Profile Completion: 0%

Coolintros.com News
New controls added to protect our members ›
We didn't create this web site to pre-judge people. We welcomed you regardless...
Welcome KRAB Listeners ›
Welcome all KRAB listeners! <b>A special welcome to the morning show, Meathead...
Who's looking at
read all messages ›

• Email
• Chat
• Instant Messenger
SUBSCRIBE TODAY AND START CONNECTING WITH PEOPLE IN YOUR AREA.
Subscribe Now!

Quick Search
I'm a Male Seeking a Female
Age Range 18 to 35
Within 25 miles

Your Current Stats
Interested:
Both said yes (0)
Members who have:
Viewed you (0)
Sent you a glance (0)

Make Money!
By joining our Associate Program
We're looking for people to promote

6. The twenty "Deal Breaker" questions are in essay form, broken down by subject. Each question is optional, but answering all of them completely will increase your chances of a successful match.

PROFILE INFORMATION Profile information including headline, date of birth, zip code, email address and password changes.		
ABOUT ME - THE BASICS General information about height, build and color of hair and eyes.		0 %
ABOUT ME - MY BACKGROUND This section covers education, ethnic and religious views as well as your views on children. Answering these question will allow us to match you with people who share simular views.		0 %
ABOUT ME - THINGS TO KNOW These are the most common questions people what to know before they meet someone.		0 %
MY ESSAYS This is one of the most important sections. Be creative and specific. You're 100 times more likely to get a response to your profile if you complete all of these questions.		0 %
MY MATCH - WHAT I'M LOOKING FOR As you're viewing other members, we compare what you're looking for with the other member's profile and, at the same time, compare what they're looking for with your profile. We call this our Mutual Match score. In order to give you the best possible results, please take the time to tell us the kind of person you're looking for in this section.		0 %
MY MATCH - MORE FOCUSED If you take a few minutes to answer these addional questions, we'll be able to give you even better results.		0 %

7. Click "Manage Your Photos?" to determine how your photos appear on your profile.

myHome | myMailbox | myProfile | Chit Chat | Search | myFriends | Who's On

Help | Logoff

perfectmatch212's Profile

Your username has not yet been approved by a Profile Administrator. For now, you will be able to modify and view your own profile settings, but other users will not be able to search for you, chat with you, or view your profile until it has been reviewed and accepted.

If your profile username is reviewed and is not accepted, your acco... and you will be notified at the email address you provided when you... profile.

Your profile has been viewed 0 times!

Your profile was last updated on October 2, 2006

Manage Your Photos ›

Click to view your detailed profile › search view ›

Online Dating... how will I stand out so that someone special will find me? amazing profiles try it now! Click Here!

Quick Search

I'm a Male Seeking a Female

Age Range 18 to 35

Within 25 miles

of the Zip Code 92310 start

switch to country search

Profile Information - *click on a topic to answer questions about yourself*

Welcome to the profile management area. This section was designed to make it extremely easy for you to describe yourself to other members. We would like to point out a couple of things before you get started:

- You don't have to answer everything now. You can update your answers as many times as you like, until your profile is perfect.
- The section is organized by categories to make it easier to follow.
- Use our unique ASK ME option on some of the questions to encourage members to send you an email to find out more about you.

You may feel that some of the questions in this section appear rather personal in nature. We have found that these questions are ones people often have, but lack the nerve to ask. It's totally your choice if you want to disclose your answers. If you do, you'll have total control over who is allowed to view the details.

hide help information

Make Money! By joining our Associate Program We're looking for people to promote Coolintros.com in metropolitan areas. more info

***Check it out:** You can assign photos a trust level, to decide when certain members have access to those photos. For instance, "Public Viewing" photos are for everyone to see, and should reveal a little bit about your personality. Full trust could be a very intimate photo to be revealed when you're ready.*

Category/ Trust Level	Description
Primary Head Shot	This is your favorite picture, which will be shown when members view your profile in search results.
Public Viewing	These are additional pictures for anyone to view. We recommend a full-length photo that gives a fair representation of what you look like. Feel free to post a picture of you dressed-up or down, or both!
Basic Trust	You might want to hold back a couple of photos for people that you're getting to know. It could be a picture of you doing your favorite hobby or your favorite pet, car, etc... Use it as a conversation piece to get to know someone.
Mid-Level Trust	This is a great spot to place photos of you working or playing that you might not want just anyone to see. Only people on your MyFriends list with Mid-Level Trust can view these pictures.
Full Trust	These pictures should be reserved only for people you're seriously considering dating. You've taken the time to get to know them via email, chat and maybe even a phone call by now. These pictures could show you with other family members, or dressed in a swimsuit or other tastefully revealing outfit.

Using CoolIntros.com

1. Click search to narrow down results based on the "Deal Breaker" selections.

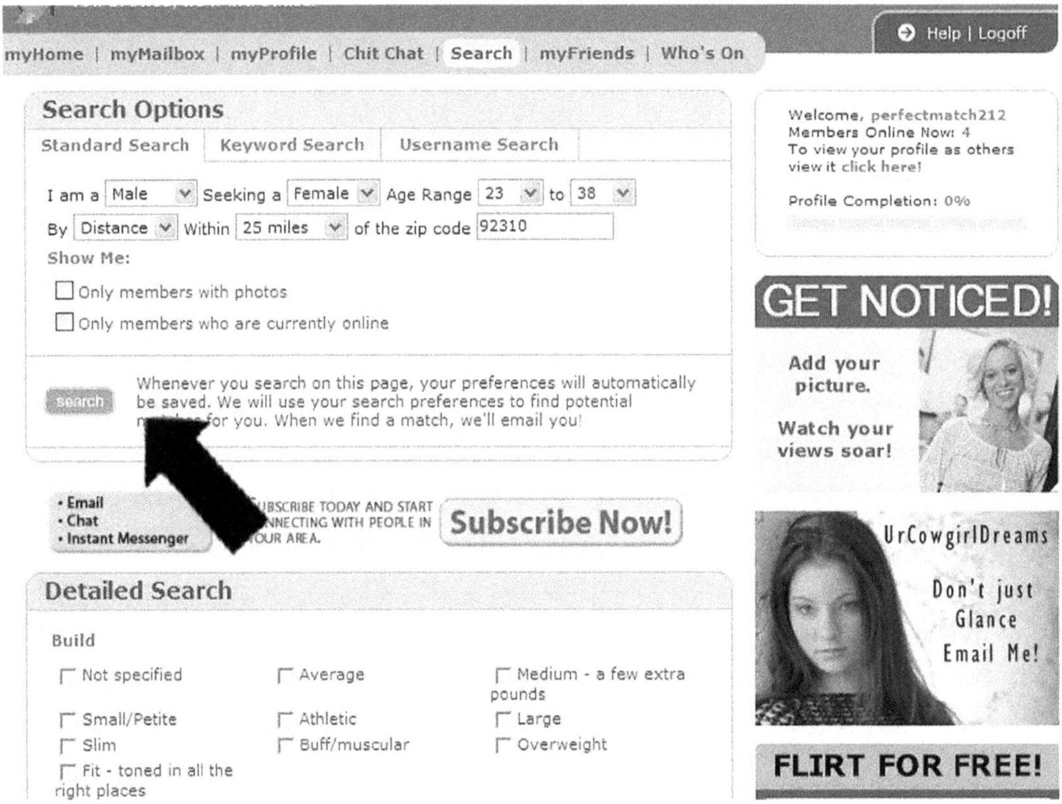

myHome | myMailbox | myProfile | Chit Chat | Search | myFriends | Who's On

Help | Logoff

Search Options

Standard Search | Keyword Search | Username Search

I am a Male Seeking a Female Age Range 23 to 38

By Distance Within 25 miles of the zip code 92310

Show Me:

Only members with photos

Only members who are currently online

search

Whenever you search on this page, your preferences will automatically be saved. We will use your search preferences to find potential matches for you. When we find a match, we'll email you!

• Email
• Chat
• Instant Messenger

SUBSCRIBE TODAY AND START CONNECTING WITH PEOPLE IN YOUR AREA.

Subscribe Now!

Detailed Search

Build

Not specified | Average | Medium - a few extra pounds
Small/Petite | Athletic | Large
Slim | Buff/muscular | Overweight
Fit - toned in all the right places

Welcome, perfectmatch212
Members Online Now: 4
To view your profile as others view it click here!

Profile Completion: 0%

GET NOTICED!

Add your picture.

Watch your views soar!

UrCowgirlDreams

Don't just Glance Email Me!

FLIRT FOR FREE!

***Check it out:** On the user Home Page, you have access to user polls, updated weekly. Also, you can view your search preferences here.*

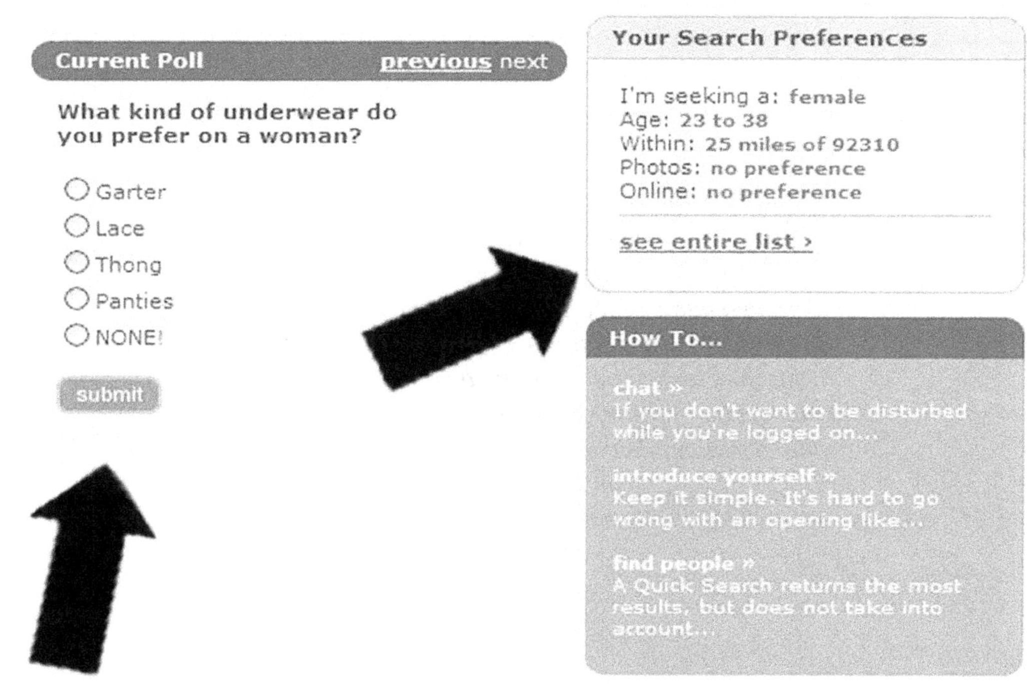

I created an online dating profile because I'm 36 years old, I want to get married, and I've run out of other ways to meet men. My friends no longer have single male friends. When I go to a bar, I get hit on by young men seeking to fulfill their older woman fantasies, or old men seeking to make themselves look good by dating a younger woman. Online, I can get all of the information I need to know about a man before deciding whether or not to date him. The best thing? I can do it anonymously.

- D.M.

MatchClick.com

Quick facts:

Year Established:	Unknown
Number of members:	1 million
Number of photos allowed:	3/less than 100KB total
Best Feature:	Easy to use, easy to view who's online
Biggest Complaint:	None identified
Cost:	Free for all but some chat rooms
Services offered:	Online personals ads, matching service, MSN and ICQ chat
Wikipedia reference:	None

MatchClick.com was designed to be powerful and easy to use. The setup process is fast, although not very thorough. One unique feature of this site is the integration with MSN messenger and ICQ. This makes it very easy to communicate with other users.

MatchClick.com also features polls, horoscopes and other content, making it well worth the price.

Signing up for MatchClick.com

1. Enter your contact information, and click "Go" to continue.

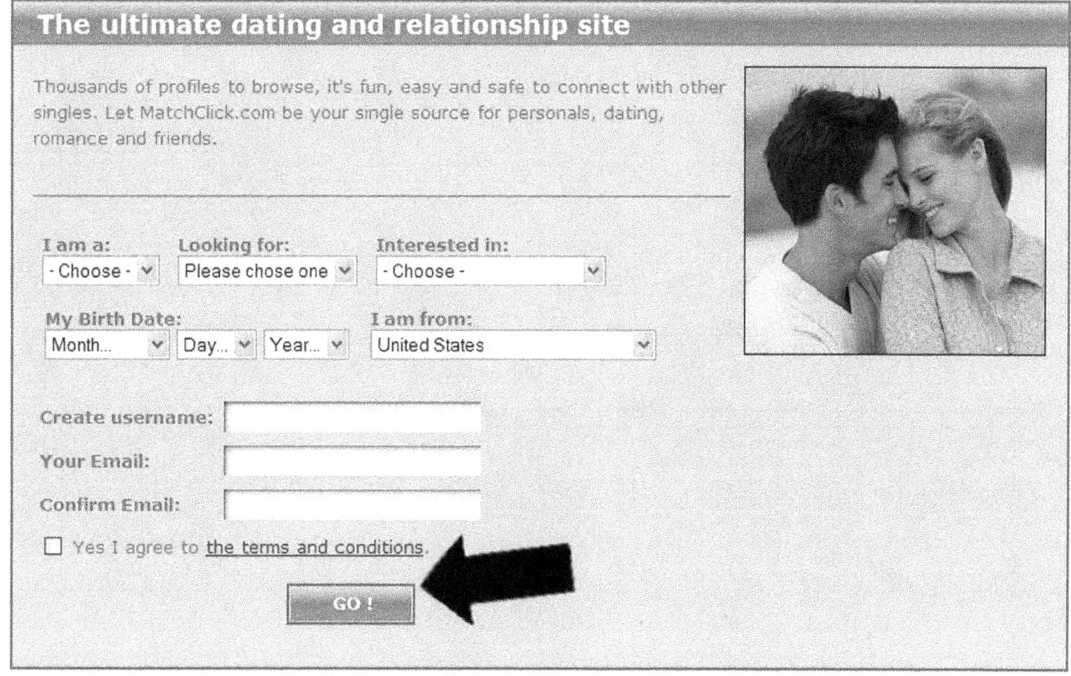

2. Introduce Yourself to MatchClick. Give your basic information.

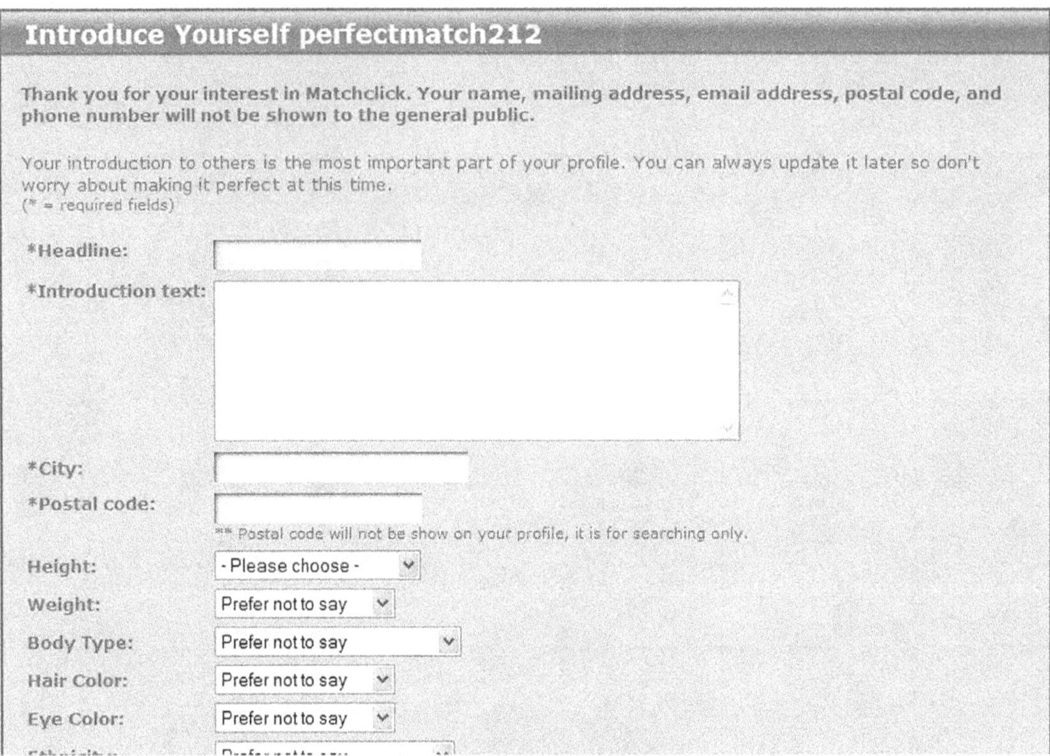

Check it out: *MatchClick asks you tell them a secret about yourself. This secret will become part of your profile and tells others a lot about you.*

Tell us a secret about yourself:

Your idea of the perfect date:

Continue to the Last Step

3. You will be prompted to choose an icon to represent yourself. You can also skip this step if you don't feel that any of these icons embody your personality.

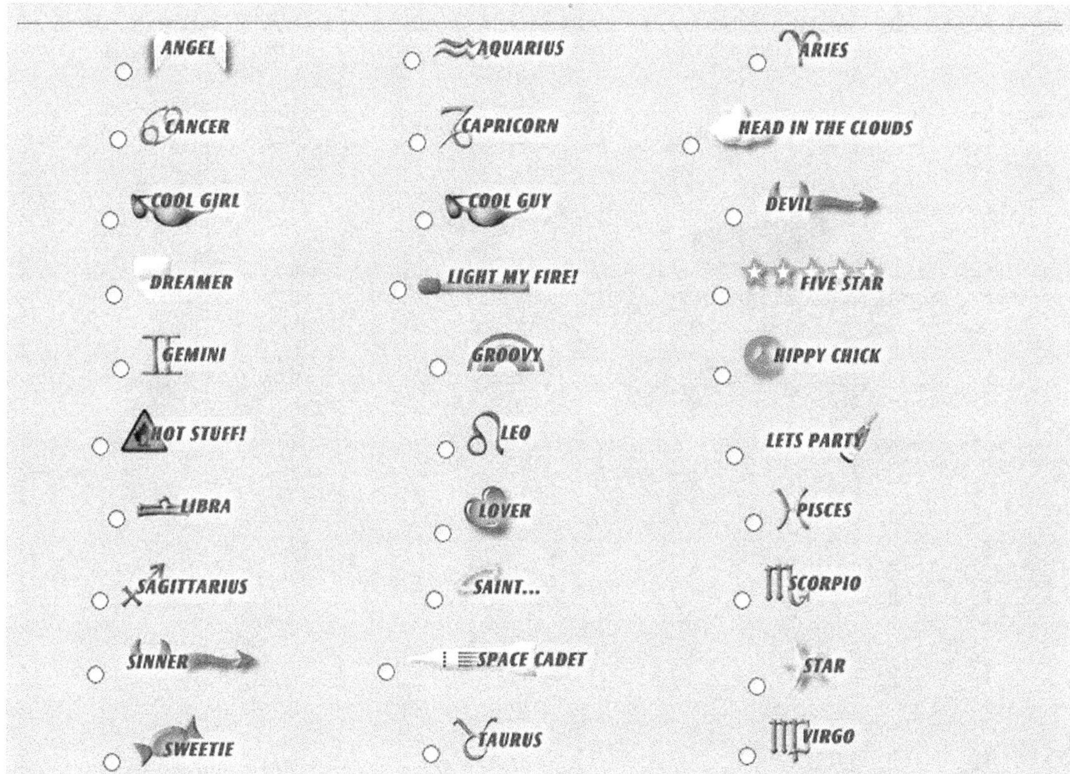

4. You will receive an e-mail with your username and temporary password. Login to the site with this information.

ï»¿
Welcome perfectmatch212 !

As the Customer Support Manager of Matchclick, I would like to warmly welcome you. To activate your account just login to Matchclick using the Username and Password below:

Username: **perfectmatch212**
Password: **igustery**

TIP: If you cut and paste the password into the password box from here, make sure there is NO trailing or invisible space as the password won't work.

Click here to login now.

Our first tip to generating responses to your profile is to add a picture to your profile either by submitting a digital picture you may have, a still grab from a web cam type device or use our free scanning service as detailed in the members' area. A picture really does say a thousand words!

Please feel free to write me if you have any questions, comments or concerns. We will keep you in touch with news and events from time to time to ensure you make the most of your membership.

Regards,

Cindy Summers
Customer Support Manager
http://www.matchclick.com
mailto:support@matchclick.com
Toll Free: 1-866-446-5129

| | Junk E-Mail | Inbox

5. Once you log back in, you will be prompted to complete your profile and add images.

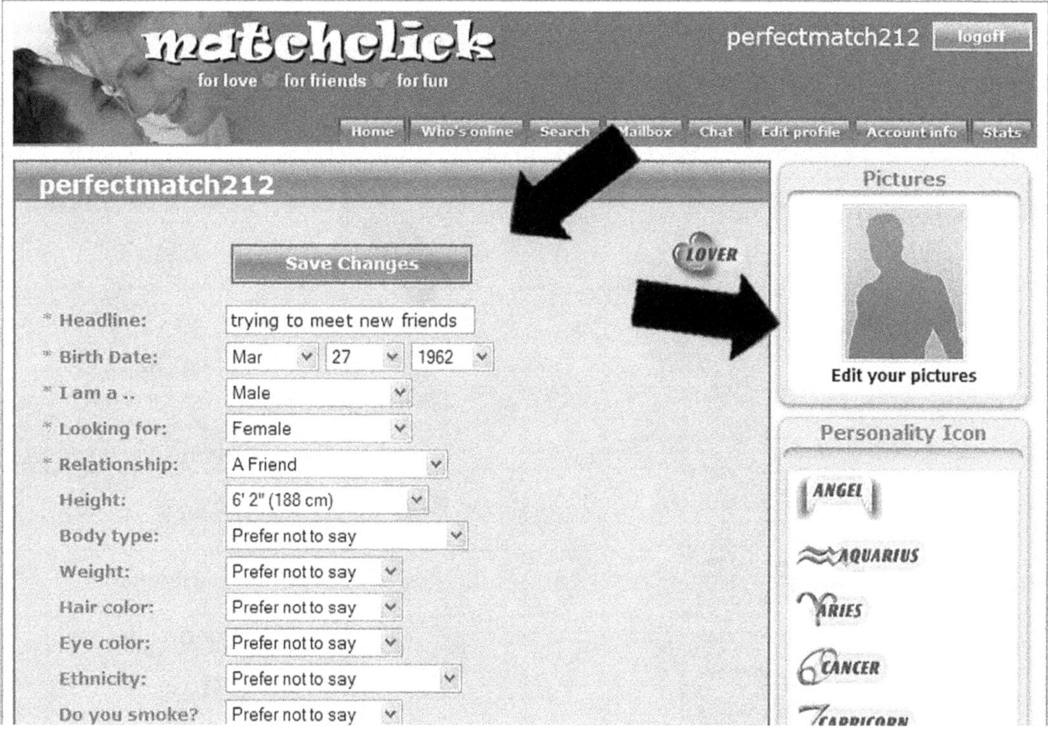

Using MatchClick.com

1. Click chat to join the MatchClick chat rooms. Note that it is required to have flash player installed to use the chat programs.

2. Clicking stats on the user bar will show you your statistics organized by month. It is here that you can see the number of views for your profile, emails sent and received and smiles sent and received.

3. Click "Who's Online" in the user bar to see who is actively online at that time. You will see images and basic information on these users, and can send them a message or engage them in chat.

Having been hurt by previous loves, I knew the importance of showing exactly who I am right up front. Creating an online profile presented the perfect opportunity to do just that. It was like saying, "This is me. Period."

- Rebekah

Cupid Junction
Your Connection Intersection
A member of the relationship exchange

Join Today and Start Connecting!

Millions of singles worldwide!
Express interest for FREE!
Post photos for FREE!
Interactive Messenger!
Receive Matches by email

Already a Member? Click here to login.

Register FREE!

I am a: seeking a:
Between the ages of: and
Username:
Password:
Confirm Password:
Email Address:
Confirm Email:
Your Birth Date:
Your ZIP/Postal Code:
Outside USA and Canada? Click here.

Inform me when I have new MATCHES or MESSAGES
Allow third parties to send me offers

Yes, I am 18+, I have read and agree to the terms and conditions of the Service Agreement, and I give consent to displaying my profile on all Relationship Exchange member sites.

Click here to Register

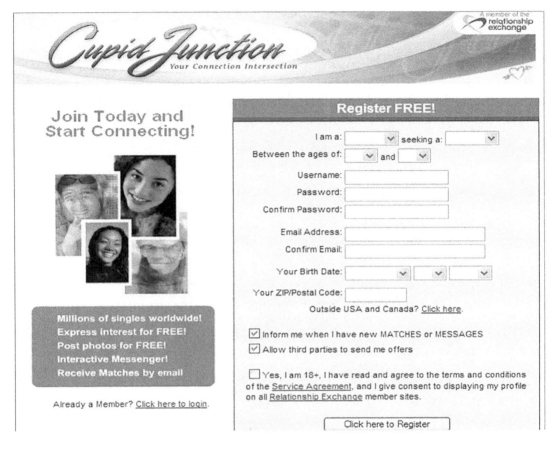

CupidJunction.com

Quick facts:

Year Established:	1995
Number of members:	2 million
Number of photos allowed:	3
Best Feature:	Great interface, strong matching system
Biggest Complaint:	None identified
Cost:	$24.95/month
Services offered:	Online personals ads, matching service, paid service "live dating pro"
Wikipedia reference:	None

CupidJunction.com, in many ways, is very similar to most dating sites. However, they offer a separate paid feature called "Live Dating Pro" that causes the site to stand out from the crowd. Live Dating Pro matches the user with a live relationship expert that is on call via email and chat to offer dating advice and tips.

The site itself is very easy to navigate, has a strong matching analysis. To back it up, all matches display a match percentage, to make it easier to determine your compatibility.

Signing up for CupidJunction.com

1. To begin, enter your basic registration information, and click "Click here to Register" to continue.

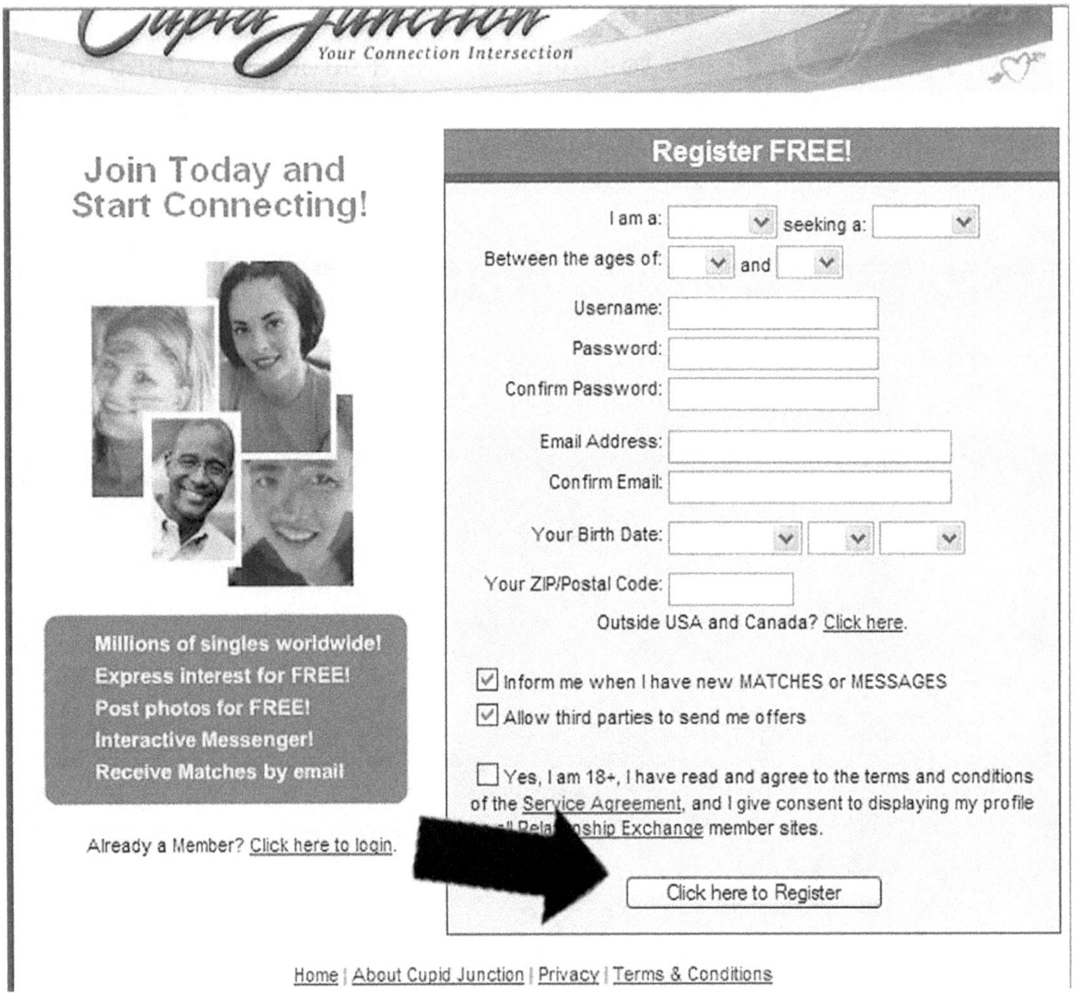

Cupid Junction
Your Connection Intersection

Join Today and Start Connecting!

Millions of singles worldwide!
Express interest for FREE!
Post photos for FREE!
Interactive Messenger!
Receive Matches by email

Already a Member? Click here to login.

Register FREE!

I am a: [ ] seeking a: [ ]
Between the ages of: [ ] and [ ]
Username:
Password:
Confirm Password:
Email Address:
Confirm Email:
Your Birth Date:
Your ZIP/Postal Code:
Outside USA and Canada? Click here.

☑ Inform me when I have new MATCHES or MESSAGES
☑ Allow third parties to send me offers

☐ Yes, I am 18+, I have read and agree to the terms and conditions of the Service Agreement, and I give consent to displaying my profile ... Relationship Exchange member sites.

Click here to Register

Home | About Cupid Junction | Privacy | Terms & Conditions

2. From the drop down menus, describe yourself in the provided categories. Also, answer the two essay questions to describe yourself and your desired match. Note that your phone number is optional, and will only be used by CupidJunction.com. Click "Create Profile" to continue.

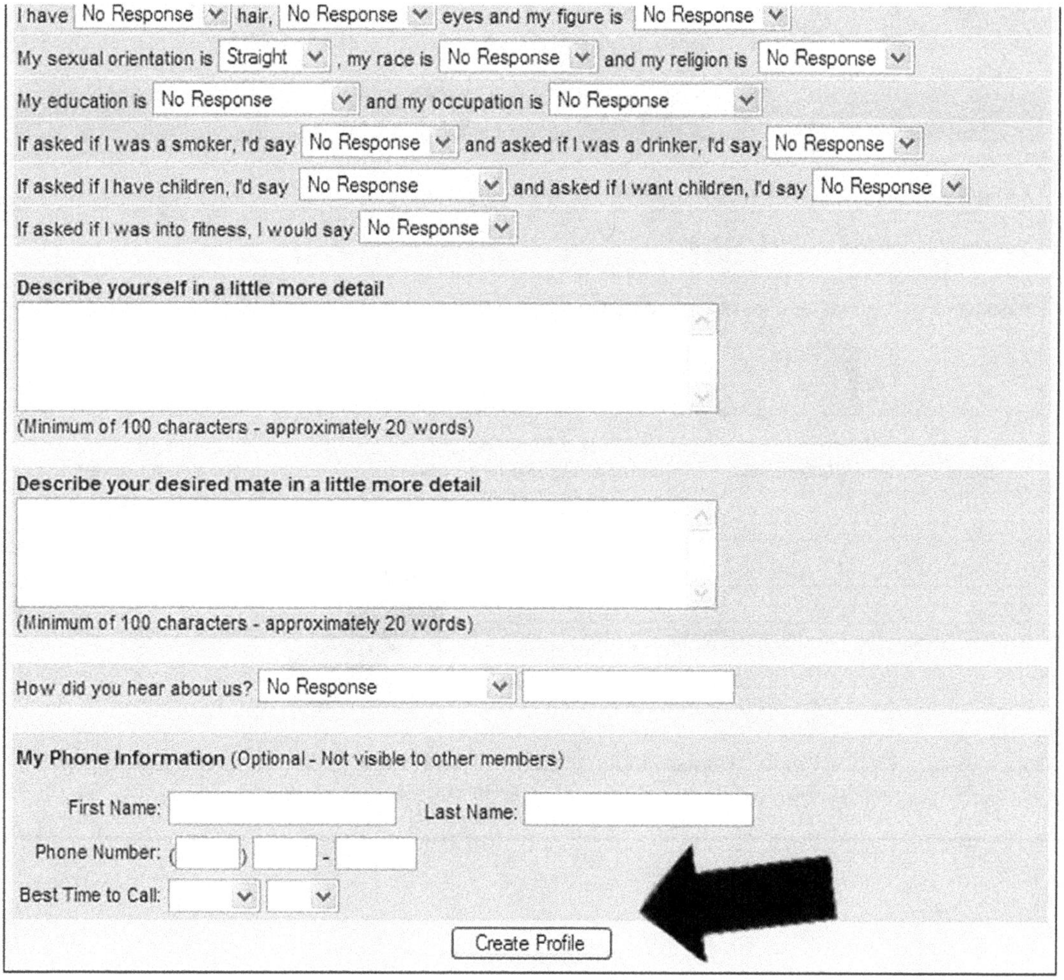

I have [No Response] hair, [No Response] eyes and my figure is [No Response]

My sexual orientation is [Straight], my race is [No Response] and my religion is [No Response]

My education is [No Response] and my occupation is [No Response]

If asked if I was a smoker, I'd say [No Response] and asked if I was a drinker, I'd say [No Response]

If asked if I have children, I'd say [No Response] and asked if I want children, I'd say [No Response]

If asked if I was into fitness, I would say [No Response]

Describe yourself in a little more detail

(Minimum of 100 characters - approximately 20 words)

Describe your desired mate in a little more detail

(Minimum of 100 characters - approximately 20 words)

How did you hear about us? [No Response]

My Phone Information (Optional - Not visible to other members)

First Name: Last Name:

Phone Number: ( ) -

Best Time to Call:

[Create Profile]

3. Select the type of relationship that you would like to find, and click "Continue".

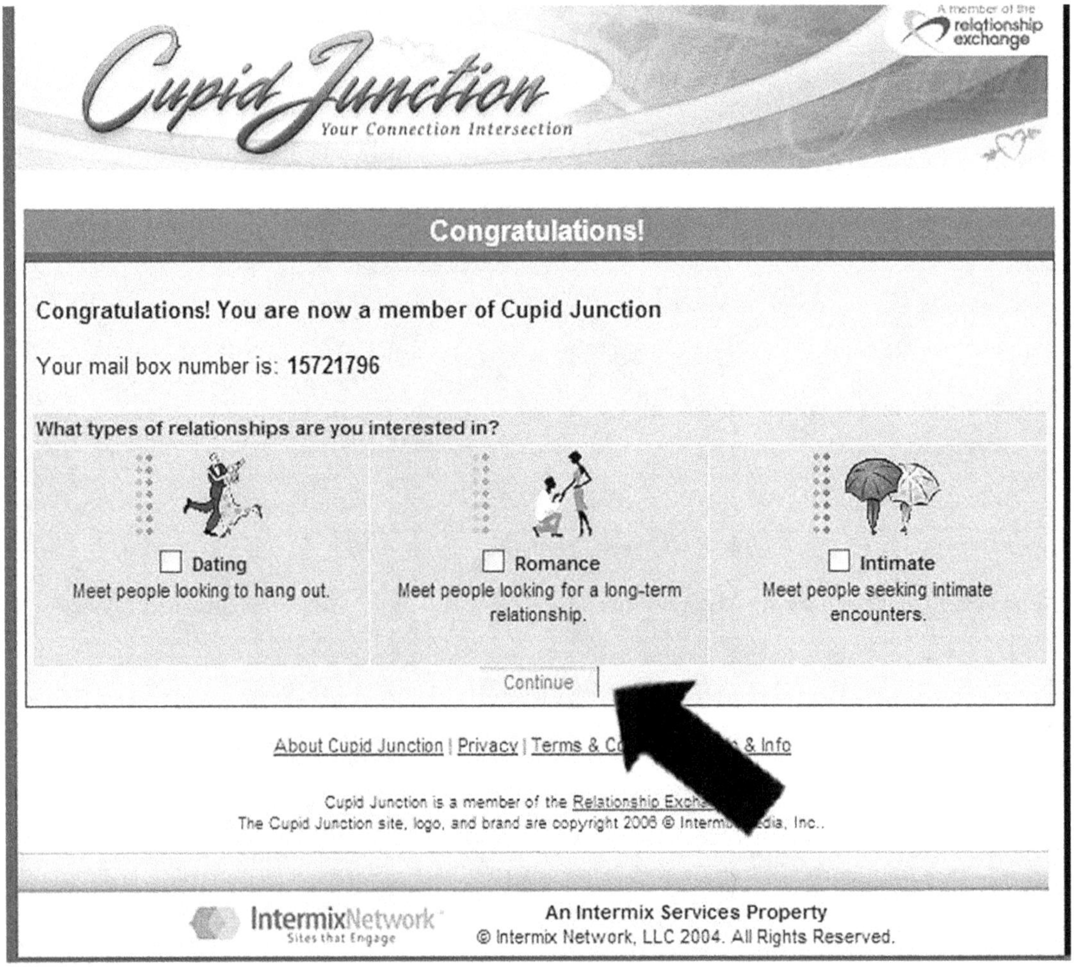

A member of the relationship exchange

Cupid Junction
Your Connection Intersection

Congratulations!

Congratulations! You are now a member of Cupid Junction

Your mail box number is: **15721796**

What types of relationships are you interested in?

☐ Dating	☐ Romance	☐ Intimate
Meet people looking to hang out.	Meet people looking for a long-term relationship.	Meet people seeking intimate encounters.

Continue

About Cupid Junction | Privacy | Terms & C... & Info

Cupid Junction is a member of the Relationship Exch...
The Cupid Junction site, logo, and brand are copyright 2006 © Interm...dia, Inc..

IntermixNetwork
Sites that Engage

An Intermix Services Property
© Intermix Network, LLC 2004. All Rights Reserved.

4. You will now be asked to select your preferences in a match. This section offers many categories, but the most unique category will be selecting the desired occupation.

Height

- ◉ I have no preference in regards to their height
- ○ I would like to meet someone who is between [ ] [ ] and [ ] [ ]

Hair color	Eye color	Figure	Smoker
☑ No Preference	☑ No Preference	☑ No Preference	☑ No Preference
☐ Black	☐ Black	☐ Slim	☐ No
☐ Blonde	☐ Blue	☐ Fit	☐ Rarely
☐ Brown	☐ Brown	☐ Muscular	☐ Socially
☐ Dirty Blonde	☐ Green	☐ Average	☐ Quitting
☐ Grey	☐ Hazel	☐ Extra Pounds	☐ Yes
☐ Red		☐ Heavy	
☐ White			

Drinker	Race	Fitness	Children
☑ No Preference	☑ No Preference	☑ No Preference	☑ No Preference
☐ No	☐ Asian	☐ Not At All	☐ No
☐ Rarely	☐ Black	☐ Rarely	☐ Yes (Live with)
☐ Socially	☐ East Indian	☐ Occasionally	☐ Yes (Don't live with)
☐ Yes	☐ Hispanic	☐ Very Much	
	☐ Native		
	☐ Caucasian		

Education (at least)	Religion	Occupation
◉ No Preference	☑ No Preference	☑ No Preference
○ High School - Some	☐ Not Religious	☐ Business Owner
○ High School - Grad	☐ Atheist	☐ Clerk/Cashier
○ College - Some	☐ Buddhist	☐ Manager/Supervisor
○ College - Grad	☐ Catholic	☐ Professional
○ University - Some	☐ Christian	☐ Sales Rep.
○ University - Grad	☐ Hindu	☐ Student

5. Before your profile is activated, you will be prompted to sign up for an affiliate site. Select "Skip this advertisement" to continue.

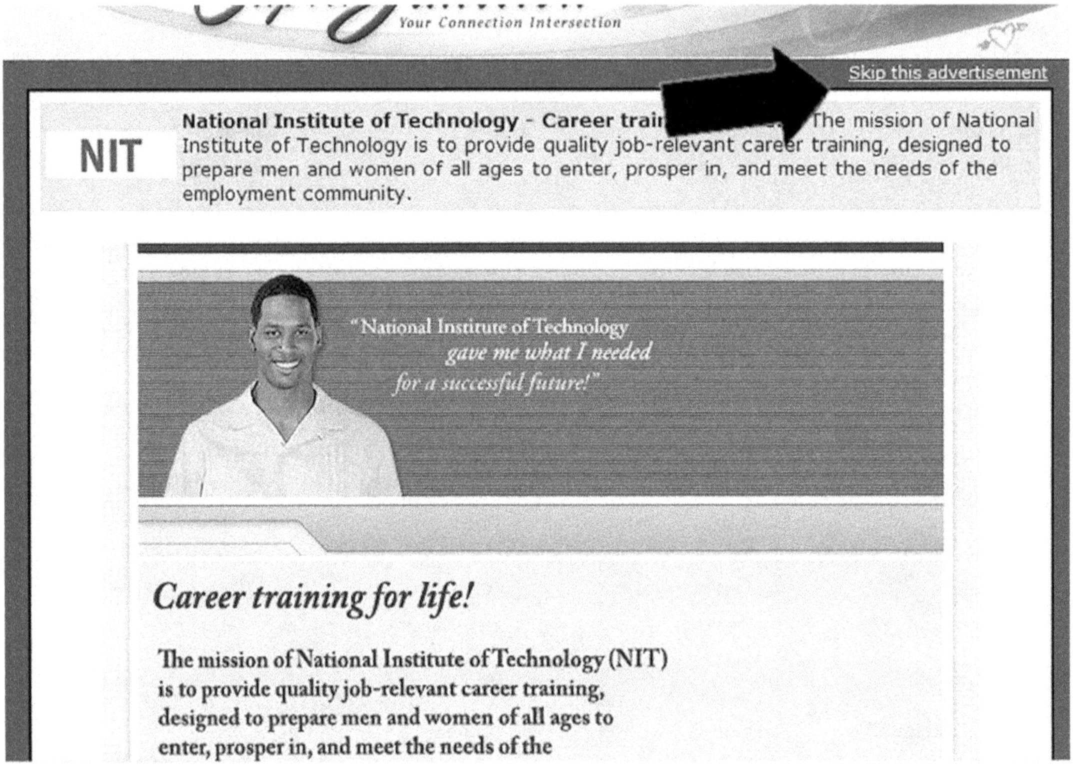

Your Connection Intersection

Skip this advertisement

NIT

National Institute of Technology - Career trai The mission of National Institute of Technology is to provide quality job-relevant career training, designed to prepare men and women of all ages to enter, prosper in, and meet the needs of the employment community.

"National Institute of Technology *gave me what I needed for a successful future!*"

Career training for life!

The mission of National Institute of Technology (NIT) is to provide quality job-relevant career training, designed to prepare men and women of all ages to enter, prosper in, and meet the needs of the

Using CupidJunction.com

1. On your user Home Page, click "View Matches" to see your system-generated matches.

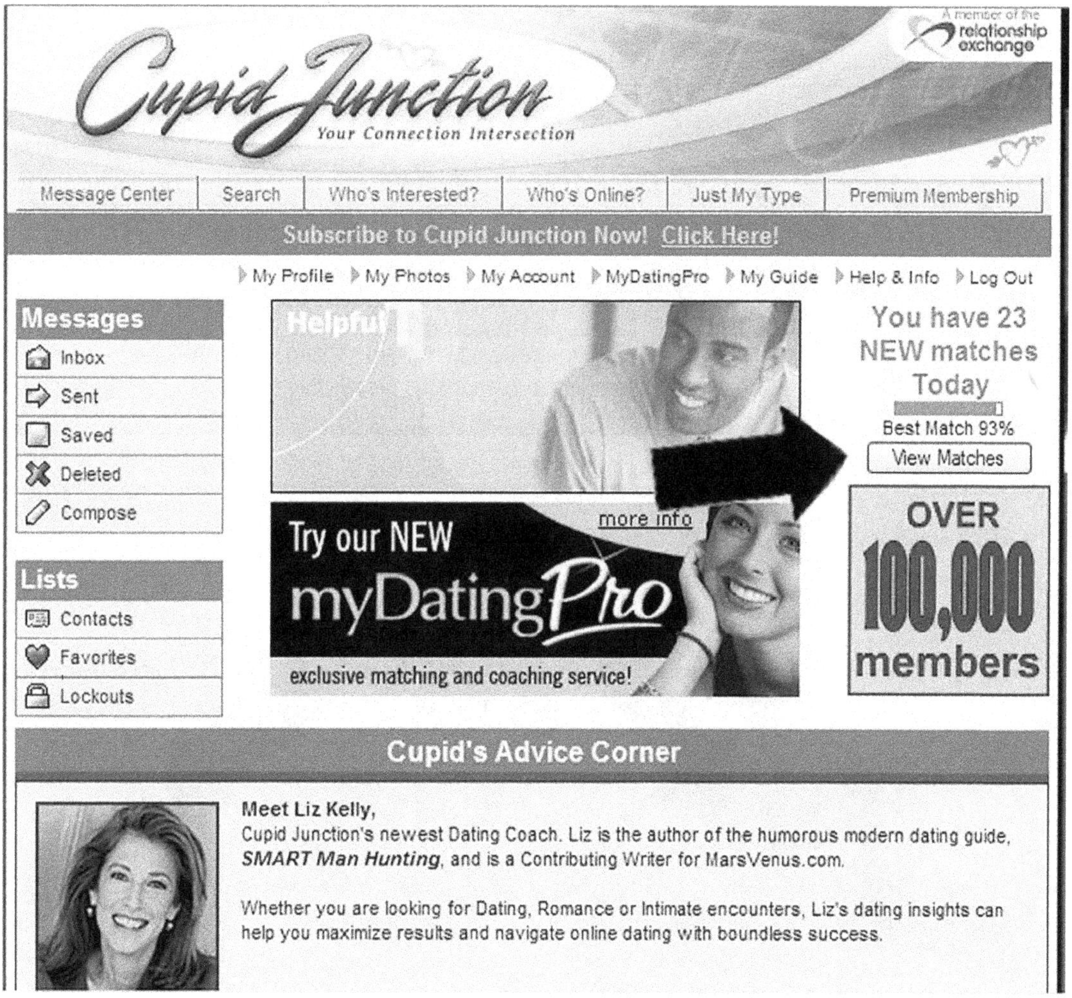

Cupid Junction
Your Connection Intersection
A member of the relationship exchange

Message Center | Search | Who's Interested? | Who's Online? | Just My Type | Premium Membership

Subscribe to Cupid Junction Now! Click Here!

My Profile | My Photos | My Account | MyDatingPro | My Guide | Help & Info | Log Out

Messages
Inbox
Sent
Saved
Deleted
Compose

Lists
Contacts
Favorites
Lockouts

Helpful

Try our NEW myDatingPro
more info
exclusive matching and coaching service!

You have 23 NEW matches Today
Best Match 93%
View Matches

OVER 100,000 members

Cupid's Advice Corner

Meet Liz Kelly,
Cupid Junction's newest Dating Coach. Liz is the author of the humorous modern dating guide, *SMART Man Hunting*, and is a Contributing Writer for MarsVenus.com.

Whether you are looking for Dating, Romance or Intimate encounters, Liz's dating insights can help you maximize results and navigate online dating with boundless success.

2. Matches will display a match percentage, showing how compatible they are to you. Also, the symbols "D" (dating), "R" (romance) and "I" (intimate) will indicate the type of relationship that user desires.

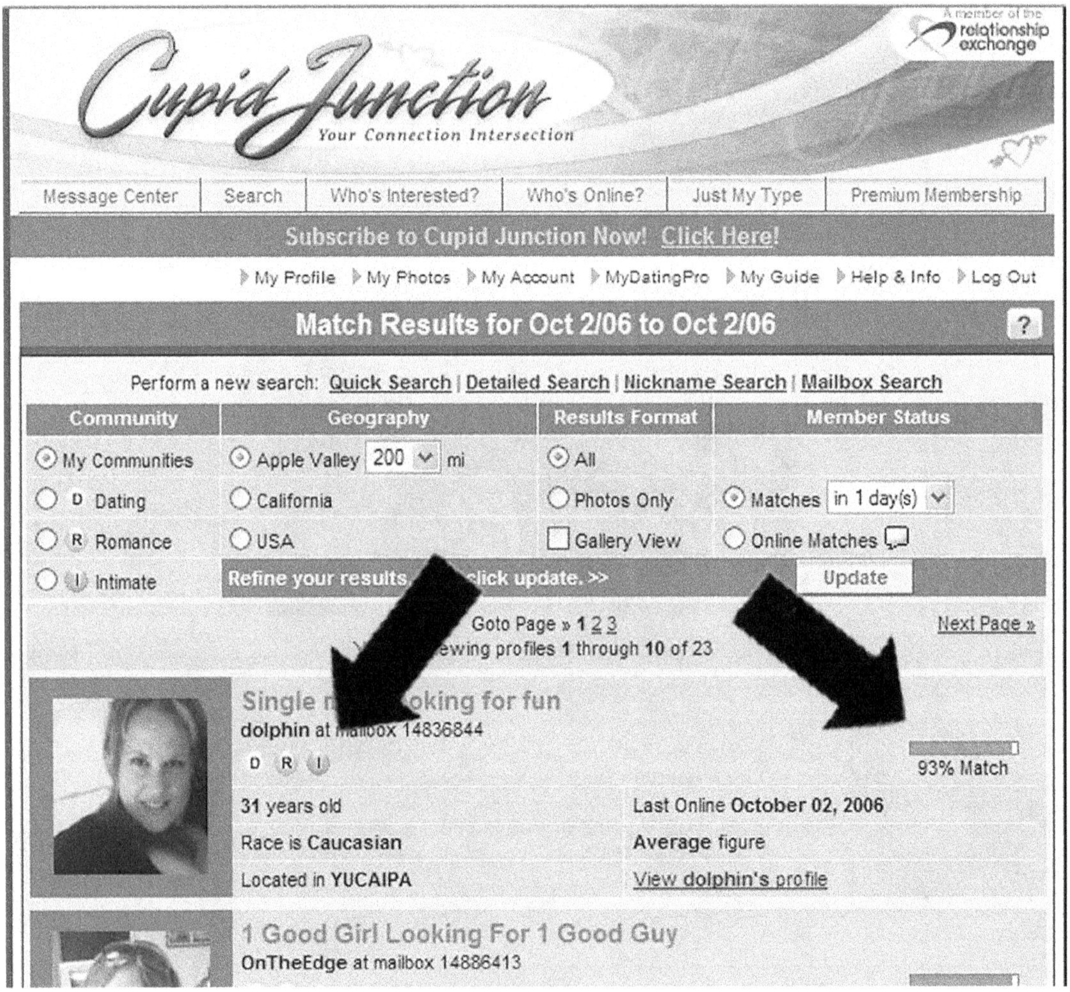

A member of the relationship exchange

Cupid Junction
Your Connection Intersection

Message Center | Search | Who's Interested? | Who's Online? | Just My Type | Premium Membership

Subscribe to Cupid Junction Now! Click Here!

My Profile | My Photos | My Account | MyDatingPro | My Guide | Help & Info | Log Out

Match Results for Oct 2/06 to Oct 2/06 ?

Perform a new search: Quick Search | Detailed Search | Nickname Search | Mailbox Search

Community	Geography	Results Format	Member Status
My Communities	Apple Valley 200 mi	All	
D Dating	California	Photos Only	Matches in 1 day(s)
R Romance	USA	Gallery View	Online Matches
I Intimate	Refine your results, click update. >>		Update

Goto Page » 1 2 3 Next Page »

ewing profiles 1 through 10 of 23

Single oking for fun
dolphin at mailbox 14836844
D R I
93% Match

31 years old | Last Online October 02, 2006
Race is Caucasian | Average figure
Located in YUCAIPA | View dolphin's profile

1 Good Girl Looking For 1 Good Guy
OnTheEdge at mailbox 14886413

3. Clicking "Who's Interested" will list members that you are interested in, members that are interested in you, and mutual interested. This makes it easy to see interested matches.

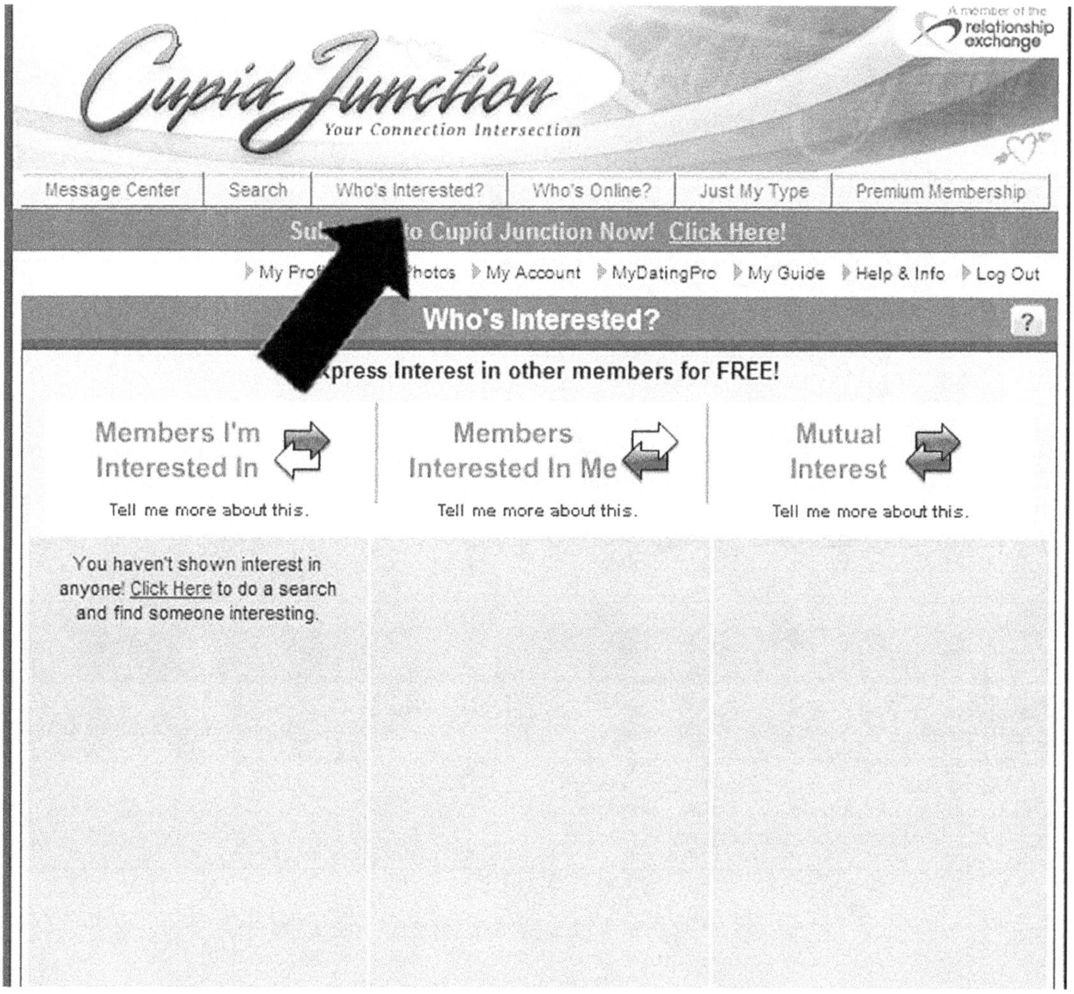

Cupid Junction
Your Connection Intersection
A member of the relationship exchange
Message Center | Search | Who's Interested? | Who's Online? | Just My Type | Premium Membership
Su... to Cupid Junction Now! Click Here!
My Pro... Photos | My Account | MyDatingPro | My Guide | Help & Info | Log Out
Who's Interested?
...press Interest in other members for FREE!
Members I'm Interested In
Tell me more about this.
Members Interested In Me
Tell me more about this.
Mutual Interest
Tell me more about this.
You haven't shown interest in anyone! Click Here to do a search and find someone interesting.

4. Although not required, you also have access to CupidJunction psychology tests on your user Home Page. These tests are designed to help you learn more about yourself and what you are seeking.

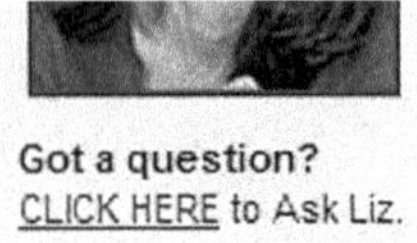

Got a question?
CLICK HERE to Ask Liz.
More...

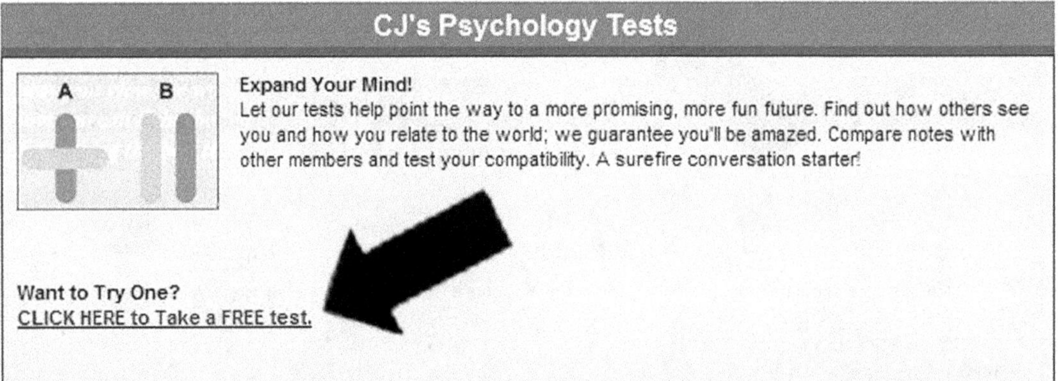

CJ's Psychology Tests
A
B
Expand Your Mind!
Let our tests help point the way to a more promising, more fun future. Find out how others see you and how you relate to the world; we guarantee you'll be amazed. Compare notes with other members and test your compatibility. A surefire conversation starter!
Want to Try One?
CLICK HERE to Take a FREE test.

Dating Tips | Feedback

Dating Tips
Consider all the things that are important to you-personality characteristics, activities and hobbies that you enjoy-and list up to twenty-five words that most describe you. Remember, these are the words that could lead your life mate to you, be sure that they are reflective of your body, mind and spirit!

Feed back
We value your feedback! Click the "Feedback" button to tell us what you think.
Feedback

About Cupid Junction | Privacy | Terms & Conditions | Help & Info

I refused to create an online dating profile, but rather used my friends sites to meet women and the rest is history. Good or bad history... well, that's all a matter of time and luck.

- Joe F.

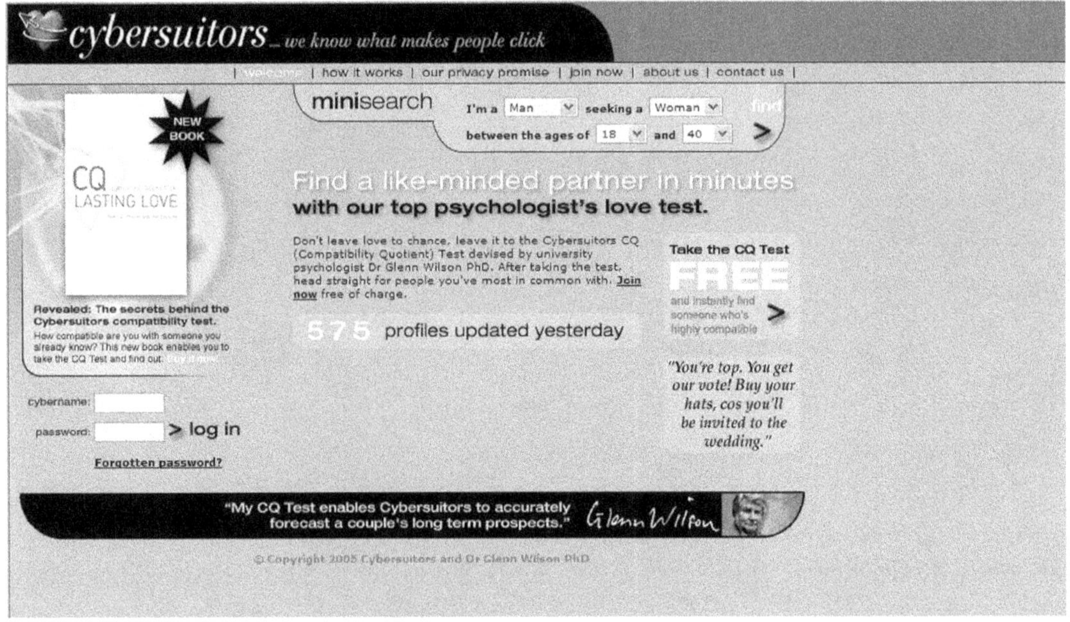

CyberSuitors.com

Quick facts:

Year Established:	2000
Number of members:	Unreported
Number of photos allowed:	1
Best Feature:	well designed site, easy to understand compatibility rankings
Biggest Complaint:	Occasional language barrier issues
Cost:	$20/month
Services offered:	Compatibility analysis, online profiles, address book
Wikipedia reference:	None

The CyberSuitors.com matching system is centered around the CQ (Compatibility Quotient) test, developed by eminent psychologist Dr Glenn Wilson. This is the only compatibility test featured that has been accepted by a peer-reviewed trade journal (sexual and relationship therapy magazine, 2003).

The CyberSuiters.com system allows you to narrow the results by preferences, and will display the remaining matches based on the results of your CQ test.

The greatest strength of CyberSuitors.com is the intuitive interface. The site is very easy to understand, and the intuitive interface makes it very easy to navigate.

Signing up for CyberSuitors.com

1. On the Home Page, select "Join Now".

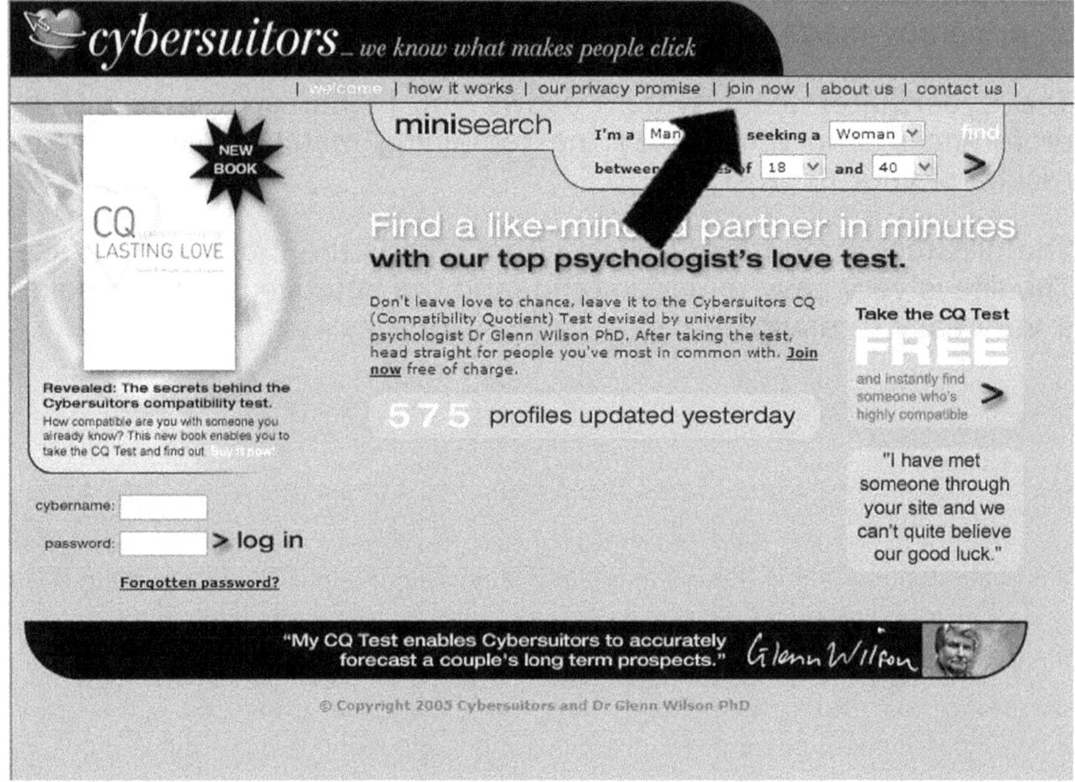

2. After reviewing the introductory information, click "Continue".

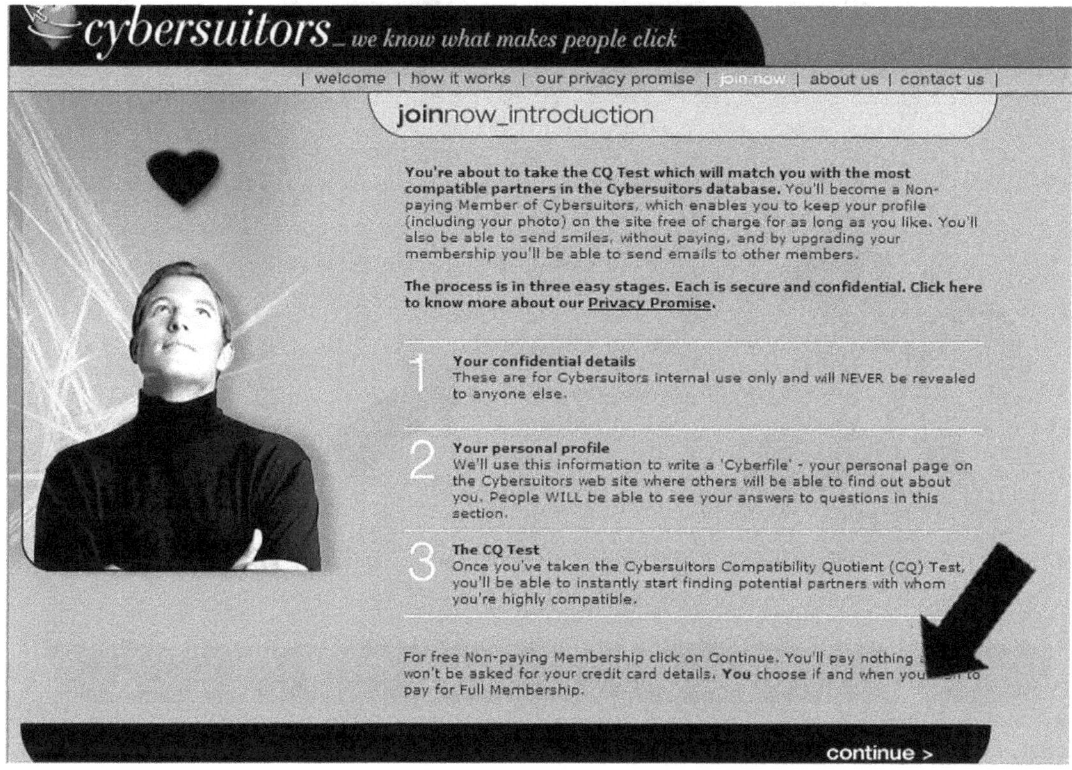

3. Click "Take the Test" to begin the CQ analysis.

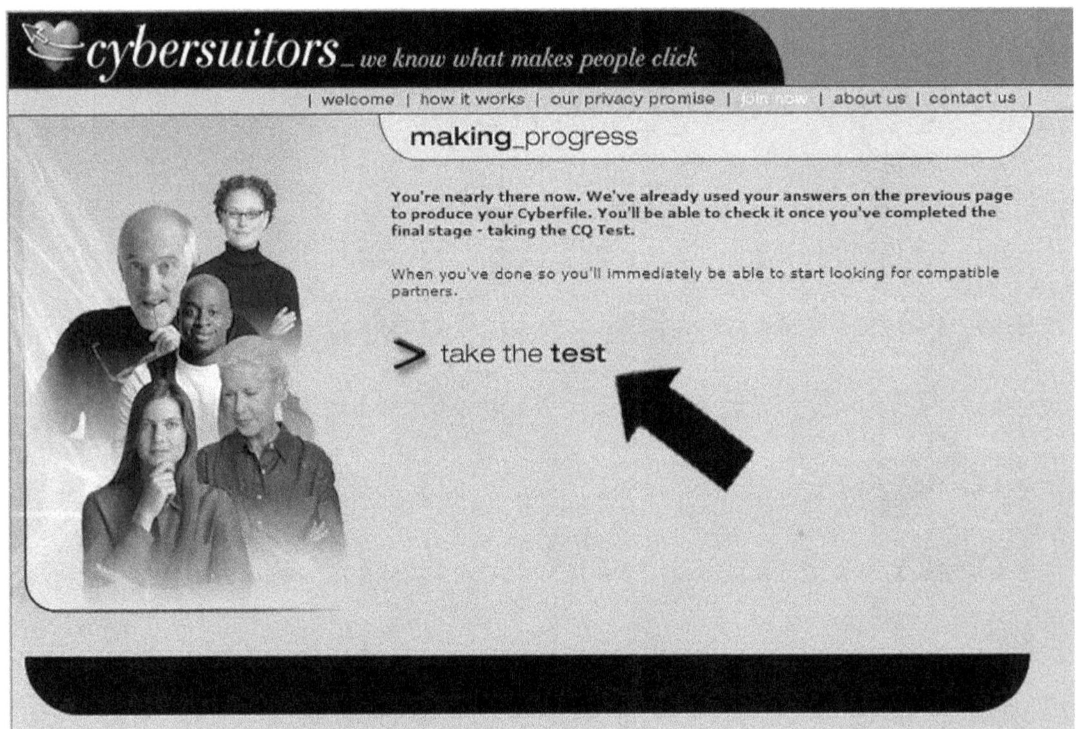

4. Your username and password will be verified on this screen. Click "My Home Page" to continue to your user Home Page.

5. On the left-hand menu, click "Add" to add your photo.

Using CyberSuitors.com

1. Select "More Search Options" to view all of the available options to narrow your matches.

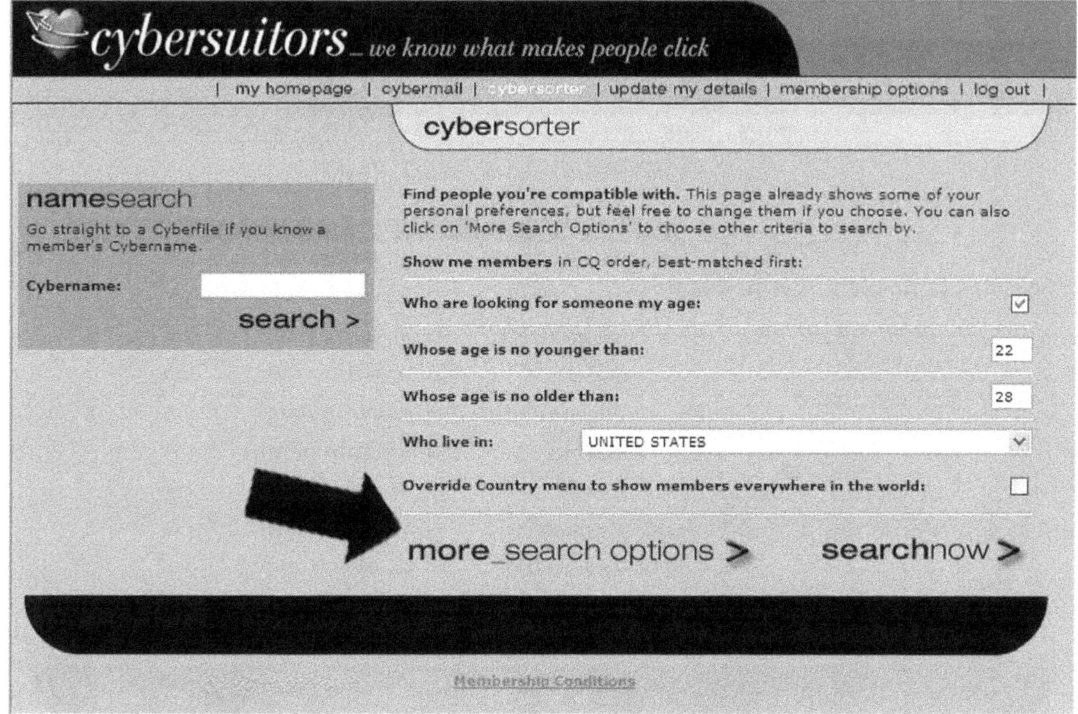

2. Your Top 10 matches will be displayed, ranked by compatibility ranking. A rating of 100 means an "average" compatibility, and 120 or more is highly compatible.

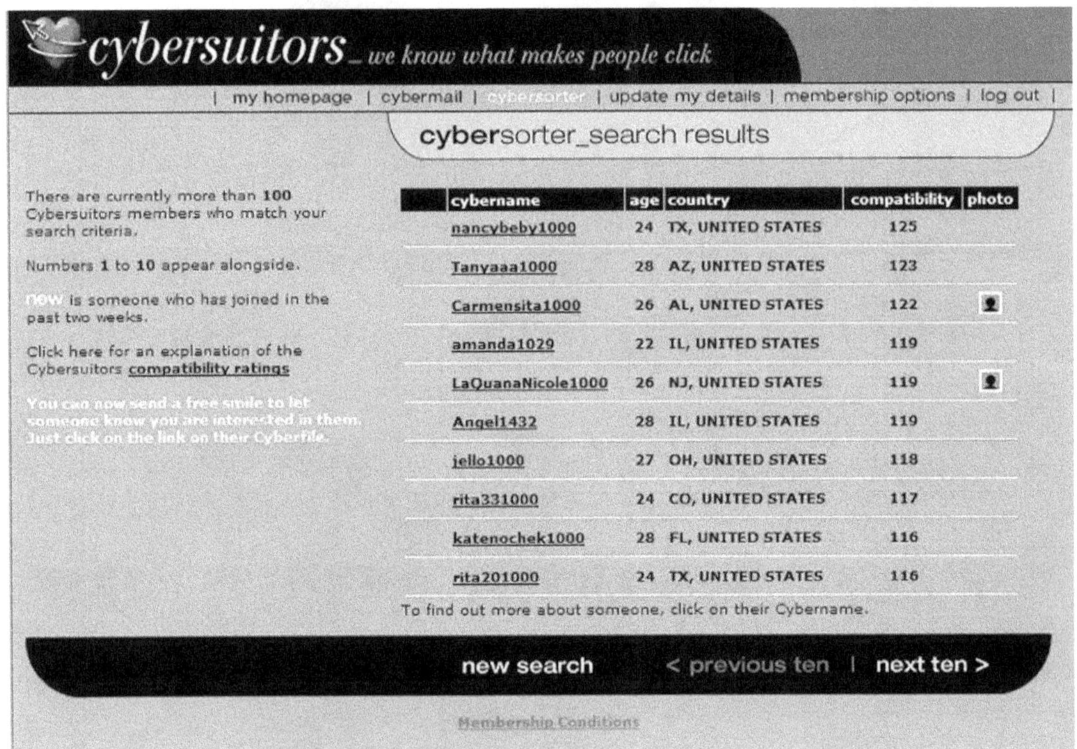

cybername	age	country	compatibility	photo
nancybeby1000	24	TX, UNITED STATES	125	
Tanyaaa1000	28	AZ, UNITED STATES	123	
Carmensita1000	26	AL, UNITED STATES	122	■
amanda1029	22	IL, UNITED STATES	119	
LaQuanaNicole1000	26	NJ, UNITED STATES	119	■
Angel1432	28	IL, UNITED STATES	119	
jello1000	27	OH, UNITED STATES	118	
rita331000	24	CO, UNITED STATES	117	
katenochek1000	28	FL, UNITED STATES	116	
rita201000	24	TX, UNITED STATES	116	

3. Clicking on a username will display the users full profile, along with the CQ rating. Click "Contact" to view contact options for that user.

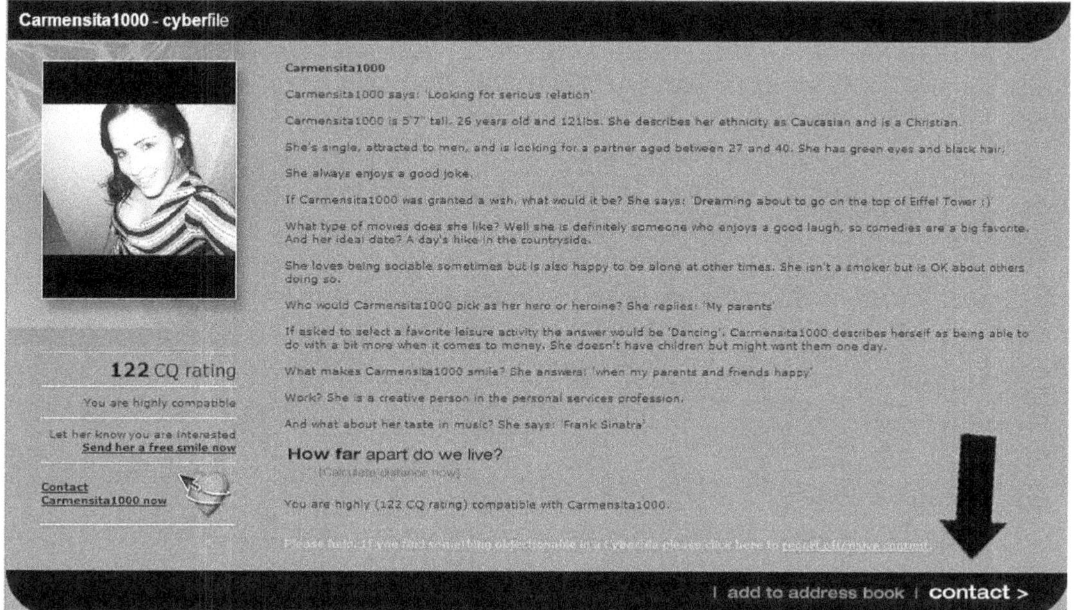

Check it out: *CyberSuitors.com recommends that you log out after using the site, to prevent others from accessing your personal information.*

The reason I started dating online was because I was attending my brother's wedding in LA, and I live in Colorado. My friends new my family would drive me crazy, and they suggested that I place a personal ad on Craigslist. I had no idea that Craigslist even had personal ads. My very first online dating ad read "Colorado Girl Coming to the Left Coast from 8/3-8/13." I got laid 350 responses and got ended up getting laid three times that week by a Chef at a W hotel, A Film Director in the back of his convertible at Venice Beach at sunset and some guy in the back of a nightclub at 5am. I was completely sold on online dating, and when I got back home to Colorado I was off and running with every site I could find related to online dating, and I have a love/hate relationship with it four years later.

- Juliette S.

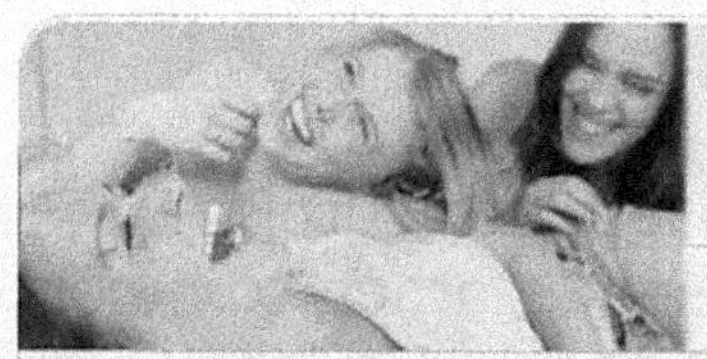

PlentyofFish

100% Free. Put away your credit card!

Free Dating Site

REGISTER | MAIL/PROFILE | HELP | NOW ONLINE (23758) | SEARCH | RATE PEOPLE | FORUMS | DATING ADVICE

Latest Online | Women Online | Men Online | Online My State | Online My City | New Users

Single in Los Angeles?
Meet quality Singles in Los Angeles Parties, Trips and Introductions
www.LASingles.org

Sarasota Singles Online
Looking For Sarasota Singles Apply For Free! Screened & Secure.
www.Great-Expectations.com

Single in Orange County?
Meet quality Singles in OC. Parties, Trips and Introductions.
www.OrangeCountySingles.org

Christian Singles
Fun, Fast, Free, In-Depth Profile. Chemistry® - New from Match.com!
www.Chemistry.com

Ads by Goooooogle

Advertise on this site

Female Seeking Male Age 25 to 35 Zip Code within 25 miles Search Now!

100% Free Dating Service - NO Charges EVER

The top 2 PAID dating sites were recently sued for massive fraud, don't be a victim join 100% FREE Plentyoffish.com today!!!

romans8 25

Woman Seeking Men - Dating

uhh...anyone there?

This reminds me of Skankin' Pickle. That should tell you something about me. I am eclectic. I am eccentric. I am intelligent. I bathe daily (most of the time). I like jokes, but not really joke book **Long Beach** California

PlentyOfFish.com

Quick facts:

Year Established:	2001
Number of members:	Unreported
Number of photos allowed:	4
Best Feature:	Free and easy to use
Biggest Complaint:	Few features
Cost:	Free
Services offered:	Instant messages, online profiles, regional searches
Wikipedia reference:	None

PlentyofFish.com is completely free, which is quite surprising. The site has as many features and quality users as other commercial sites. PlentyofFish.com is very easy to use, and has a lot of users, making it a seemingly great place to get a good catch.

Using the built in filtering functions, you can chat with members in your region, either city, state, country or world. There is no commitment with signup, which makes PlentyofFish.com a great place to start your search.

Signing up for PlentyofFish.com

1. On the PlentyofFish homepage, you can browse members for free. To register, click "Register".

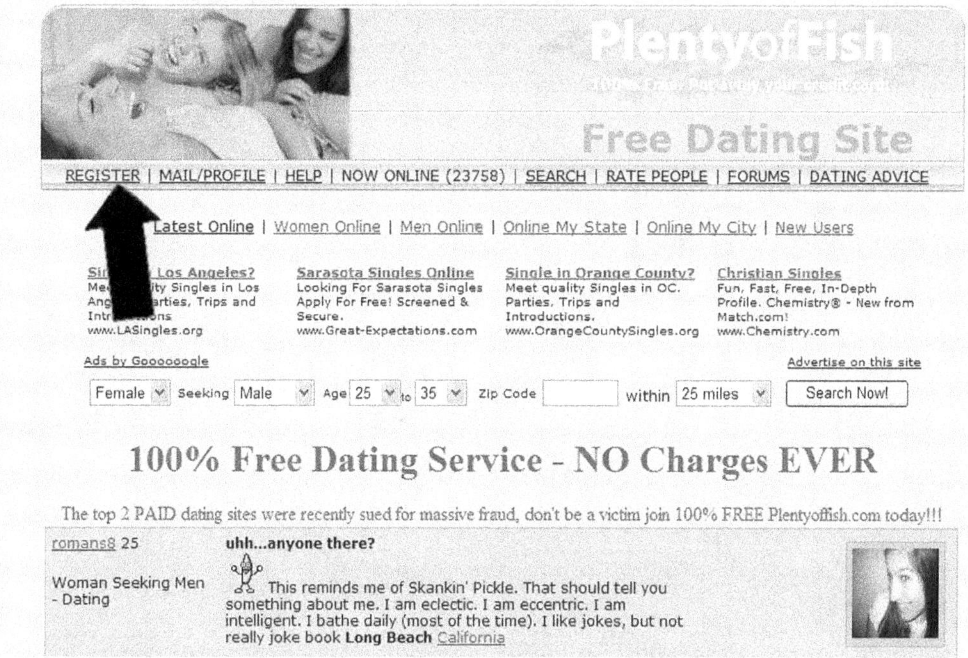

2. Complete the basic two step registration process.

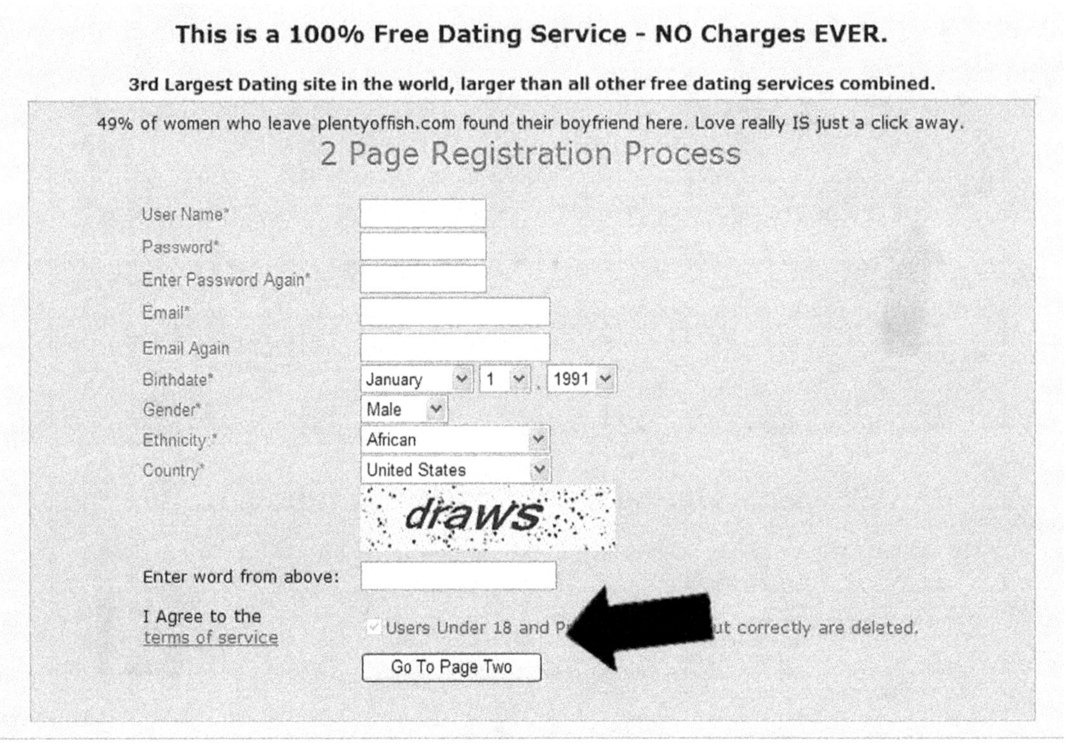

This is a 100% Free Dating Service - NO Charges EVER.

3rd Largest Dating site in the world, larger than all other free dating services combined.

49% of women who leave plentyoffish.com found their boyfriend here. Love really IS just a click away.

2 Page Registration Process

User Name*
Password*
Enter Password Again*
Email*
Email Again
Birthdate* January 1 1991
Gender* Male
Ethnicity:* African
Country* United States

draws

Enter word from above:

I Agree to the terms of service — Users Under 18 and P ... ut correctly are deleted.

Go To Page Two

3. Describe yourself using dropdown fields and a textbox. In the text box, select smilies where desired.

Postal Code		**state**	Alabama
City		**Do you want children?**	Prefer Not To Say
My Gender	Male	**Marital Status**	Prefer Not To Say
Seeking a	Female	**Do you have children?**	Prefer Not To Say
Height	< 5' (< 152 cm)	**Do you smoke?**	Prefer N[illegible]
Body Type	Prefer Not To Say	**Do you do drugs?**	Prefer N[illegible] Say
Hair Color	Black	**Do you drink?**	Prefer Not To Say
Interests		separate interests with commas	
I Am Looking for	Hang Out	**Religion**	non-religious

Headline(ex. looking for good hearted man)

Description (Mandatory)
For your own safety, do not include your name, phone number or address. This is the section where you tell the world about yourself. Include your likes/dislikes, aspirations, the type of person you'd like to meet etc. You can also put smilies in your messages and headline. Click on the smilies to add them or type its shortcut ex typing :devil: in the headline adds a devil icon. One final note, don't enter your email address below, because spam bots on the internet will find your email address and send you spam.

Using PlentyofFish.com

1. Review your profile, and then click "My Matches" to view the matches based on your profile.

2. The closest matches with the most recent activity will be displayed. You can also click "Refine Matches" to narrow the search results.

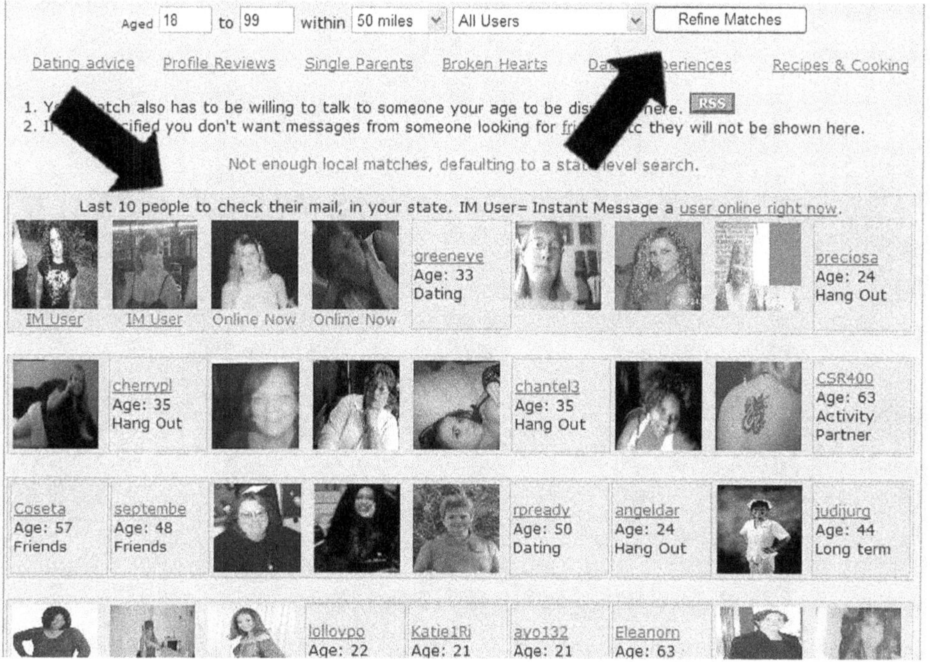

***Check it out:** Clicking on a username will display that user's profile. In addition, you will be able to see how many other members are interested in that user.*

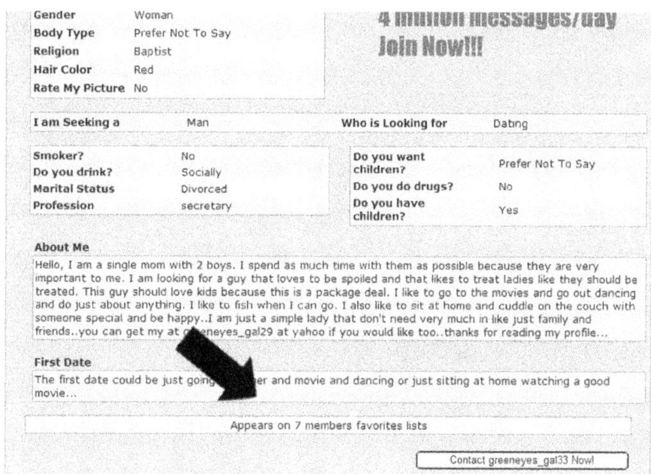

3. Click "Now Online" to view members that are online at that time. You can contact and chat with those members right away.

At the time I created my online dating profile I was in college. My last boyfriend had been over a year previous and I wasn't meeting anyone at school that I was interested in dating. My mom was starting to tease me about how long it had been since my last date, so I thought I'd give a chance to the fates of cyberspace. It all worked out great!

- April N.

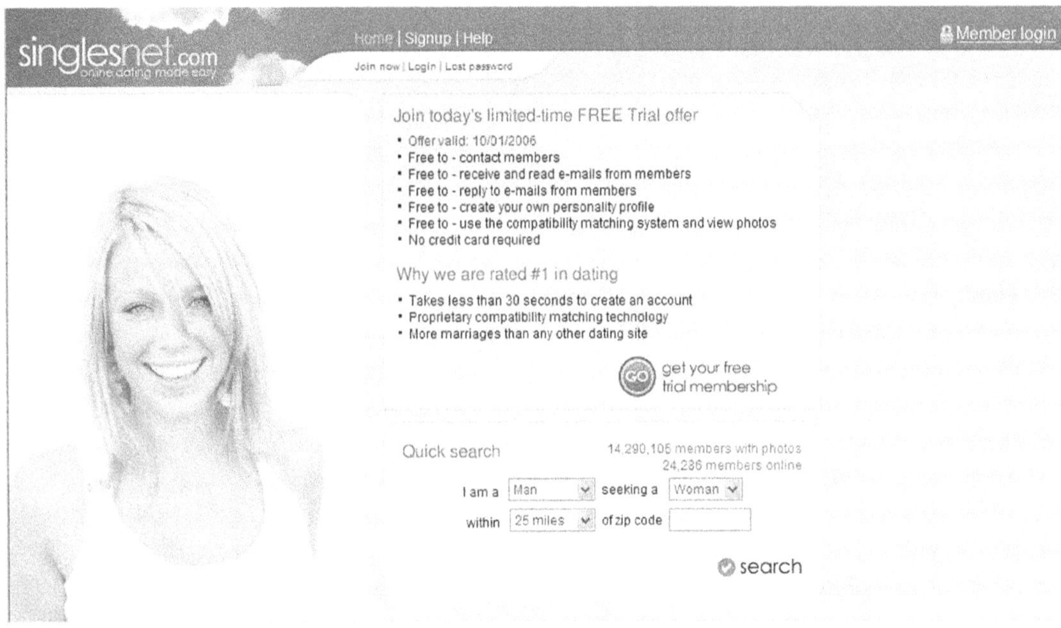

SinglesNet.com

Quick facts:

Year Established:	2001
Number of members:	14 million
Number of photos allowed:	3
Best Feature:	Easy to navigate, many members
Biggest Complaint:	Poor search capabilities
Cost:	$7.49-$24.95 month
Services offered:	Online profiles, custom chat rooms, instant messaging
Wikipedia reference:	None

SinglesNet.com is among the easiest dating sites in terms of navigation and use, and the capability to create custom chat rooms make communication with other members private and fun. Although there are relatively few features, the volume of members makes finding compatible matches a near certainty.

Unlike some sites, removing your profile is very easy: simply clicking "remove" in the account settings automatically removes your profile.

Signing up for SinglesNet.com

1. On the SinglesNet.com Home Page, click the "Go" button to register for your free trial.

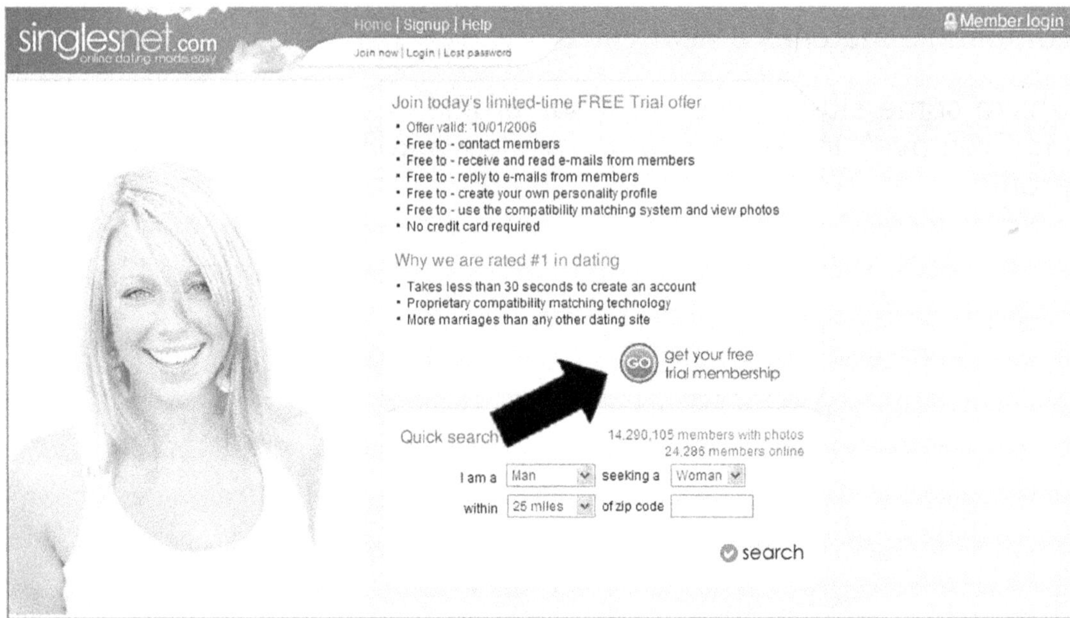

2. The registration process takes about 30 seconds to complete. The first section covers your basic information.

3. The second section will identify your personal information and preferences.

yes no Would you consider dating someone from a different country?

yes no Do you smoke?

yes no Do you drink socially?

yes no Do you have a strict diet?

Tell us about your past relationships

yes no Have you ever had a serious relationship?

yes no Do you have any children?

yes no Would you date someone who has children?

Tell us about your education and career

yes no Did you attend high school?

yes no Did or do you attend college?

What is your occupation?

<select one>

Tell us more about yourself

yes no Would you like to write something about yourself and who you're looki

next

Using SinglesNet.com

1. SinglesNet.com will display compatible matches in your geographic region. Note the checkboxes with each profile. Checking these boxes will allow you to make use of the "Actions" screen on the right-hand panel. Using the actions menu, you can send a flirt or save the checked profiles.

2. Each profile also gives you shortcuts to email the match, flirt with the match or view the full profile.

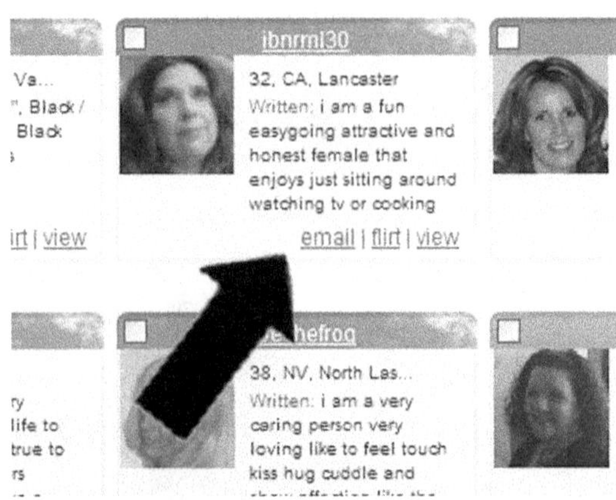

I created a dating profile because I lived on an island millions of miles away from the mainland USA!-----aloha!

- Marci W

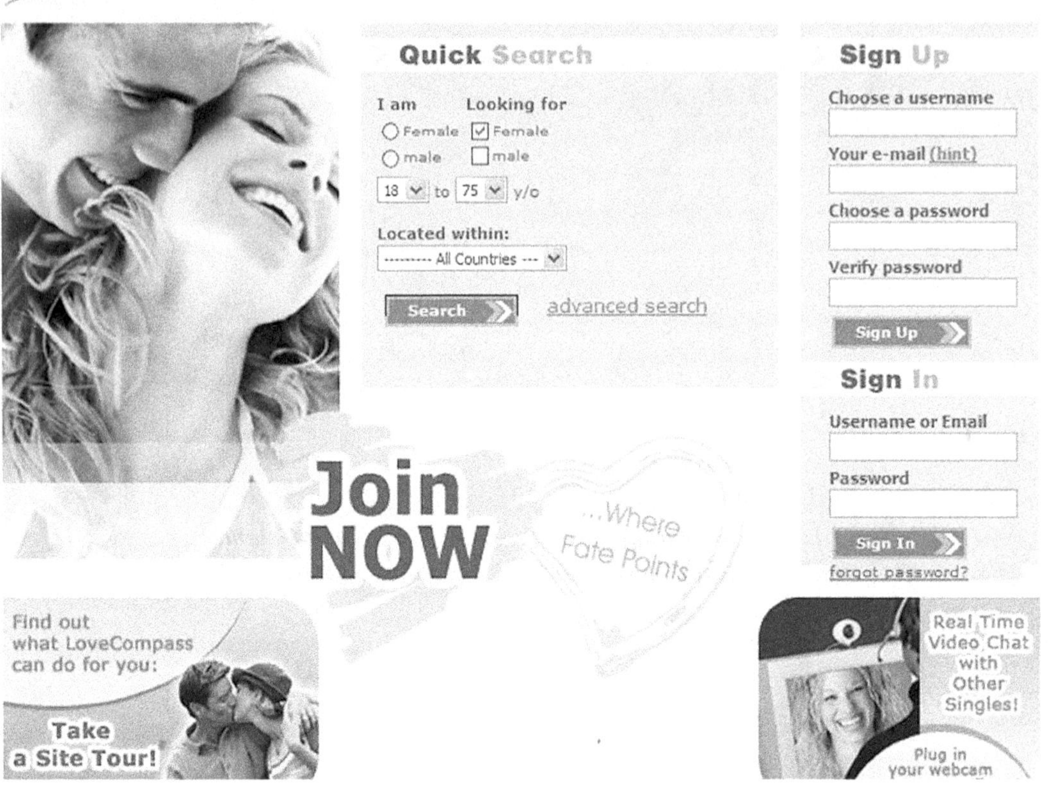

LoveCompass.com

Quick facts:

Year Established:	2002
Number of members:	Unreported
Number of photos allowed:	5
Best Feature:	Easy signup and use
Biggest Complaint:	Few features for free members
Cost:	$19.95/month
Services offered:	Online profiles, personals, live chat
Wikipedia reference:	None

LoveCompass.com merges online and real-world dating. Your profile available worldwide on the site, and optionally, locally via local dating service.

Although LoveCompass.com is based in Australia, it maintains servers in the U.S. for quick access to American singles. The site is easy to use and features a one page signup procedure.

Signing up for LoveCompass.com

1. Click "Join Now" to begin.

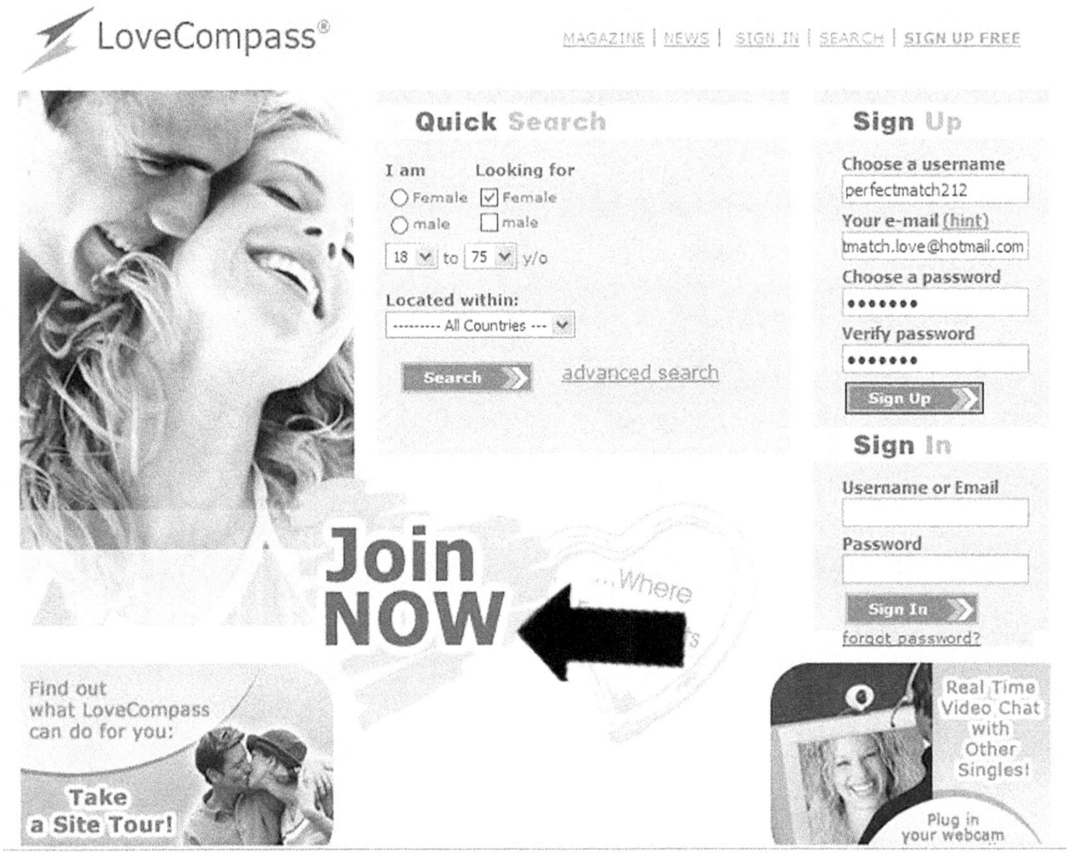

LoveCompass®

MAGAZINE | NEWS | SIGN IN | SEARCH | SIGN UP FREE

Quick Search

I am Looking for

Female Female

male male

18 to 75 y/o

Located within:

--------- All Countries ---

Search

advanced search

Sign Up

Choose a username

perfectmatch212

Your e-mail (hint)

tmatch.love@hotmail.com

Choose a password

Verify password

Sign Up

Sign In

Username or Email

Password

Sign In

forgot password?

Join NOW

...Where

Find out what LoveCompass can do for you:

Take a Site Tour!

Real Time Video Chat with Other Singles!

Plug in your webcam

2. Complete the easy, one page profile.

Join Personals & Dating Online - LoveCompass

Real Name	
You are	○ Female ○ Male
Looking for	☐ Female ☐ Male
Your Date of Birth	Year: - Month: - Day:
Desired Relationship	☐ Activity Partner ☐ Friendship ☐ Marriage ☐ Relationship ☐ Romance ☐ Casual ☐ Travel Partner ☐ Pen Pal
Country of residence	USA
ZIP/Postal code	Please enter your US ZIP or click here to select it from the list
Your life motto or introductory line	

3. After registration, you will be taken to your user Home Page. In the left-hand column, click to add your photo.

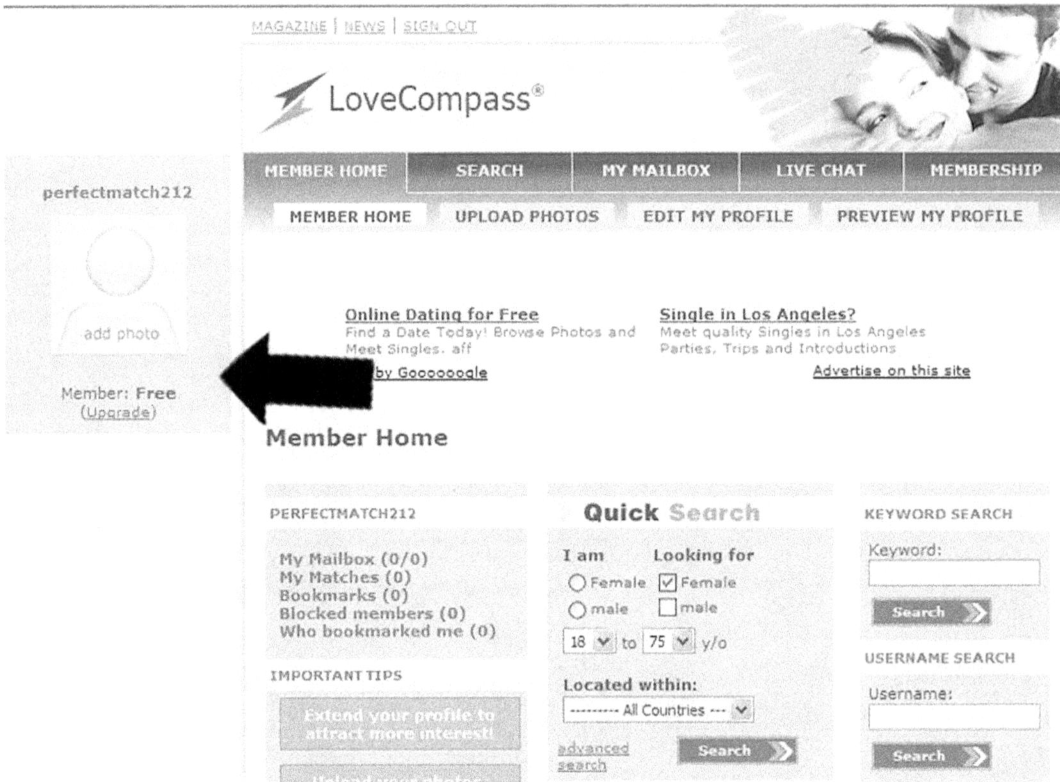

Using LoveCompass.com

1. Search for matches using the checkboxes and drop-down menu

2. You can refine your results using the left-hand menu.

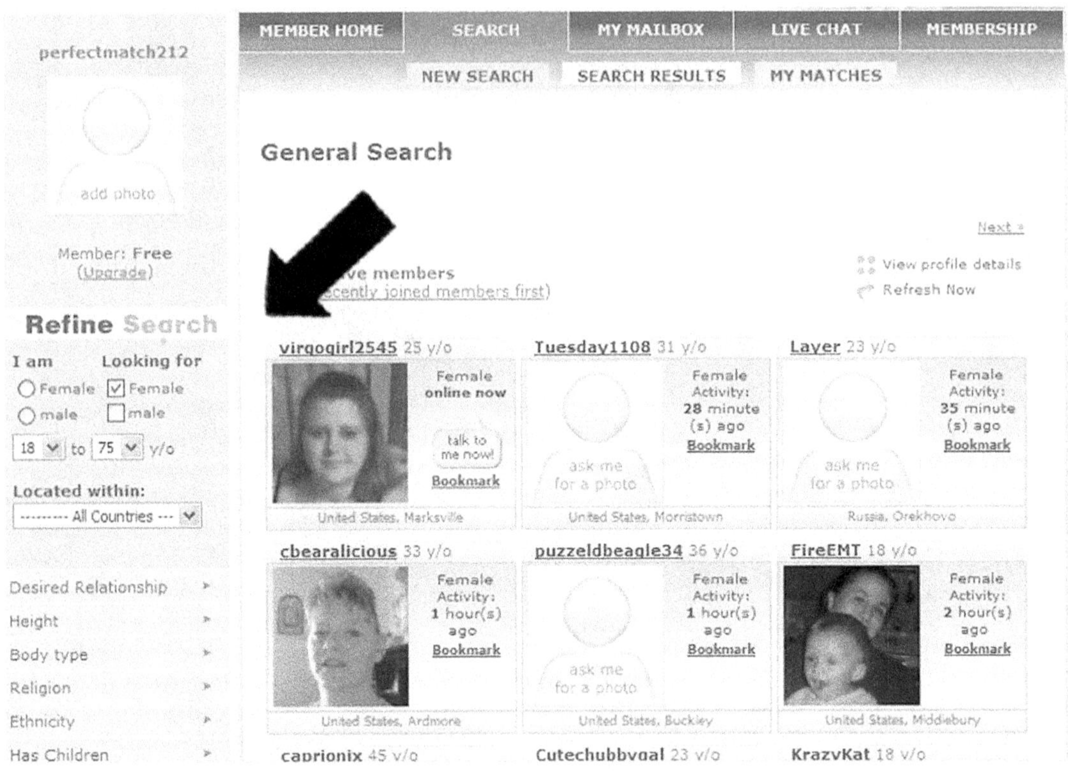

3. After selecting a profile, you can bookmark the match, block them from your searches, email the match or forward the profile.

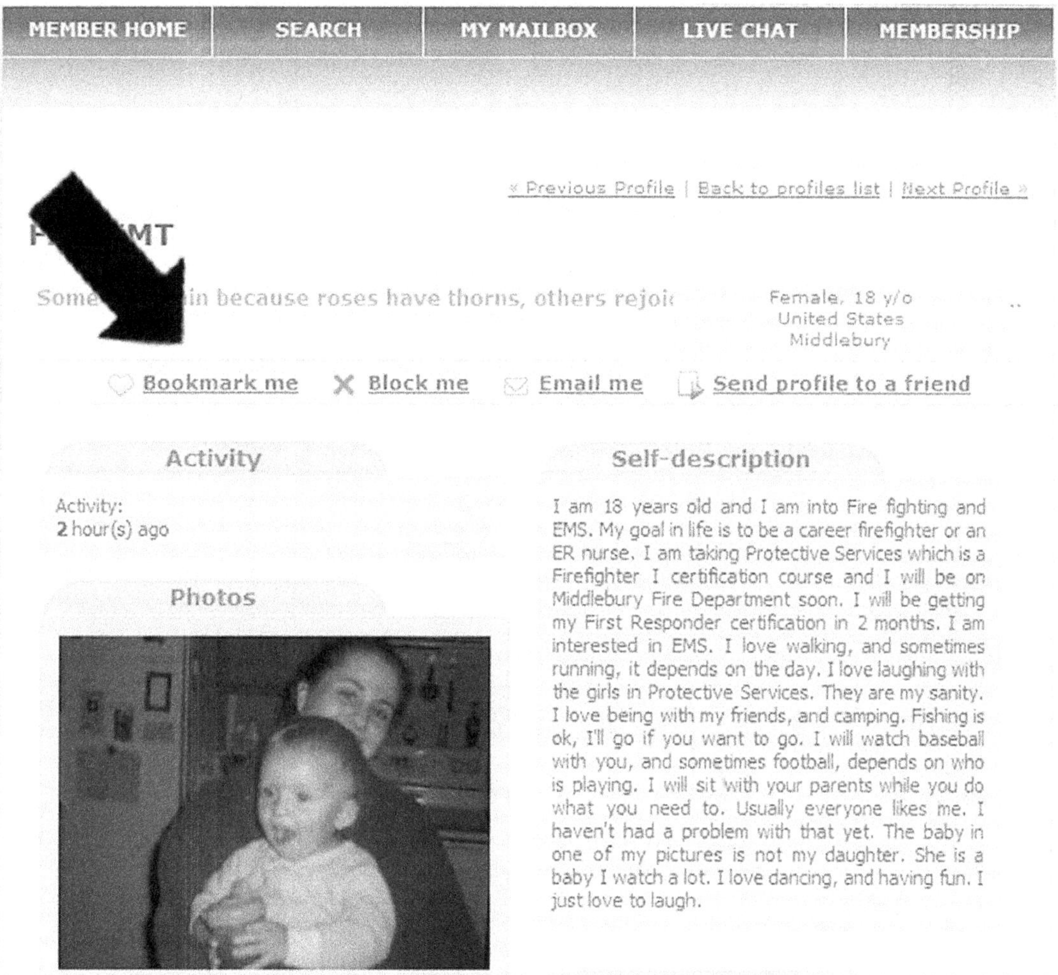

MEMBER HOME | SEARCH | MY MAILBOX | LIVE CHAT | MEMBERSHIP

« Previous Profile | Back to profiles list | Next Profile »

F...MT

Some... in because roses have thorns, others rejoi...

Female, 18 y/o
United States
Middlebury

Bookmark me | Block me | Email me | Send profile to a friend

Activity

Activity:
2 hour(s) ago

Photos

Self-description

I am 18 years old and I am into Fire fighting and EMS. My goal in life is to be a career firefighter or an ER nurse. I am taking Protective Services which is a Firefighter I certification course and I will be on Middlebury Fire Department soon. I will be getting my First Responder certification in 2 months. I am interested in EMS. I love walking, and sometimes running, it depends on the day. I love laughing with the girls in Protective Services. They are my sanity. I love being with my friends, and camping. Fishing is ok, I'll go if you want to go. I will watch baseball with you, and sometimes football, depends on who is playing. I will sit with your parents while you do what you need to. Usually everyone likes me. I haven't had a problem with that yet. The baby in one of my pictures is not my daughter. She is a baby I watch a lot. I love dancing, and having fun. I just love to laugh.

Sites Summary

Site	URL	Year Established
Match.com	www.Match.com	1996
EHarmony	www.eHarmony.com	2000
Perfect Match	www.PerfectMatch.com	2002
Yahoo Personals	http://personals.yahoo.com	1996
American Singles	www.AmericanSingles.com	1996
Black People Meet	www.BlackPeopleMeet.com	2000
Chemistry.com	www.Chemistry.com	1995
Lavalife.com	www.LavaLife.com	1987
Date.com	www.Date.com	1997
Craigslist	www.Craigslist.com	1995
FriendFinder	www.FriendFinder.com	1995
Imatchup	www.Imatchup.com	1993
Metrodate	www.MetroDate.com	1998
CoolIntros	www.CoolIntros.com	unreported
Matchclick	www.MatchClick.com	unreported
Cupid Junction	www.CupidJunction.com	1995
CyberSuitors	www.CyberSuitors.com	2000
PlentyOfFish	www.PlentyOfFish.com	2001
SinglesNet	www.SinglesNet.com	2001
LoveCompass	www.LoveCompass.com	2002

Number of photos	Cost	Members
1	$14.99/month- $29.99/month	8 million
1	$59.99.month for singles. Flat rate if married	8 Million
1	$19.95/month	3 million
5	$24.95/month	9 million
4	$29.99/month	4 million
6+	$9.95/month	7 million
26	$49.95/month	unspecified
10	$14.99/50 "credits"	unspecified
4	$24.95/month	2 million
4	free	varies
20	$22.95/month	3.5 million
5	$24.95/month	3 million
5	$14.95month	3.5 million
4	$9.99month	unspecified
3	Free + extras	1 million
3	$24.95/month	2 million
1	$20.00/month	unspecified
4	free	unspecified
3	$7.49-$24.95/month	14 million
5	$19.95/month	unspecified

Niche Dating Services

These dating sites provide services to people with special interests or conditions:

http://www.datemypet.com/

"DateMyPet.com is the leading online dating website created exclusively for pet lovers. Whether you are looking for a life partner, a buddy for your pet or just someone to hang out with, here you'll be able to find exactly who you are looking for - pet lovers like yourself. It's fun, interactive, safe and anonymous - until you decide to take it further. Our website offers numerous interesting and comfortable approaches for our members to meet and get to know each other, from our pet buddy communities to pet dates."

http://www.militarysinglesconnection.com/

"Military Singles Connection is a singles online community dedicated to helping men and women meet other singles in a comfortable online environment. Our personals community is a source for creating relationships ranging from companionship to friendship, romance to marriage. Military singles enjoy chat rooms, message boards, photo personals, a photo gallery, anonymous private mailboxes, and much more."

http://www.seniorfriendfinder.com/go/p16002

"The purpose of the Senior FriendFinder site is to make it as easy as possible for you to meet people, using the power of the internet. At Senior FriendFinder, you'll find a community of people using the site as a tool to make connections and find partners for dating, romance, friendship, and a variety of encounters. To find your match, we offer several powerful features, which allow you to narrow your search so that you are able to find exactly the kind of person you, are looking for. On various occasions, we also add new features to make your time at Senior FriendFinder a successful and fun experience."

http://www.positivesingles.com/

"Welcome to the best, easiest and largest dating site for STD singles and friends in the world! 70 million are afflicted with STDs in the U.S. alone and an estimated 200-400 million worldwide. Are you one of them? When you have Herpes, HIV/AIDS, or any other STD, it can feel like you are all alone in the world. Do you wish there was a place where you didn't have to worry about being rejected just because of something beyond your control? This is an exclusive community for singles and friends with STDs. Here you can get on with your life and meet new friends, partners or potential spouses. If you just need to find someone to talk to or give them help or advice, this is the best place. Never feel lonely again!"

http://www.whispers4u.com/

"Whispers4u was founded in 2002 when all the major dating sites seemed to ignore the needs of disabled people - We started as a small business and have really grown into something unique that others are now trying to emulate. We now have **24098** registered men and women looking for love, the majority of which have some form of disability. Our user base is growing rapidly day by day, and we are established as the Internet's number 1 dating service for disabled or handicapped people. Hundreds of people have found new friends or started relationships through our site, just by chatting in the live webcam chatroom. We even have our own Casino for our members to enjoy, with up to $100 sign up bonus!!"

http://www.deafsinglesconnection.com

"Deaf Singles Connection is a singles online community dedicated to helping men and women meet other singles in a comfortable online environment. Our personals community is a source for creating relationships ranging from companionship to friendship, romance to marriage."

http://www.gothicmatch.com

"Welcome to the largest and most successful dating site for Gothic friends and singles in the world! Do you live the Gothic lifestyle? Do you wish there was a place where you could make new friends, chat, or hook up with other members of the gothic community? GothicMatch was set up to help those in the Gothic lifestyle find each other. Whether in your local community or around the world. Join GothicMatch to find someone to share your interests, your problems, your music and your spirit or even the perfect darkchylde to bring back to your lair. It's free to join the hundreds of thousands who have already made this dark little corner of the net their home. Never be alone in the dark again."

http://www.largefriends.com

"Largefriends.com, the best and most successful website for meeting plus-size singles and friends."

Trademarks

All of the trademarked names, images, or likeness that have been used in this book are properties of the respective owners.

eHarmony

PerfectMatch

Yahoo Personals

American Singles

Black People Meet

Chemistry.com

Lavalife

Date.com

Craigslist

FriendFinder

Imatchup

Metrodate

Cool Intros

MatchClick

Cupid Junction

Cyber Suitors

Plenty Of Fish

SinglesNet

LoveCompass

Datemypet.com

Militarysinglesconnection.com

Seniorfriendfinder.com

Positivesingles.com

Whispers4u.com

Deafsinglesconnection.com

Gothicmatch.com

Largefriends.com

Match.com

www.ingramcontent.com/pod-product-compliance
Lightning Source LLC
Chambersburg PA
CBHW080407060326
40689CB00019B/4165

* 9 7 8 1 4 1 9 6 5 1 2 3 6 *